SEX LAW IN ENGLAND

SEX LAW
IN ENGLAND

Tony Honoré
Regius Professor of Civil Law
in the University of Oxford

Archon Books

First published in 1978 in Great Britain by
Gerald Duckworth & Co. Ltd.
The Old Piano Factory
43 Gloucester Crescent, London NW1
and in the United States of America as an Archon Book, an
imprint of The Shoe String Press, Inc. Hamden, Connecticut
06514

© 1978 by Tony Honoré

Archon ISBN 0-208-01764-X

Made and printed in Great Britain by
The Garden City Press Limited
Letchworth, Hertfordshire SG6 1JS

Contents

TO NIKI
AND FRANK

Introduction

For most people sex is an important interest. It is true that on the whole men are, on the evidence of opinion surveys, more likely than women to rank it above love, security or a home.[1] But a book like Nancy Friday's *My Secret Garden*[2] will convince the male doubter that sexual fantasies and obsessions are not confined to men.

For laymen sexual experience is an aspect of life which possesses a certain unity. Sex inside or outside marriage, within or against the criminal law, is part of a single segment of existence, just as eating at home or in a restaurant or snack bar or in violation of the Mosaic law is part of a single activity which may be more or less enjoyable, obsessive or guilt-ridden according to the slant of the person who does it. Lawyers, however, tend to overlook this, since their minds are formed by the technical divisions of their subject—criminal law, family law and so on—and their books follow suit. Hence there are not many law books about sex as opposed to special aspects of sex, like rape or prostitution. In the United States there is at least one such book, Judge Ploscowe's *Sex and the Law*,[3] a wise and readable distillation which draws on the author's years on the bench in New York. There is nothing similar for the law of England, and I hope that a simple account, which combines an outline of the law with a sketch of the social and moral background, may be of general interest.

The subject possesses a genuine unity, not merely one resting in the eye of the man or woman whose itches and urges have to be expressed or controlled. From the point of view of Western morality sex is an area of conduct to which special rules and

---

[1] S. Cronan, 'Notes from the Third Year', *Women's Liberation* (1971) 62–5, cited in Davidson, Ginsberg and Kay, *Text, Cases and Materials on Sex-based Discrimination* (1974) 176.

[2] Nancy Friday, *My Secret Garden* (1973).

[3] M. Ploscowe, *Sex and the Law* (1951).

principles apply. Indeed, in the ordinary speech of Western peoples, including the English, morality is almost exclusively concerned with sex. An 'immoral woman' may be truthful, upright, a good cook and an excellent mother. If she sleeps around she is 'immoral'. On the other hand if she is faithful to her husband she can be sluttish and neglectful and spend her spare time shoplifting, yet nothing will be said against her 'morals'.

Philosophers talk differently. To them morality is concerned with preserving life, respecting property, keeping promises. Indeed, for reasons which are a little mysterious, they say very little about sex. Perhaps one clue is that about three-quarters of the great philosophers from Descartes to Wittgenstein have been unmarried. Their writings rarely contain serious discussions of sex.

So we must work out for ourselves what are the underlying themes and aims of that Western sexual morality which underlies much of our law about sex and which has for some time been challenged in the name of freedom and 'doing your own thing'. In the Jewish and Christian[4] thought (followed by Marxism) on which the traditional rules rest, four aims stand out—and by 'aims' I mean rational purposes which could account for the rules, even if the rules have not been consciously adopted or retained for these reasons. One is the need of groups in a hostile world to maintain and increase their numbers. This need makes for rules which forbid those forms of sex which cannot or do not ordinarily lead to children being conceived. These include forms of sex like masturbation or homosexual relations which would not ordinarily be called contraceptive. To violate these rules is thought of, or at least was thought of in early times, as a sort of treason to one's group or race, which in its religious form becomes a tendency to forsake one's own gods or god and go whoring after the gods of strangers.

A second aim of traditional sexual morality is to strengthen the family as the unit within which children are to be reared and which gives society its main structure. The children which the society needs to maintain its identity are to be brought up in a stable environment. This is, on the traditional view, provided by

[4] For a Christian philosopher's view, see A. T. Kolnai, *Sexualethik* (1930).

marriage,[5] by which I mean a permanent union of man and woman of the Western type, or by some similar relation which lasts as long as is necessary for the children to be brought up. Indeed it should last longer, since, in most societies hitherto, women, especially if they devoted many years to bearing and rearing children, could not compete economically with men, and needed support both during the child-bearing years and after. From this point of view those forms of sex which are not consistent with, or do not tend to promote, marriage and the support by a man of his wife and family are condemned. All forms of sex outside marriage are therefore wrong, but especially those which, like pimping and homosexuality, stop men supporting women or make it less likely that they will do so.

A third strand in the traditional morality, not so important as the other two, but quite prominent in religious thinking, is an ascetic one. It is best to abstain from sex altogether, or reduce it to a minimum. This may be connected with a pessimistic view of life, or with an attitude, such as that of early Christianity, which foresees an imminent end to the world. What point is there in marrying or taking on family responsibilities if life as we know it is shortly to end? This ascetic strand merges in another, which is specially prominent in protestant Christianity and Marxism. According to this view indulgence in sex should be minimised because it interferes with the production of material things, which is the main business of life. As the *Peking Workers Daily* puts it, 'Love between man and woman . . . consumes energy and wastes time. On the other hand, love of the party and of the chairman, Mao-Tse-tung, takes no time at all and is in itself a powerful tonic.'[6]

Though the aims of traditional sexual morality are not generally spelled out they will be found for the most part to consist in a desire to promote population growth, marriage or production. But not everyone thinks these objectives important, or at any rate so important that they should override others. There are two competing ideas which have some influence on present-day thinking about sexual morality. One is the idea (generally called

[5] For the difficulties in defining marriage across cultures see P. G. Rivière, 'Marriage: a Reassessment', in *Rethinking Kinship and Marriage* (1971) 57.

[6] Cited by M. Schofield, *Promiscuity* (1976) 89.

utilitarian) that we should adopt those moral principles which
are likely to increase pleasure—either the pleasures of the majority
or the minimum pleasures of all. But far more weighty in Western
societies today is the idea of human rights, especially the right of
each human being to express and develop his or her own personality. In this way of thinking sex, which is an intimate and
sometimes deep expression of one's personality, must have a
prominent place. It is by no means a new thought that we only
live once, and that our basic wants should not be sacrificed to
the demands of society (which in effect means other people). But
this manner of thinking has been given a stimulus by three
relatively new developments.

One of these is the growth of population to a point at which,
all over the world, there are doubts about the need or wish for
a further increase. Is it really necessary for nearly everyone to
marry and have children? Another new factor is the improve-
ment in methods of contraception, which are now more secure
than they once were, and to a lesser extent in techniques of
abortion. If men and women can have sex together with little
likelihood of a child being conceived or, if conceived, being born,
do the traditional rules about sex outside marriage continue to
apply? The third new factor is the growing economic emancipa-
tion of women in industrial societies. If women can support themselves, is it so important that men should marry in the sense in
which marriage carries with it a lifelong duty of support? Would
some more limited or temporary arrangement meet the case?
These three developments make people ask questions which were
hardly asked a hundred years ago. Will the family remain as
central to our society in the new age as in the old? Will marriage
give way to informal living together (cohabitation)? Will marriage, on the contrary, adapt itself so as to cope with the problem
of boredom and the fact that a marriage is now likely to outlast
by many years the period of having and bringing up children, if
indeed the married couple do decide to have children? Or will it
remain essentially unchanged, a rock that outlasts the passing
storms?

No one moral theory has a monopoly of the law, which is a
patchwork of statutes and cases put together at different times
and by people of varying outlook. Some bits reflect one moral
viewpoint, others a different one. Some legislators and judges

think that the law should be neutral in moral questions, others that it should afford a guide to citizens but enforce only minimum standards, others again that it can go further by way of enforcement, at least when strongly supported by public opinion.

As readers of this book will find out, my own view is the second. Law is, I believe, deeply concerned with questions of right and wrong. As Ulpian long ago put it, it is the lawyer's job to cultivate justice, to disseminate a knowledge of what is good and equal, to distinguish the lawful from the unlawful and to profess true philosophy.[7] But the lawyer and legislator must be cautious, in a society in which moral views conflict, in coming to conclusions about where the right lies. He must guard against two dangers. One is the danger of pitching the required standard of conduct too high. The other is that of enforcing rules which serve no reasonable aim, though they may have done so in the past. Sex law in Western Protestant countries has in the past often fallen into disregard through making extreme demands on its subjects.

On the other hand I entirely reject the argument that law should be neutral in moral questions, that it should not seek to enforce morals except when to fail to do so would demonstrably lead to harm. This approach to the subject, though eloquently captured in the debate between Hart and Devlin on the legal enforcement of morals,[8] seems to me misleading, at least so far as sex is concerned. The battle between tradition and freedom in matters of sex is a battle between conflicting notions of morality and social health, not a demarcation dispute between law and morals. How much importance should we attach to population as opposed to copulation, to family life and to the production of things as opposed to pleasure and self-expression? Whatever the balance, law cannot be morally neutral in matters of sex any more than in relation to property or violence.

For these reasons I have prefaced the legal matter in each chapter of the book with a brief outline of the social facts, so far as they could be discovered, and followed it with an account of the moral arguments bearing on the topic under discussion. If that makes an unusual sort of law book my defence is that the

---

[7] Justinian, *Digest* 1.1.1.1.
[8] P. Devlin, *The Enforcement of Morals* (1965); H. L. A. Hart, *Law, Liberty and Morality* (1963); *The Morality of the Criminal Law* (1965).

subject demands it and that lawyers should be readier than they are to cut across the bounds of convention.

One such boundary is that between civil and criminal law. This book mixes them and starts with the civil law of marriage, because marriage is the institution which traditional sexual morality is mainly concerned to uphold. It is only against the background of marriage that one can understand the law about those who deviate and dissent : rapists, prostitutes, homosexuals, pimps. We move, then, from civil to criminal law, leaving aside the fringe industries of pornography and abortion, and end with a chapter on the right to decide for oneself what form of sex life to adopt —what the Germans call the right of sexual self-determination— and the measures to protect the young and weak that are needed to give this right a real content.

This book does no more than broach a vast and, strange as it may seem, neglected subject. I hope that those, from teenage to dotage, who read it will find in it something of interest. It is easy to be silly, romantic or trivial about sex. It is impossible for a man to write about it from a woman's point of view. If any of the many pitfalls have been avoided this is largely due to Ruth Deech, Catherine Collis, Dan Prentice, Peter Skegg, Roger Hood, Stephen Cretney, David Rosettenstein, Adrian Zuckerman, Ken Shelton, Rupert Cross, Hugh Collins and other friends of both sexes, including my children, who have helped me with my inquiries, and also to Barbara Hunter, who typed and retyped the various drafts with speed and stoicism.

I

Marriage

'Sometimes all I need is the air that I breathe and to love you'

  (Hammond/Hazlewood : *The Air that I Breathe*)

1. THE PURPOSE OF MARRIAGE

A book on sex law must start with marriage, because the rules of sexual morality with which Western peoples are familiar are rules which are intended to strengthen marriage as an institution and encourage people to marry and bring up children.

That a male and female who have had a child should remain together until the child is old enough to fend for himself is a feature of many, though not all, animal societies. The link which keeps them together is generally called pair-bonding. The fact that it can exist helps the species to survive since it makes it more likely that the young will live to maturity and will learn to cope with the outside world before they are on their own.

Human children take longer to grow to maturity than other animals and so the need for pair-bonding is that much stronger. There may well be an inborn, genetic basis for our tendency to form these bonds, but they need to be reinforced by social links if they are to be strong enough. Something in the nature of a domestic partnership is needed. Marriage, of the type here considered, is basically an arrangement, varying greatly from one people to another, which gives a social and legal frame to human pair-bonding. It links husband and wife as partners in making and keeping a home. Thus united, husband and wife are intended to remain together and educate their children. But marriage involves two elements which are not always found among other animals. Because it takes children so long to grow up, and because the burden of having and educating children falls mainly on the mother, she needs protection and support both during the period when she raises a family and afterwards.

So that she may be looked after in her later years marriage in Western societies is lifelong, in the sense that it is intended to last until either husband or wife dies. Law and custom vary a great deal in the protection they give married women against desertion and loss of support, but at least where the economic position of women is weak a wife is generally entitled to be supported by her husband until one of them dies, and sometimes after his death. In Western industrial societies, for instance, a wife can generally (in law at least) obtain maintenance if her husband leaves or divorces her. In England, a wife also has a claim that her husband (or former husband) should make reasonable provision for her when he dies.[1] But as women acquire a status more equal to men, and as social security develops, the picture in many countries is changing. In Denmark, for example, it has now become rare for a divorced woman to claim maintenance. In Australia[2] and in some states of the USA, laws provide that a wife has no claim to maintenance during or after marriage unless she can show need. In England today, whatever may be the position during a marriage, it has been said that when the property rights of married people are adjusted on divorce 'husbands and wives come to the judgment seat on a basis of complete equality', so that, for example, a wife can be ordered to transfer part of her capital to her husband.[3] Indeed, if the proposals of the English Law Commission are accepted, there will even during marriage be a duty on each spouse to support the other on a basis of equality.[4] The main impact of this principle, if it is adopted, is likely to be on childless marriages or those where the children are grown up.

Apart from the raising of children and the support of women, marriage has a third purpose which is closely connected with

[1] Inheritance (Provision for Family and Dependants) Act 1975 s. 1(1)(e).
[2] Family Law Act 1975 s. 72, 75(2); P. E. Nygh, *Guide to the Family Law Act 1975* (1975) 96, 98–107.
[3] *Calderbank* v. *Calderbank* 1975 3 All ER 333.
[4] *Family Law: Report on Matrimonial Proceedings*, Law Commission 77 (1976) p. 9.

the theme of this book. Men and women are in sexual competition. Several men often want one woman, or several women one man. Social life would suffer great stress if there were a lifelong sexual league in which everyone played everyone else. One point of marriage, as a social arrangement, is to limit the competition. A man chooses a woman, a woman a man (or they are chosen by parents or in some other way). Thereafter no one is entitled to compete with the husband for the wife or with the wife for the husband.

In the sexual competition marriage is a restrictive practice. A practice of this sort, which implies that husband and wife owe one another a duty to be faithful (at least in a monogamous country) and, equally important, owe it to other husbands and wives not to poach, makes it possible for a couple to be both secure in their minds and relaxed in their bodies.

There is another side to the coin. As a return for the security which each spouse gives the other, each takes the other as he or she is, with all faults, and with the risk that accident, illness or misfortune may pare away the pleasure they take in one another. Though one judge called the words 'for better for worse, for richer for poorer' in the Anglican marriage service a 'cynical jest',[5] they express one of the most treasured aims of marriage: that husband and wife insure one another against the chances of life.

Though the reasons given—child rearing, the support of women, security and mutual commitment—explain why there is such a thing as marriage, they do not ensure that married people will live together until one of them dies. No acceptable motive would be strong enough to secure this. Though in nineteenth-century England decrees for the 'restitution of conjugal rights' were enforceable by imprisonment, according to current ideas of personal freedom husband and wife cannot be compelled to stay together.

The traditional rules of sexual morality, however, go some way towards giving married people a motive to remain together, and unmarried people a motive to marry. These rules, in effect, ban all sexual relations outside marriage.

The ban is backed to a greater or less extent, according to the country, by the sanctions of the criminal law. Some states of the

[5] *Buchler* 1947 P. 25, borne out by *Thurlow* 1976 Fam. 32.

USA go close to making all sex outside marriage a crime, little though they enforce their own laws. In England the area of what the criminal law permits is wider. But even when sex outside marriage is not a crime it is not 'lawful'. This has the result that one cannot make a binding contract to have sexual relations outside marriage.

Sex outside marriage is not necessarily a crime, but marriage is the only relation in which sex is positively lawful. Marriage is also a contract, some of whose elements in English law we must now look at.

2. THE CONTRACT OF MARRIAGE

Marriage is a contract by which a man and a woman undertake to live together until of them dies. An informal agreement whereby a man and a woman agree to live together indefinitely is not a marriage in modern English law, and a formal contract between persons of the same sex, or one of whom is neither a man nor a woman does not make a marriage (living together and homosexual marriage are dealt with in Chapter 2).

The partners must be a man and a woman. A purported marriage between people of the same sex or one of whom has no sex is void and may be declared void even after the death of both parties, at the instance of any interested person, e.g. a later husband or wife of one of them. Generally it is easy to discover a person's sex from physical signs, but there are borderline cases of three sorts. A man should have male chromosomes, male gonads (i.e. testes) and male genital organs. In that case he is legally male even if he would like to be and thinks of himself as a woman. This was decided in the leading case of *Corbett* v. *Corbett*[6] where it was held that April Ashley, the model, was a man for purposes of marriage, though she had a 'sex-change' operation by which an artificial vagina was cut, with which she was able to have intercourse. Hence she could not marry a man. Similarly a woman normally has female chromosomes, female gonads (ovaries) and female genital organs and in that case counts as a woman even if she thinks of herself as a man. The border-

[6] 1971 P. 83; D. K. Smith, 'Transsexualism, sex reassignment, surgery and the law', 56 *Cornell* LR (1971) 963.

line cases occur, first, when a person is male by one test and female by another, for example having a penis but also ovaries. The *Corbett* case suggests that the law of marriage will here go by the external organs.[7] Another type of borderline case is where a person has, according to one test, the features of both sexes, for example both testes and ovaries. In that case, if the external genitals do not decide the matter, the person (a true hermaphrodite) may have neither sex for purposes of marriage and so may not be able to marry. The same is true of persons who lack the features of both sexes, for example having neither testes nor ovaries. It should be noted that this need not prevent a person of doubtful physical make-up being a man or woman for other purposes, such as employment or social security. Nor need the sex be the same for marriage and for the other purposes, since in employment and many other spheres of life what is decisive is not the physical facts but whether a person regards himself as male or female and whether he or she is accepted as such.[7a]

Given that the marriage is not void, what sort of contract is it and what are its terms as they bear on sexual relations?

It is sometimes said that a contract of marriage is unlike an ordinary contract in that (i) many of its standard terms cannot be altered at the will of the parties, (ii) the courts will not enforce it specifically by ordering husband or wife to perform their duties or indirectly by giving damages for the breach of their duties, and (iii) the parties to it cannot bring it to an end by consent. But in fact a contract of marriage is not so different from an ordinary contract as at first sight appears.

Certain terms of the marriage contract cannot be altered in advance. Thus, an engaged couple cannot validly agree not to live together when married.[8] But once they are married they can, if they wish, separate and enter into a valid agreement regulating their separate life.[9] What is more, there are other contracts of which some important terms cannot be altered by the parties, for

---

[7] *Corbett* 1971 P. 83, 106.

[7a] But under the Sex Discrimination Act 1975 ability to bear children is said by one Industrial Tribunal to be the test: *White* v. *British Sugar Corp.* 1977 Ind. Rel. LR 121.

[8] *Brodie* 1917 P. 271.

[9] *Wilson* (1848) 1 HLC 538.

instance hire-purchase contracts.[10] To a certain extent the law of
contract protects us against ourselves.

As regards enforcement, a contract of marriage is in some
ways like a contract of employment. Courts will not order
an employee to work for the employer he has agreed to work for,
nor (generally speaking) order an employer to keep a workman in
his employment against his will.[11] In a like way courts will not
in modern England order a man and a woman to marry, and if
they are married will not order them to perform the sexual duties
they have undertaken. They will not be ordered to consummate
the marriage or to abstain from committing adultery. So much
for the sexual sphere. But in money matters the position is different. A husband can be ordered to pay his wife maintenance
and, in exceptional cases, a wife can be ordered to pay maintenance to her husband.[12] It would not be correct to say, therefore,
that the duties arising from marriage are not legally enforceable.
Some are not, but others are.

It is normally implied in the marriage contract that the husband will support the wife and that the wife will look after the
house, care for the children and feed the family. Why is this not
a contract of employment? A number of reasons can be given.
There is usually no fixed wage. Any informal arrangement as to
housekeeping allowance is not legally binding.[13] The wife's duties,
though extensive, are not precisely defined. Indeed this is precisely the complaint of some supporters of women's liberation.[14]
There are no fixed hours, no overtime. But above all the marriage
contract is not a labour contract because to treat it in this way
would be to demean it. The right of support is not simply a return
for services given, but exists independently of it. It continues even

---

[10] Hire-Purchase Act 1965 s. 17(1)(b), 18(3).

[11] M. R. Freedland. *The Contract of Employment* (1967) 272f; Trade
Union and Labour Relations Act 1974 s. 16; Employment Protection Act
1975 s. 71, 72.

[12] Matrimonial Proceedings (Magistrates' Courts) Act 1960—hereafter
MPA—s. 2(1)(b), (c); Matrimonial Causes Act 1973—hereafter MCA—s. 27;
Gray 1976 3 WLR 181.

[13] *Balfour* 1919 2 KB 571.

[14] S. Cronan, 'Notes from the third year', *Women's Liberation* (1971)
62–5.

[15] Not mere sluttishness according to *Bartholemew* 1952 2 All ER 1035,
but this case, which turns on the fact that the wife did not *intend* to drive
the husband away, is now of doubtful authority.

if for some reason a wife is unable to look after the house or children. For all that, a wife's refusal to perform her duties, like a husband's refusal to support her, would amount to behaviour which is not reasonably tolerable and so ground a divorce.[15] The contract of marriage can, in effect, be set aside when one of the parties has committed a fundamental breach of his or her duties. In the case of marriage, however, as opposed to employment, only the court can set aside the contract, not the parties themselves. But there is nothing unusual about this. For there are systems of contract law, such as the French, under which only the court can set aside an ordinary contract.[16]

Although it is technically true that the parties cannot bring a marriage to an end by consent a divorce has been available since 1971 after two years' separation if the spouses consent and after five years' separation if one of them petitions for it without the other's consent.[17] It is the court, not the parties, that grants the divorce, and the court will not do so if it is satisfied that the marriage has not broken down irretrievably.[18] Though the court is not supposed to be a rubber stamp, under the 1977 Practice Direction it will in most cases virtually become one in undefended divorces in which the special procedure is used.[19] Indeed the marriage contract is in this respect like a contract of partnership, which one partner can dissolve without the consent of the other, rather than most other contracts which remain binding until both or all parties agree that they should end.

Most features of the marriage contract therefore find their parallel in other contracts, such as employment or partnership. But marriage differs from the other contracts in that the ordinary remedies, such as damages, are not available for breach of the contract of marriage. So there has been little occasion for the courts to explore the exact terms of the marriage contract. Nevertheless, the law can with some trouble be extracted from cases and statutes which deal with the matrimonial remedies: nullity, separation, maintenance and divorce. The lawyer must not shy away from the task with the excuse that it is impossible to express

[16] Code civil art. 1184 (3).
[17] MCA 1973 s. 1(2)(d), (e).
[18] MCA 1973 s. 1(4).
[19] *Santos* 1972 Fam. 247; Matrimonial Causes (Amendment No. 2) Rules 1976; Legal Aid (Matrimonial Proceedings) Regulations 1977; Practice Direction Matrimonial Causes Special Procedure No. 2) 1977 1 WLR 320.

the duties of husband and wife precisely. To make the vague less vague is one of his professional duties.

Before setting out the law about sex and marriage four warnings are needed if the cases are to be given their proper value. Until 1948 the courts tended to see the procreation of children as the dominant purpose of marriage. Since then it has been treated as important but not dominant. Until 1964 conduct counted as 'cruel' only when it was aimed at, or intended to injure, the spouse who complained of it. Since then cruelty, and its successor, behaviour which is not reasonably tolerable, has been seen as the sort of behaviour which the other partner cannot reasonably be expected to live with. If, taking account of the personalities of both, the one cannot be expected to put up with the other's behaviour, it does not matter that the offending husband or wife is, through mental disease or for some other reason, not fully responsible.[20]

Since 1971 the grant of a divorce turns on whether a marriage has irretrievably broken down. If it has not, a maintenance or separation order (sometimes called a non-cohabitation order) may be granted, but not a divorce. If on the other hand there is acceptable evidence of a final breakdown of the marriage, then, subject to certain safeguards, divorce is available. It is true that, even for divorce, the old matrimonial offences, adultery, desertion and cruelty (or behaving in such a way that your husband or wife cannot reasonably be expected to live with you)[21] remain in a new role, that of evidence of breakdown. Even so, the change has had an important and beneficial effect on the outlook of courts and lawyers.

Cases decided before 1948, 1964 or 1971 may, therefore, have lost some or all of their force. More generally, ideas about marriage and sex have been changing rather quickly since the Second World War. Whereas once it was thought much worse for a wife to refuse her husband sexual intercourse than for a husband to refuse his wife, and the most recent decisions still reflect this

[20] *Thurlow* 1976 Fam. 32.

[21] Now in MCA 1973 d. 1(1), 1(2)(b). If this conduct is to be described in a word it should be called 'intolerable'. The judicial preference is for 'unreasonable'. It is unreasonable, but not intolerable, to put four spoons of sugar in one's tea: no good reason for the non-sugaring spouse to leave. It is intolerable, but not unreasonable, to behave in a paranoiac way, since a paranoiac cannot behave reasonably.

view,[22] the courts will surely move towards treating the two more equally. Once any variation from the man-on-top 'missionary' position was regarded as unnatural, if not unmentionable, but now sexual variety is openly discussed and all sorts of experiments are common. Though the standard of behaviour in matters of sex remains that of the individual married couple, their standards are apt to be influenced by the freer attitude to sex which now prevails.

3. THE SEXUAL DUTIES OF HUSBAND AND WIFE

Pre-marital sex

Neither husband nor wife is bound to come to marriage a virgin and neither is bound to disclose to the other before or after marriage his or her sexual experience, if any, before marriage.[23] But if either party was at the time of marriage suffering from venereal disease in a communicable form the marriage is voidable and the other spouse may within three years petition for a decree of nullity.[24] The effect of this is to set aside the marriage from the date at which the decree is granted. The same is true if the wife was at the time of marriage pregnant by someone other than her husband.[25] In both these cases a decree of nullity may be granted although the pregnant wife or the spouse suffering from venereal disease did not know her condition at the time of marriage. In neither case can the time limit of three years be extended because the other partner did not learn the facts in time, though if he knew them at the date of marriage his petition will fail.

New Zealand has not for the first time taken the lead in putting women on an equal footing to men. There a 1963 statute lays down that if another woman is pregnant by the husband at the time of marriage the wife can have it set aside.[26]

---

[22] Compare *P.* 1964 3 All ER 919; *B(L)* v. *B(R)* 1965 3 All ER 263 on the man's refusal to have sex with *P(D)* v. *P(J)* 1965 2 All ER 456; *Evans* 1965 2 All ER 789 on the wife's.

[23] 'En mariage trompe qui peut' (in marriage you deceive if you can), says the French proverb.

[24] MCA 1973 s. 12(e).

[25] MCA 1973 s. 12(f).

[26] New Zealand MPA 1963 s. 18(2)(d).

If the husband learns of his wife's pregnancy later and nevertheless confirms or 'approbates'[27] the marriage, his petition will also fail. Approbation bars all claims for nullity on the ground that the marriage is voidable. A spouse is said to approbate when he or she knows that it is open to him or her to have the marriage voided and nevertheless behaves to the other spouse in a way which leads the other reasonably to believe that he or she will not seek to have it set aside. Approbation is no bar unless the court is also satisfied that it would be unjust to the other spouse to grant a decree of nullity.

Generally, when the ground for nullity is pregnancy by another man or venereal disease, the pregnant or diseased partner knows the facts at the time of marriage. She or he ought then to disclose them. If they have not been disclosed before marriage, to fail to make them known to the other *after* marriage may amount to cruelty or behaviour which is not reasonably tolerable and so ground a maintenance or separation order or a divorce.

After marriage

So much for pre-marital sex. During marriage husband and wife have a duty:

(a) To consummate the marriage by having sexual intercourse at least once.

(b) To develop and maintain a mutually tolerable sexual relationship.

(c) To be faithful to one another in matters of sex.

To these can be added two duties specially laid down by statute at present (though they are also implied in (b) and will be absorbed in (b) if the recommendations of the Law Commission are carried out).[28]

(d) A spouse who knows he or she is suffering from a venereal disease must not insist on or, when the other spouse is not aware of the disease, permit sexual intercourse between them.[29]

[27] MCA 1973 s. 13(1).
[28] Family Law: Report on Matrimonial Proceedings: Law Commission 77 (1976) p. 9–11, 154.
[29] MPA 1960 s. 1(1)(e).

(e) A husband must not compel his wife to submit herself to prostitution or be guilty of conduct which is likely to result in and does result in the wife's submitting herself to prostitution.[30]

These will be dealt with in turn.

(a) *The duty to consummate the marriage*

A marriage which has not been consummated is voidable. This means that it can be set aside by the court if the reason why it has not been consummated is (i) the wilful refusal of one spouse to consummate it and the other petitions for court for a decree of nullity,[31] or (ii) that one or both of the spouses is incapable of consummating it and either of them petitions for nullity.[32] The legal effect of a decree of nullity is again to set aside the marriage from the date of the decree.[33]

Both husband and wife have a duty to consummate the marriage. Though not explicitly set out, this is assumed in the cases and shown by the phrase 'wilful refusal' and the fact that a spouse can have the marriage set aside because of the other spouse's wilful refusal to consummate, but not of his own.

Sexual intercourse. To consummate the marriage means to have sexual intercourse at least once. The requirements for this are stricter than are needed to establish a case of rape. The husband's penis must penetrate the wife's vagina if not to its full extent at least to a certain depth,[34] and he must be able to keep up the penetration for a reasonable length of time.[35] A slight penetration, or one which lasts only a moment or two, is not enough. But it is not necessary that the husband or wife should have an orgasm.[36]

---

[30] MPA 1960 s. 1(1)(g).

[31] MCA 1973 s. 12(b).

[32] MCA 1973 s. 12(a).

[33] MCA 1973 s. 16; J. Jackson, *The Formation and Annulment of Marriage* (1969) 306. For canon law, P. Flood, OSB, *The Dissolution of Marriage: Non-Consummation as a ground for Annulment or Dissolution of Marriage* (1962).

[34] *D---e* v. *A---g* (1845) 1 Rob. Eccl. 279; 163 ER 1030.

[35] *W* v. *W* 1967 3 All ER 178.

[36] *R* v. *R* 1952 1 All ER 1194. The contrary has been held for the husband in Ontario: *Miller* 1947 3 DLR 354 (influenced by *Cowen* 1946 P. 36 below n. 45).

It has been said that intercourse must be 'ordinary and complete, not partial and imperfect'.[37] The reason given is that neither husband nor wife would generally speaking be satisfied with less, so they would resort to adulterous relations unless the marriage could be set aside.[38] In the case of rape or adultery, on the other hand, any such reason is beside the point, and so the slightest penetration is enough.[39] Besides being 'complete' in this limited sense, the intercourse must be 'ordinary'. Hence though a woman with a vagina too short for complete intercourse may consummate the marriage when she has had it artificially lengthened,[40] a marriage cannot be consummated with a vagina which is wholly artificial[41] or, if it comes to that, a dildo.

On the other hand, the intercourse does not have to be such that a child could be conceived.[42] Although procreation is an important aim of marriage, it is not so overwhelmingly important that a marriage can be annulled merely because the couple cannot have children, or must be affirmed merely because they can. A marriage can be consummated though husband or wife is not fertile. Even if the wife has no uterus, the marriage can be consummated, provided that her vagina is big enough for proper intercourse.[43]

From this it follows, if the law is consistent, that a marriage can be consummated even if husband or wife use contraceptives and even if, as with a sheath, the contraceptive prevents (or usually prevents) the husband's semen from being deposited in the wife's vagina. This was finally decided by the House of Lords in *Baxter*[44] in 1948, after earlier cases, especially *Cowen*,[45] in which it was held that, because procreation was unlikely (though not actually impossible), sex with a sheath could not amount to consummation. The same principle applies to *coitus interruptus*,[46] when the husband withdraws before orgasm (the 'British Rail' technique), and to other forms of contraception, whether they

[37] *D---e* v. *A---g* (1845) 1 Rob. Eccl. 279, 297.
[38] Ibid.
[39] *Dennis* 1955 P. 153.
[40] *D---e* v. *A---g* (1845) 1 Rob. Eccl. 279.
[41] *SY* v. *SY* 1963 P. 37.
[42] *Baxter* 1948 AC 274.
[43] *SY* v. *SY* 1963 P. 37.
[44] 1948 AC 274.
[45] 1946 P. 36.
[46] *White* 1948 P. 330.

work, like the oral pill, by preventing ovulation, or mechanically. It will also apply to a spouse who has himself sterilised before or after marriage but remains capable of erection and penetration. A contrary decision in 1947 reflects the greater importance attached by the courts before 1948 to the possibility of having children.[47]

Just as a marriage can be consummated though contraceptives are used, so it may not have been consummated though the wife conceives a child by the husband. If the husband does not enter the wife, but makes her pregnant by having an emission while he is lying between her legs, this (fecundation *ab extra*) does not amount to consummation.[48] Nor, on this reasoning, is a marriage consummated if the wife is artificially made pregnant from her husband's semen (AIH),[49] or from a mixture of her husband's and a donor's. Still less, of course, is the marriage consummated if the wife is inseminated by seed from a donor alone (AID). But if the husband agrees to these methods of insemination, whether by himself, a donor or a mixture, he is likely to be held to have 'approbated' the marriage.

If, then, sexual intercourse takes place, the marriage has been consummated; if not, it has not been, even if the wife bears the husband's child. But, despite consummation, if one of the spouses insists on using contraceptive methods against the will of the other, he or she may have broken the duty to maintain a mutually tolerable sexual relationship, and have behaved in a way which is not reasonably tolerable.[50] In principle a refusal to use a reasonably safe contraceptive method when there is a good reason to avoid pregnancy may have the same legal effect. A decision which denied this on the ground that the husband's religious scruples made it reasonable for him to refuse[51] seems to confuse the question whether it was reasonable for the husband to act as he did with the question whether it was reasonable to expect the wife to tolerate his behaviour.

Wilful refusal. Wilful refusal to consummate a marriage means a settled and definite decision arrived at without just excuse not to

[47] *J.* 1947 P. 158.
[48] *Clarke* 1943 2 All ER 540. Cf. *Russell* 1924 AC 687, *Ampthill Peerage Case* 1976 2 WLR 777.
[49] *REL* v. *EL* 1949 P. 211.
[50] *Baxter* 1948 AC 274, 290.
[51] *Archard, The Times* 19 April 1972.

have intercourse.[52] Such matters as health, or the fact that one spouse promised the other to go through a separate religious ceremony and has not done so, may make it reasonable to postpone consummation until there is no danger to health in consummating it, or until the religious ceremony has been held.[53]

Can an agreement not to consummate the marriage amount to a just cause for not consummating it? In general such an agreement if made before or after marriage is void for the same reason that an agreement before marriage not to live together after marriage is void.[54] But in both cases this is subject to qualification:

(a) An agreement to live apart for a time while there is a good reason for doing so, for example because the husband's or wife's employment requires it, may be valid.

(b) Though a woman of 62 may be 'very keen on sexual intercourse',[55] in the case of an elderly couple there is no objection to a companionate marriage, and so no reason why they should not properly agree to live 'as brother and sister',[56] but a mental reservation on the part of one spouse is not enough.[57] The same is true if one spouse is impotent or incapable at the time of marriage and the other after marriage approbates the marriage.[58] If this is the position, a decree of nullity will be refused, and the marriage will continue in existence, but the spouse who has approbated the marriage cannot then insist on consummation. There is therefore in effect a valid agreement between the spouses not to consummate.

(c) In other cases an agreement before marriage not to consummate it is invalid and either spouse may insist on its being consummated.[59] But he (or she) may instead after marriage accept the agreement and approbate the marriage.[60]

---

[52] *Horton* 1947 2 All ER 871 (HL). A Manitoba case says this can be inferred from refusal to live together: *G* 1974 1 WWR 79.

[53] *Jodla* 1960 1 All ER 625.

[54] *Brodie* 1917 P. 271.

[55] *Slon* 1969 P. 122, 131. There is no need for older people to give up sex: L. D. Scheingold and N. N. Wagner, *Sound Sex and the Aging Heart* (1974).

[56] *Morgan* 1952 P. 92, 101; *Scott* 1959 P. 103n.

[57] *Morgan* 1952 P. 92, 102.

[58] *Morgan* 1952 P. 92, 102; MCA 1973 s. 13(1).

[59] *Brodie* 1917 P. 271.

[60] *Scott* 1959 P. 103n.; *Finegan* 1917 33 TLR 173.

(d) After marriage spouses who are living together cannot validly agree to live apart or not to have sexual intercourse. But if they have already separated or are on the point of separation they can settle between themselves the terms of the separation and of any future separation.[61]

Incapacity to consummate. If either or both spouses are incapable of consummating it, the marriage is voidable, and either may petition for nullity.[62] The incapacity or impotence must exist at the time of the marriage. If the spouses were capable, it makes no difference that one became incapable later,[63] and if they were incapable then, it makes no difference that they had intercourse, or even a child, before marriage.[64] The cause may be physical or mental. A wife who has an 'invincible repugnance' to intercourse with her husband is incapable of consummating the marriage.[65] But the incapacity must be permanent and incurable. If it could only be cured by a dangerous operation, or one which the impotent spouse refuses to undergo, it counts as 'incurable'.[66] The incapacity need not, however, amount to being unable to have sexual intercourse with *anyone*. It is enough if the husband cannot have intercourse with the wife or the wife with the husband: the incapacity may be relative to her or him (*quoad hanc, quoad hunc*).[67] Impotence is not made out simply because the first attempt at intercourse, or the first few attempts, fail.

Following canon law, an incapable spouse may petition on the ground of his or her own incapacity.[68] But this is subject to the rule of approbation, which also applies, of course, to a petition by the spouse who is capable of consummating the marriage.[69]

---

[61] *Wilson* (1848) 1 HLC 538; *Harrison* 1910 1 KB 35, *Re Meyrick's Settlement* 1921 1 Ch. 311;
[62] MCA 1973 s. 12(a).
[63] *Brown* (1828) 1 Hag. Eccl. 523.
[64] *Dredge* 1947 1 All ER 29.
[65] *G* 1924 AC 249 (Scotland).
[66] *W* v. *H*(1861) 2 Sw. and Tr. 240; *G* (1908) 25 TLR 328–9; *M* 1956 3 All ER 769 (vaginismus: wife incapable, though operation and psychiatric treatment might cure it); contrast *S* 1954 3 All ER 736 (only removal of hymen needed).
[67] *Bury's Case* (1558) 2 Dyer 179 a; *N* (1853) 2 Rob. Eccl. 625; 163 ER 1435; *G* 1924 AC 349.
[68] MCA 1973 s. 512(a); *Harthan* 1949 P. 115.
[69] *Nash* 1940 P. 60.

(b) *The duty to develop and maintain a mutually tolerable sexual relationship*

This duty, which I shall call the mutual duty, was hardly recognised until recently and even now is nowhere set out in so many words. A critic might argue that the law of marriage recognises only the negative duty not to behave in matters of sex in an unreasonable way. But it is better, surely, to put it positively. In the contract of employment the 'principle of cooperation', first set out by an American writer, has been adopted by the courts as a guide to the duties of employers and employees.[70] Marriage can hardly involve less of a duty to cooperate than employment, and sex is central to marriage. It is this duty of cooperation as applied to sex in marriage that I propose to describe as the duty to develop and maintain a mutually tolerable sexual relationship. The duty has a positive and a negative side. The positive side is that each must adjust to the needs of the other partner so far as he or she reasonably can. The negative side is that each must refrain from imposing on the other demands which the other finds intolerable. Such a duty was certainly not recognised a hundred years ago. According to Victorian standards, a wife was simply expected to 'submit to her husband's embraces' and was not thought to have any rights in matters of sex except perhaps the right to have children if she wished. She was held to consent to sexual intercourse when she married. This consent could not be withdrawn and so a husband, apart from exceptions, could not (and still cannot) be guilty of raping his wife, however unsuitable the time and place in which he forces her to submit. According to a decision which must mark the summit of the English disregard for logic he can, however, be found guilty of indecently assaulting his wife.[71]

Although the rule about rape survives, it can now only be justified on the basis that it is undesirable for the criminal courts to pry into the exact degree of force or pressure used by a husband in order to have intercourse with his wife. Such matters are best raised, if at all, in matrimonial proceedings under the

[70] *Secretary of State for Employment* v. *ASLEF* (No. 2) 1972 ICR 19; M. Freedland, *The Contract of Employment* (1976) 27–32.

[71] Hale 1 PC 627: *Miller* 1954 2 QB 282. She should be thankful for small mercies. Her husband may not kidnap her: *Jackson* 1891 1 QB 671.

heading of cruelty or conduct which it not reasonably tolerable. Once matrimonial proceedings have been started in which a wife claims divorce or separation, this reason does not apply, and it would be rational to say that she has thereby withdrawn her consent to intercourse. It has, however, been held that while a husband can be guilty of rape once a decree nisi has been granted[72] or a court has made an order for judicial separation, if the parties are actually living apart,[73] merely to begin proceedings for divorce or separation does not revoke the wife's consent.[74] If the spouses separate under a voluntary agreement, the wife can presumably be raped, since, depending on the terms of the agreement, she has no duty to live with her husband and so no duty to submit to sexual intercourse.

The talk of 'consent' is of course pure fiction. A wife does not, merely by going through a ceremony of marriage, consent to sexual intercourse at any time or place which her husband may choose. What she and he agree to do is to develop and maintain a mutually tolerable sexual relationship. It may seem a little unambitious to put the duty so low. But the law is here concerned with minimum standards of conduct, not with the conduct of the ideal husband or wife. For that reason it is put as a duty to try to ensure a tolerable relationship, not to satisfy the other partner. The duty is framed with a view to the sort of behaviour which is commonly taken by courts to be a breach of marital obligations, which can be best summed up in the phrase 'highly inconsiderate'.[75] For example, refusal of sexual intercourse by a wife over a period and without good reason is a breach of marital duty,[76] and despite cases which seem to deny this,[77] in equity the same must be true of the husband. Though a man cannot get an erection to order, he can be responsive to his wife's wishes in matters of sex. It is a breach of duty to make excessive demands on the other spouse, as when a husband insists on sex after every

---

[72] *O'Brien* 1974 3 All ER 663.

[73] *Clarke* 1949 2 All ER 448.

[74] *Miller* 1954 2 QB 282. By Michigan Crim. Cod. s. 520J(3) spouses can be guilty of sexual assault (including what we call rape) against one another if living apart and if one has filed suit for maintenance or divorce.

[75] 'Grave lack of consideration', *Holborn* 1941 1 All ER 32.

[76] *Synge* 1900 P. 180; 1901 P. 317; *Hutchinson* 1963 1 All ER 1; *Slon* 1969 P. 122.

[77] *P* 1964 3 All ER 919; *B(L)* v. *B(R)* 1965 3 All ER 263.

meal or fails to take into account that at 57 his wife's desires have faded, or a wife badgers her man by pulling his hair and ears in the early hours of the morning in order to arouse him.[78]

It will likewise be a breach of marital duty to insist on having intercourse in a way which shows a lack of consideration for the other spouse. An example is when a husband persistently uses contraceptives though he knows that his wife is very keen to have a child.[79]

For the sake of variety one partner may ask the other to try a new position or to experiment with sex in the mouth (fellation), or in the anus (buggery), or licking (cunnilingus), or masturbation or a 'swinging' form of sex in which the spouses exchange partners with another couple or group. Merely to make a suggestion of this sort is not the breach of any marital duty.[80] If the other partner is willing, there is no reason why spouses should not experiment. To this buggery or sodomy is an exception, because by a strange legal quirk sodomy between man and woman, including husband and wife, remains a crime punishable with life imprisonment.[81] Indeed a sentence of eighteen months for this crime was passed as recently as 1971.[82] Even so, a wife who agreed to sodomy could not, when sodomy was a distinct ground of divorce, later complain of it as a matrimonial offence, though courts were reluctant to hold that an inexperienced wife had really consented.[83]

The general principle that a spouse cannot later complain of a sexual experiment to which she or he has agreed is not in doubt. What is debatable is whether, if she (or he) changes her mind and refuses to experiment, this can amount to a breach of marital duty. Perhaps the safest view is that agreement in a matter of sexual experiment is never final. If it is withdrawn, because one of the partners finds that, after all, he or she does not like the idea, the other spouse should accept this. To pester or insist beyond the point at which it has become clear that the other finds

[78] *Holborn* 1947 1 All ER 32; *Chapper, The Times* 25 May 1966; *Willan* 1960 1 WLR 624.
[79] *Knott* 1955 P. 249 (withdrawal); *P* 1965 2 All ER 456; *Rice* 1948 1 All ER 188, 191.
[80] *Holborn* 1947 1 All ER 32.
[81] Sexual Offences Act 1956 s. 12(1).
[82] *Harris* (1971) 55 CAR 290.
[83] *Statham* 1929 P. 131; *Bampton* 1959 1 WLR 842; *T* 1964 P. 85.

• •

the experiment revolting or simply unnatural may be a serious breach of the mutual sexual duty. It is to seek to impose on the other spouse a sexual relationship which she (or he) does not find tolerable and which her husband (or his wife) knows she (or he) finds intolerable.[84]

In sum, the duty of mutual adjustment requires each partner to take the other's temperament into account and, so far as physique (falling short of incapacity or impotence) is concerned, to take him or her as he or she is.[85] The same is true of mental traits, like wanting children, but not, it seems, of neurotic dislike for sex or for the other spouse. Given the temperaments of the spouses, each must meet the other some of the way. Thus, an oversexed husband should reduce his demands, an undersexed wife accept more than she would be inclined to. But there is no 'reasonable' standard of sexual behaviour such as the intercouse twice a week of the old maxim.[86] As Lord Merriman put it, 'there is the greatest diversity of standards between one set of spouses and another as to what is a normal standard of sexual intercourse. What will be regarded as grossly excessive demands by one wife will be regarded as quite normal and reasonable by another wife ... There are things strictly outside what may be called normal sexual intercourse which will be regarded by one wife as so revolting as to be unmentionable, whereas other couples will regard them as nothing more than natural, normal love-making.'[87] The same is true of the wife's demands on the husband.

Are there any limits to the principle that the spouses must take account of one another's temperament in matters of sex and must take one another 'for better for worse'? Neither can complain of an impotence which did not exist at the time of marriage but which comes on later through age, disease or accident. But what of mental changes? Suppose that, as sometimes happens after childbirth, a wife conceives a settled dislike of sexual intercourse with her husband. Though there is a decision which holds that a wife's refusal of intercourse, based on 'invincible repugnance',

[84] *Holborn* 1947 1 All ER 32; *Raw* 1947 WN 96 (insistence on masturbation).
[85] *White* 1948 P. 340; *King* 1953 AC 124, 147.
[86] *Bis ruere in hebdomade.*
[87] *Holborn* 1947 1 All ER 32–3.

does not amount to cruelty,[88] this perhaps reflects an outdated view of cruelty (or now behaviour which is not reasonably tolerable).

Suppose, again, that the mental quirk consists in the desire of the husband to be a woman (transsexual) or to dress like a woman (transvestite)? Assuming that his wishes are beyond control, it was decided by the Court of Appeal that a husband who tried to conceal them from his wife was not guilty of cruelty. But this also fails to recognise that behaviour which would be cruel or not reasonably tolerable in a responsible husband or wife is no less so because the spouse is not fully responsible.[89]

A breach of the mutual sexual duty, for example a persistent refusal of sexual intercourse without good cause, has, if it is serious, or as lawyers said in relation of cruelty, 'grave and weighty',[90] the following legal consequences :

(i) It amounts to behaviour such that the other spouse cannot reasonably be expected to live with the spouse who is at fault, and will ground a divorce unless the court is satisfied that the marriage has *not* broken down irretrievably.[91]

(ii) It amounts to cruelty and, if it affects the health of the other spouse, grounds a matrimonial order in the Magistrates' Court, separation or maintenance.[92] If the Law Commission proposals[93] are enacted, it will be treated as conduct which is not reasonably tolerable and will ground an order for maintenance, but, in the absence of violence of threats of violence, not a 'personal protection' or 'exclusion' order.

(iii) It affords a good cause for the other spouse to leave, so that the separating spouse is not guilty of desertion.[94]

(iv) It may amount to 'constructive desertion', so that, if the other spouse leaves, the spouse at fault, who remains behind,

[88] *Fowler* 1952 2 TLR 143, distinguished in *Forbes* 1956 P. 16; cf. *Beevor* 1945 2 All ER 200 (husband not justified in leaving—also an outmoded decision); *Katz* 1972 3 All ER 219.
[89] *Bohnel* 1960 1 WLR 590.
[90] *Saunders* 1965 P. 499; *Mulhouse* 1966 P. 39.
[91] *Walsham* 1940 P. 350 (refusal, withdrawal); *Sheldon* 1966 P. 62 (refusal).
[92] MCA 1973 s. 1(2)(b), 1 (4).
[93] Law Commission 77 p. 154f.
[94] *Sheldon* 1966 P. 62; *Hughes* (1966) 110 Sol. Jo. 349 distinguishing *Weatherley* 1947 AC 628.

is treated as guilty of desertion.[95] Desertion is, in turn, a basis for a matrimonial order or, if it lasts for two years immediately before the other spouse presents a petition, for divorce.[96]

(c) *The duty to be faithful in matters of sex*

'Let mutual fidelity continue until death.'[97] The duty of each partner to be faithful to the other in his or her sexual behaviour is one of the marks of (monogamous) marriage and, in a different form, it exists even when a man is allowed several wives or a woman several husbands. In English law the breaches of this duty fall into three groups: adultery, sexual intimacy other than adultery and provocative friendships. These will be discussed in turn.

(i) *Adultery.* A husband or wife commits adultery if he or she voluntarily has sexual intercourse during marriage with a person of the opposite sex other than his or her spouse.[98] Sexual intercourse for purposes of adultery is defined in the same way as for rape. Some penetration by the man's penis of the woman's vagina is required, but it need not be a full or deep penetration, nor need it last for more than a moment.[99] Part entry is enough, and adultery has been found when the husband and the other woman occupied the same bedroom and were on close terms, though the woman's hymen was (according to the evidence) intact.[100] If the man tries but fails to enter the woman, the married partner to the act is guilty of a breach of his or her marital duty but not adultery.[101] Again, for a wife to allow herself to be artificially impregnated by someone other than her husband is a breach of her marital duty, but a Scottish court has held that since there is no penetration, it does not amount to adultery.[102]

Sexual intercourse is not adultery unless the married partner to the act consents. If a married woman is raped, she does not

[95] *Slon* 1969 P. 122.

[96] MPA 1960 s. 1(1)(a), MCA 1973 s. 1(2)(c).

[97] Laws of Manu 9.101.

[98] *Rayden on Divorce* (12th ed. 1974 by J. Jackson and others) 189.

[99] *Rutherford* 1923 AC 1, 11 as explained in *Dennis* 1955 P. 153.

[100] *Thompson* 1938 P. 162.

[101] *Sapsford* 1954 P. 394, 399, but Karminski J. found, not very convincingly, that adultery had been committed in this case.

[102] *Maclennan* 1958 Scots LT 12.

commit adultery.[103] If a married man rapes a woman, he commits adultery but she, even if married, does not. But since sexual intercourse is usually voluntary, it is for a wife who has had intercourse with a man who is not her husband to prove that she did not consent.[104] Though a 1962 decision held that a woman was not guilty of adultery when through mental disease she did not know that she was doing wrong,[105] this is probably a mistake. The test is whether the conduct would amount to adultery in a responsible person. It will not do so if the wife's resistance has been overcome as a result of drink or drugs which have been given her against her will.[106] But if she takes drink or drugs voluntarily, knowing that she may feel amorous as a result, she will be held to have consented to the intercourse, though at that later stage she did not realise what she was doing.[107]

In many societies adultery is one of the most serious crimes, and often carries the death penalty. This is because adultery is conceived as an offence, not just against the other spouse, but against the family and society. It is an offence against the family because it leads to the danger that the children of strangers will be accepted as members of an adulterous wife's family, and for this reason among others a double standard has long been, and to some extent still is, accepted. According to this, it is far more serious for a wife than for a husband to commit adultery.[108] A second reason for severe penalties against adultery is that it leads to family feuds which threaten the peace of society. But though adultery is (theoretically) a crime in many states of the US,[109] and was made one in several British colonies, it was never a common law offence but only one punishable in the church courts. It still has important effects in civil law.

First, adultery is a ground on which a spouse may petition for divorce provided that he or she also shows that he or she finds

[103] *Redpath* 1950 1 All ER 600.
[104] *Redpath* 1950 1 All ER 600.
[105] *S* 1962 P. 133. Rayden 190 holds that this case is wrongly decided. Even if such conduct is not adultery it may amount to behaviour which is not reasonably tolerable.
[106] *Benton* 1958 P. 12, 21, 31–3.
[107] *Goshawk* (1962) 109 Sol. Jo. 290.
[108] The Divorce and Matrimonial Causes Act 1857 s. 27, 33 adopted the double standard for adultery. See also P. Devlin, *The Enforcement of Morals* (1965) 70.
[109] R. M. Perkins, *Criminal Law* (2nd ed. 1969) 378.

it intolerable to live with the partner who has committed adultery.[110] In this case the court must grant a divorce unless it is satisfied on all the evidence that the marriage has *not* broken down irretrievably. The bars which at present prevent a matrimonial order from being made in the Magistrates' Court—connivance, conduct conducing to adultery, condonation and the adultery of the complaining party—do not prevent a decree of divorce or judicial separation from being granted. Does this mean that it makes no difference if the spouse who petitions for divorce or separation has consented to the adultery in question?

At first sight it seems to make no difference. Though the point has not finally been settled, it seems that the adultery complained of does not have to be the reason why the spouse who brings the petition finds it intolerable to live with the other. All that is necessary is that he or she, in his or her own mind, does find the common life unbearable.[111] The test is subjective, and though one can imagine a case in which a spouse *pretended* to find life intolerable (for example, in order to obtain the tax advantages of a divorce), if he or she is honest, a statement that he or she finds it intolerable to live with the other spouse settles the matter. It may be said, then, that since it does not matter whether it was the adultery that made life seem intolerable or something else, trivial or important, like picking one's nose or taking hard drugs, it can make no difference whether the adultery was committed with the consent of the complaining spouse. But this is surely wrong. Though the adultery need not be the reason why the other spouse finds continued life together intolerable, it is mentioned because it is the sort of behaviour which in general (though not necessarily in this particular case) may have that effect. Adultery committed with consent need not have any such tendency. The husband and wife may just be looking for variety. If, after one has learned of the other's adultery, the spouses live together for periods which together make up six months or more, the adultery cannot be relied on in a petition for divorce.[112] Apart from this, however, the fact that they live together after the adultery has become known to the other spouse is not to be taken as evidence

---

[110] MCA s. 1(2)(a).

[111] *Goodrich* 1971 1 WLR 1142; *Cleary* 1974 1 All ER 498; *Carr* 1974 1 WLR 1534.

[112] MCA s. 2(3).

that the other partner finds it tolerable to live with the spouse who has committed adultery.

Whatever the court in which proceedings are brought, clear proof of adultery is demanded. In the absence of a confession the evidence may consist of the transmission of VD from one spouse to the other, the statement of an inquiry agent, a blood test on an illegitimate child, or the birth of a child to the wife too long after the husband could have had intercourse with her.[113] Some cases have laid down that adultery, or other issues in matrimonial cases, must be proved beyond reasonable doubt,[114] as in a criminal trial. The contrary view, long adopted in Australia,[115] is now probably law in England[116] and has common sense on its side, since divorce or separation is not a punishment, and for a court to find that someone has committed adultery is a serious matter, but no more so than finding that a doctor has been guilty of professional negligence, which can be settled on a balance of probabilities.[117]

Secondly, adultery is a ground on which the other spouse (in practice the wife) may apply to the Magistrates' Court for a matrimonial order (viz. for maintenance of separation).[118] If the Law Commission proposals are enacted, adultery will no longer be a separate ground for an order, nor will the applicant's adultery be a bar. Adultery will simply be behaviour which by itself or with other incidents may amount to behaviour which is not reasonably tolerable and so ground a maintenance order. The applicant's adultery will be part of the 'conduct of the parties in relation to the marriage' which the court must take into account in deciding whether to order maintenance and how much, 'so far as it is just to take it into account'.[119]

Under the present law, however, the court must not make a maintenance or separation order on the ground of adultery unless it is satisfied that there are no bars. There is a bar if the complaining spouse has condoned or connived at, or by wilful neglect

---

[113] *Preston-Jones* 1951 AC 391 (360 days).

[114] *Ginesi* 1948 P. 179.

[115] *Watts* (1953) 89 Commonwealth LR 200.

[116] By inference from Family Law Reform Act 1969 s. 26 (rebutting presumption of legitimacy).

[117] Cross, *Evidence* (4th ed. 1974) 102.

[118] MPA 1960 s. 1(1)(d).

[119] Law Commission 77 p. 9, 154.

or misconduct conduced to, the act of adultery complained of.[120] Nor can the court make an order if the complaining spouse is proved to have committed an act of adultery during the marriage unless, again, the other spouse has condoned or connived at or conduced to the adultery in question.[121]

A full discussion of this rather technical branch of the law would be out of place, especially as the bars are likely to be abolished when the jurisdiction of the Magistrates' Court is next reformed. Connivance means consent.[122] Condonation is a reinstatement of the spouse who has committed adultery such as indicates forgiveness.[123] But to resume living together, to 'kiss and make up' for up to three months, does not amount to condonation.[124] Wilful neglect or misconduct which contributes to adultery by the other spouse is said to 'conduce' to it.[125] Refusal of sexual intercourse without good cause may 'conduce' to adultery;[126] so may the conduct of a husband who tells his wife to leave, knowing that she is likely to live with another man, even though he may not want her to do so.[127]

(ii) *Sexual intimacy other than adultery.* Apart from adultery, a husband who has sexual relations with someone other than his wife and a wife who has relations with a person other than her husband is guilty of a breach of marital duty, unless the other spouse consents. It does not matter whether the relations are with the same or the other sex. Thus, it is not permissible for a wife to masturbate a man other than her husband or for a husband to allow a woman other than his wife to masturbate him.[128] The same is true, in principle, of other sexual acts. Indeed, even to kiss, flirt or pet in such a way that the sexual organs are not involved may be a breach of the duty of fidelity which husband and wife owe one another. Whether they are in a particular case will depend on such points as whether the kiss was passionate, the

[120] MPA 1960 s. 2(3)(a).
[121] MPA 1960 s. 2(3)(b); *Gray* 1976 3 WLR 181.
[122] *Godfrey* 1964 P. 287.
[123] S. Cretney, *Principles of Family Law* (2nd ed.) 112–15.
[124] MCA 1965 s. 42(1)(2).
[125] *Brown* 1956 P. 438.
[126] *Callister* (1947) 63 TLR 503.
[127] *Haynes* 1960 2 All ER 401.
[128] *Sapsford* 1954 P. 394.

flirtation serious, the conventions in the social circle in which the spouses move strict and the other partner sensitive or jealous.[129]

As in the case of adultery these sexual intimacies have a different legal effect in the Magistrates' Court and before a court which has power to grant a divorce.

On a petition for divorce or judicial separation a sexual infidelity other than adultery may be shown to amount to behaviour such that the petitioning spouse cannot reasonably be expected to live with the other spouse.

If, however, they amount to persistent cruelty to the other spouse, they form a ground on which a Magistrates' Court may grant a 'matrimonial order' for maintenance or separation. Cruelty has been found when a husband attempted to commit sodomy with a man,[130] when he was convicted of an indecent assault on the wife's child,[131] and when he was sentenced for incest and indecent exposure.[132]

If the Law Commission's proposals become law, the Magistrates' Court will be able to grant a maintenance order if the infidelities amount to conduct which by itself or together with other incidents is such that the other spouse cannot reasonably be expected to live with the spouse who is guilty of them.[133]

(iii) *Provocative friendships.* Even if a husband or wife is not committing adultery or some other sexual act outside marriage he may create in the mind of his wife or of other people the impression that he is. What is in fact only a strong friendship may look like a sexual relationship. For a spouse openly to behave in this way is a breach of the duty to be faithful, since that includes a duty not to appear unfaithful, or at least not to flaunt an apparently intimate relationship. Thus it may amount to cruelty (or behaviour which is not reasonably tolerable) for a wife to form a friendship with another woman such that, though lesbianism cannot be proved, her husband reasonably suspects it and suffers grave anxiety as a result.[134] While the other partner's

[129] *Ash* 1972 Fam. 135.
[130] *Moss* 1916 P. 155.
[131] *Cooper* 1955 P. 99.
[132] *Boyd* 1955 P. 126; cf. *Crawford* 1956 P. 195.
[133] Law Commission 77 p. 154.
[134] *Spicer* 1954 3 All ER 208; *Windeatt* 1962 1All ER 776.

belief must be a reasonable one based on evidence and not on hearsay, the conduct is none the less cruel, or not reasonably tolerable, because the spouse affected by it is sensitive or highly strung. In *Buchler*,[135] a decision which has been criticised on the facts, a farmer husband formed an intimate friendship, which was not shown to be homosexual, with his pigman. This was held not to amount to cruelty to his neglected wife, but the principle was accepted that it may be cruelty (and so now conduct which is not reasonably tolerable) to form such a provocative friendship.

(iv) *Duty in regard to venereal disease.* It is a marital wrong for a spouse who knows he or she is suffering from venereal disease to insist on sexual intercourse with the other, or to permit it when the other spouse is not aware of the presence of the disease. It does not matter how serious the disease is.[136] If the duty is broken, a Magistrates' Court may at present make a matrimonial order for separation or maintenance. If the proposals of the Law Commission become law, however, the breach of this duty will, in the absence of violence or threatened violence, ground only a maintenance order, and then only if it amounts to conduct which is not reasonably tolerable by the other spouse.[137]

The existing statute mentions sexual intercourse, but other sexual contacts falling short of intercourse may also spread venereal disease. In such cases insistence on sexual contact, or allowing it without mentioning the VD, may, at least if the disease is syphilis or, perhaps, gonorrhoea, amount to conduct which is cruel or not reasonably tolerable. Such deliberate conduct is also, in my opinion, a civil wrong (tort) if serious harm is caused by it, and will give rise to a claim for damages unless the other spouse knows and consents.[138] The fictitious consent prevents a husband from being charged with the rape of his wife should surely not be extended to actions in tort. A husband in any case is not deemed, even by a fiction, to consent to intercourse with his wife at all times and in all circumstances.

---

[135] 1941 P. 25.
[136] MPA 1960 s. 1(1)(e).
[137] Law Commission 77 p. 154.
[138] Cf. *Clarence* (1888) 22 QBD 23, 52 indicating that such conduct by a husband, if malicious, may amount to rape.

(v) *Duty in regard to prostitution.* As will be seen in Chapter 4, a husband whose wife is a prostitute is presumed to be living on the earnings of prostitution (which is a serious offence) if he lives with her or is habitually in her company.[139] Apart from this, a husband who compels his wife to submit herself to prostitution, or who is guilty of conduct which is likely to result in and does result in her submitting herself to prostitution (e.g. by sending her to live in a brothel), commits a breach of marital duty for which the wife can obtain a matrimonial order in the Magistrates' Court. Under the statute the duty is confined to husbands.[140] It would be unusual, though possible, for a wife to force her husband into prostitution. If she did, her behaviour would amount to conduct which is not reasonably tolerable, and if he forces or coerces her into prostitution his conduct may amount to cruelty (for purposes of the Magistrates' Court jurisdiction) or conduct which is not reasonably tolerable. If the Law Commission's proposals are made law the special duty with regard to prostitution will fall away and the Magistrates' Court will simply have to consider, when deciding whether to grant a maintenance order, whether the conduct of husband or wife in regard to the other's prostitution was reasonably tolerable, having regard so far as is just to the conduct of the other spouse.[141]

We have examined the duties of husband and wife in matters of sex. It may be worth mentioning some matters which fall outside them. Just as neither is bound to disclose to the other their sexual activities before marriage, so neither is bound to make a clean breast of their unfaithfulness during marriage. Indeed to blurt out the fact that he or she has been unfaithful might, with a sensitive partner and in the wrong surroundings, amount to cruelty or intolerable conduct. But a wife who is pregnant by another man ought to let her husband know, since he will be liable to support the child unless its paternity is settled.

[139] Below, ch. 5 p. 128.
[140] MPA 1960 s. 1(1)(g).
[141] Law Commission 77 p. 154.

2

Living Together

'Knowing me, knowing you, it's the best I can do'
(Andersson/Anderson/Ulvaeus:
Knowing me, knowing you)

I. MARRIAGE CRITICISED

Marriage is popular. It seems that in England 95 per cent of men and 96 per cent of women between 45 and 49 years of age have been or are now married.[1] Marriage has grown more popular over the last two centuries, as men and women have come to demand more in the way of personal fulfilment,[2] as young people have been able to earn more, and as young married women without families have been better able to help support themselves and sometimes their husbands. Some decline may, however, now be expected, since between 1972 and 1974 the marriage rate in England fell by about 10 per cent (8.6 to 7.8 per 1,000). This agrees with the trend in the seventies in some like-minded countries such as Australia, Denmark, France, New Zealand and West Germany, but not with the path of love in the cold climates of Canada and Sweden.[3] In England as in other countries people are marrying younger. While in 1957 of all brides under 29 26 per cent were under 20 when they married, in 1975 the figure was 31 per cent. So there has been a sharp increase in the

[1] G. Cole, 'The legal implications of cohabitation', 1976 Poly. LR 28, citing *Proceedings of the Royal Society*, Series B Vol. 159 (1964) 180; Bernard (below, n. 11) 172.

[2] E. Shorter, *The Making of the Modern Family* (1976), but he overstates the case.

[3] The figures for recent trends in English marriage and divorce are taken from a forthcoming book by John Eekelaar, to whom I am indebted.

proportion of young women, especially of the working class, who hurry to get married. Though this is sometimes because they are pregnant, the bun-in-the-oven marriage by no means explains the whole increase in early marriages. Later on these young brides or their young husbands may regret having married so young. Looking back, it may seem that the best years of youth were wasted. A bride who marries under 20 has about twice the chance of seeing her marriage end in divorce of a bride of 20 to 24 and three times the chance of a bride of 25 to 28. It is also the case that a pregnant bride has about twice the chance of a bride who is not pregnant of finding that her marriage ends in divorce. The divorce rate has risen with the marriage rate, and in one sense the rise in marriage accounts for the rise in divorce, because the more people marry who would not have done so fifty years ago the more likely it is that they will be people who are unsuited to such a long-lasting and intimate relationship. It is not easy to give a figure for the likelihood that an English marriage will end in divorce, because the position is changing from generation to generation and year to year. In the USA between a third and a quarter of women who marry by the age of 30 are now likely to be divorced sooner or later.[4] In England the comparable figure is probably lower but rising. Nine per cent of those married in 1957 had been divorced fifteen years later, but when allowance is made for those who divorce after fifteen years and for the greater readiness to divorce which the figures show for those who have married more recently than 1957, there is no doubt that the chances that a couple who marry in 1978 will be divorced are at least one in six and perhaps as much as one in four.

So it is not surprising that marriage does not please everyone and that there are those who cast about for alternatives. The critics of marriage fall into three groups. Some regard it as a one-sided arrangement, with the advantages on the side of husband or wife according to one's point of view. Another group thinks that, even if the balance is level, the rules are too strict: marriage is too difficult to dissolve and requires too exclusive a commitment to one person. There is a third group which thinks that the advantages and prestige of marriage are such that they should be extended to couples of the same sex and who therefore favour homosexual marriage.

[4] P. C. Glick and A. J. Norton, *Demography* 10 (1973) 301–14.

This chapter deals with the criticisms and the suggested alternatives, especially with the alternative of living and having sex together without being married.

Supporters of women's liberation see in marriage the model for all other forms of discrimination against women.[5] The marriage contract is the only important contract in which the terms are not listed, or are expressed so vaguely that there is no clear limit to what a wife must do in order to fulfil them. A wife must perform the domestic chores (cleaning, cooking, washing, etc.) necessary to maintain the home and must care for her husband and children.[6] She must 'perform her household and domestic duties . . . without compensation therefor. A husband is entitled to the benefit of his wife's industry and economy'.[7] A wife's effective working week is longer than her husband's.[8] No union would accept such conditions for its members. The fact that she is bound to allow her husband sexual intercourse is itself a one-sided feature of marriage. Men value sex above love, affection or sentiment, while opinion surveys show that women put sex at the bottom of a list in which love, security, companionship, home, family and social acceptance rank higher.[9] There is a close parallel, it is argued, between marriage and slavery.[10] What is more, the inferior legal and social position of wives has a baneful influence on relations between men and women outside marriage. A man will expect his girl-friend to type his papers, iron his shirts, cook his dinner and even clean his apartment. While marriage on the whole makes both husbands and wives happy, careful US studies seem to show that the husband's marriage is, relative to the unmarried, better than the wife's. Married men are healthier and live longer than bachelors, but unmarried women are sounder in mind than their married sisters.[11]

[5] S. Cronan, 'Notes from the third Year'. *Women's Liberation* (1971) 62–5.

[6] R. T. Gallen, *Wives' Legal Rights* (1967) 4–5; H. Clark, *The Law of Domestic Relations* (1968) 181. I have used American writing and case law when it is more explicit than, but not substantially different from, the English.

[7] *Rucci* v. *Rucci* 181 Atl. 2d 125, 257 (1962 Conn.).

[8] When both are employed, four to nine hours longer in the US: Weitzman (below, n. 37) 1190, n. 110.

[9] Cronan 176.

[10] Cronan 177.

[11] J. Bernard, *The Future of Marriage* (1976) 309–30.

A point of view which reverses that of women's liberation sees in marriage, at least in its middle-class form, an arrangement for exploiting men. The middle-class husband is made to strain himself to the point of ulcers and heart attacks to earn extra money which is spent by his wife. The player who in a spectacular reversal of roles protests against women exploiters is the pimp. The pimp is a hero in the ghetto because he controls women. He makes them support him, rather than the other way round, and he does so in a way which underlines their servile status.[12]

In a less violent form, some men protest against the idea that marriage is a lifelong bread-ticket for the wife. As women become better able to support themselves, courts are looking for a new test to apply to fix their economic claims when a marriage breaks down. Some ask how much a wife has changed her position through marriage: on this view her age and the length of time the parties lived together are important.[13] Others look to her expectations, so that a woman who made a catch by marrying a rich man is entitled to a good share of his wealth even if their time together was brief.[14]

The criticisms have some foundation. Husband and wife form a very small group, and in such a group it is easy for one to dominate the other. It is made easier by the fact that the relations of husband and wife are mostly not governed by legal rules, and even social pressure usually stops at the front door of the neighbour's house. The fact that married people do not for the most part run their lives according to rules is not an accident. An arrangement which is meant to last a lifetime must be flexible and able to adapt to new situations. For this purpose very general guides—trust, mutual support, consideration—are better than detailed rules to the effect that shopping is the wife's and gardening the husband's chore. If the couple want to they can, and some do, post up in the kitchen a list of the jobs to be done by Him and Her. The fact that detailed rules imposed from outside are not usually wanted or effective is parallel to the fact that relations between colleagues at work, or indeed in any lasting enterprise in which mutual support is needed, are difficult to reduce to a formula. Indeed, between equals, a formula is not

[12] C. and R. Milner, *Black Players* (1973) 271–3.
[13] *Krystman* 1973 2 All ER 247 CA; *Taylor* (1975) 119 SJ 30.
[14] E.g. *Brett* 1969 1 WLR 487 CA.

generally necessary. The trouble about marriage is that it easily
turns into a unequal relation, since the husband generally earns
the family living, and, on the whole, the more he earns, the more
he makes the important decisions.[15] Of course there are exceptions. Sometimes temperament overrides the economic factor, and
makes the economically weaker spouse dominant.

But can the law do anything to redress the balance? Unlike
slavery, marriage cannot be abolished. It is a needed framework
for having and bringing up children. The question is whether the
rules can be changed so that, in a small housebound unit, there
is a fairer distribution of chores between husband and wife or so
that the unit becomes less isolated.

At first sight the answer is No. Laws cannot be effective inside
the home without a degree of intrusion on privacy which would
not be accepted or acceptable, and this is true whether the couple
is married or living together unmarried.

On the other hand the law has long regulated the ending of
marriage, whether by separation or divorce, and changing views
of the duties of husband and wife, intended to make it a real
partnership rather than merely a shell, can be taken into account
at the stage of break-up, if break-up there is. Can anything be
done by legal techniques while man and wife continue to live
together? Perhaps it would help to a limited extent if wives had
certain legal rights, for instance to a percentage of their husband's
earnings, and if there was a legal duty on both to disclose the
amount of earnings or income. The example of the contract of
employment shows that, even if the main role of the law is to
make rules for the case where a complicated relation comes to an
end (redundancy, dismissal), it may also have a supporting role
while the relation continues. Yet it must be admitted that the
inequality which may exist in a marriage is not likely to be set
right in this way.

A second set of criticisms of marriage holds that it is too much
of a closed institution : too difficult to end, too restrictive in
denying sexual variety or even, in some cases, friendship with
members of the opposite sex. In short, it is suffocating. 'Spouses
are now asked to be lovers, friends, mutual therapists, in a society
which is forcing the marriage bond to become the closest, deepest,

---

[15] D. L. Gillespie, 'Who has the power? The marital struggle', in *Family,
Marriage and the Struggle of the Sexes* (ed. H. P. Dreitzel 1972) 133-5.

most important and putatively most enduring relationship of one's life. Paradoxically, then, it is increasingly likely to fall short of the emotional demands made upon it.'[16] Various experiments have been and are being made to open the locked doors. In some of them, for example the O'Neills' 'open marriage',[17] the stress is on better communication between husband and wife and less sense of exclusive possession. Other new ideas put the emphasis on sexual variety. In its formal, middle-class, 'swinging' version in the US husband and wife agree that they owe one another a paramount loyalty[18] but that, subject to this, they will engage in the exchange of partners or group sex with other couples. Neither may telephone or meet another partner outside the rather formal swinging sessions, nor may they become emotionally involved with the others. In some groups a strict rotation is laid down, so that no husband may show a preference for a particular wife other than his own. The sex is impersonal, and is tolerated for much the same reason as prostitution, only by both spouses.[19]

The research into swinging or co-marital sex in America yields ambiguous results. Those who remain in the group say the experience has done them good and improved their marriage.[20] Those who leave tell their psychiatrists that swinging led to jealousy, guilt and a threat to their marriage.[21] The evidence is that husbands are keener than wives to try swinging or swapping, and that wives are keener to stop.[22]

The swinging groups are meant for a monogamous society in which each husband has a single wife and each wife a single husband. There have been still more ambitious attempts to replace monogamy by group marriage, in which each husband has several wives and each wife several husbands all forming part of the

[16] P. E. Slater, 'Some social consequences of temporary systems', in *The Temporary Society* (1968).

[17] N. and G. O'Neill, *Open Marriage: A New Life Style for Couples* (1972).

[18] D. Denfield and M. Gordon, 'The sociology of mate swapping', in *Beyond Monogamy* (ed. J. R. Smith and L. G. Smith 1974) 68, 81.

[19] K. Davis, 'Sexual behaviour', in *Contemporary Social Problems* (ed. R. K. Merton and R. A. Nisbet 1966) 371.

[20] C. A. Varni, 'An exploratory study of spouse swapping', in *Beyond Monogamy* (1974) 246, 256.

[21] D. Denfield, 'Dropouts from swinging: the marriage counsellor as informant', in *Beyond Monogamy* (1974) 261, 263.

[22] Denfield 265.

same group, or by living in communes.[23] These are unstable. Most of us need to depend on a particular person for support and reassurance.[24] A group cannot fulfil this need, though it may provide variety.[25]

It is safe to predict that monogamy will hold its ground. But it may be that the balance between its two main forms—marriage and living together—will shift, so far as childless couples are concerned, towards informal cohabitation. It is also possible that among married couples agreements for adultery by consent will become commoner. When there is an agreement of this sort neither spouse can complain, in proceedings for maintenance, separation or divorce, of *that* adultery. At most a court may be slow to agree that a wife has really consented to the swinging or group arrangement. The duty to be faithful remains. It is broken if a spouse commits adultery with a person who is not a member of the group, or with a member of the group outside the regular swinging sessions, or if he or she breaks the other rules of the group.[26] Consent to adultery in these conditions is not a general licence to have sexual relations with everyone.

We have dealt with the point of view of those who find marriage too lopsided or too closed. Some homosexuals think that it should be possible for members of the same sex to marry. The argument is that since a marriage between a man and a woman who cannot have or do not intend to have children can be valid the same should apply to people of the same sex.[27] Apart from overcoming the legal difficulties about a contract which involves sexual relations outside marriage, the motive for wanting homosexual marriage is religious, social, legal, or some combination of these. Some want to be bound by a religious sacrament. This is surely the concern of the churches rather than of the state. It is for them to decide whether to bless such unions. The social motive is a desire for recognition, a wish to be treated like

[23] J. W. Ramey, 'Communes, group marriage and the upper-middle class', in *Beyond Monogamy* (1974) 214.

[24] J. Bernard: 'Infidelity: some moral and social issues', in *Beyond Monogamy* 138, 156–7.

[25] M. P. Sapirstein, *Emotional Security* (1948).

[26] L. G. and J. R. Smith, 'Co-marital sex', in *Beyond Monogamy* (1974) 84, 99.

[27] On the legal invalidity of homosexual marriage in the US see *Baker* v. *Nelson* 191 NW 2d 185 (1971 Minn.) appeal dismissed 409 US 810; 82 Yale LJ (1973) 573, 583–8.

man and wife, invited out together and so on. Whether the fact that the couple was formally married would win a degree of social approval is uncertain. It may be that public opinion is more likely to be influenced by the stability of the union than by its formal status. But the main difficulties concern the roles of husband and wife and the existence of a differential between marriage and unmarried cohabitation. The legal rules about married couples' rights of support, tax relief, inheritance, rights in the matrimonial home, social security and the adoption of children depend on two ideas. One is that normally couples marry with a view to having children and that this role entitles a wife to special rights and privileges, for example the right of support. The second is that, because normally a married couple intend to have a family, which is something to be encouraged but which entails burdens, there should be a differential in favour of married people, so that, for instance, a special right to live in the home is given to a husband or wife and not to others who are living together unmarried.

It may be that the differential which has long existed in favour of marriage rather than living together is now breaking down. Living together is thought of as acceptable so long as the couple do not have children, and are prepared to marry if they do have children. But many married people now choose not to have children either, at least for some years, and there has in consequence been a sharp drop in the birth rate in England in the seventies. If a substantial percentage of married people do not have children the difference between marriage and living together is blunted, and the legislator may in due course take the view that rights which in the past were confined to married people, such as rights of inheritance, should extend to those who live together. If that happened the objection to homosexual marriage would be much weaker. To refuse it would be to discriminate against couples of the same sex simply because their form of sex was disapproved.

But, as we shall see, the distinction between marriage and living together is still a fairly sharp one, both socially and legally.

2. COHABITATION

Cohabitation is the name given to the arrangement by which a man and a woman live and have sex together without being married. This arrangement may be intended to last for a definite period, for example so long as they are both students, or until a certain event takes place, for instance until the woman becomes pregnant, or indefinitely. They may or may not make a formal agreement about sharing expenses, about their living accommodation and so forth.

Cohabitation is simply a form of domestic partnership. There are several sorts of domestic partnership (using the term partnership in a social, not a legal sense). One is the setting up of home by people who do not have a sexual relation, for example men or women who are simply friends. A second is marriage and a third is cohabitation. Cohabitation is like marriage in that so long as it lasts it is meant to be exclusive, not in the sense that the couple are necessarily faithful to one another, but in the sense that they are a couple, sharing and living together, to the exclusion of other partners, so long as the cohabitation lasts : one man, one woman, at any one time. The men and women who cohabit are sometimes called cohabitors.

It is not easy to estimate the number of couples living together unmarried. In England, it seems, nearly 40 per cent of illegitimate births (about 26,000) are registered on the joint information of both mother and father.[28] To this one must add many couples who are not married but who do not have children, or not in a particular year. There are also a small number of cases where the couple think they are married but are not (putative marriages).[29] On the basis of these figures, and taking account of the fact that many unmarried couples will take special care not to have children, one may estimate that about 10 per cent of all couples who are living together are unmarried.

The reasons for cohabiting are various. The most obvious is that the couple are not certain whether they wish to enter on a partnership which, like marriage, is in principle lifelong. Again, they may wish to marry, but only after finishing their training or getting a job, or one may wish to marry and the other not. One or both may already be married to someone else. They may

[28] V. Wimperis, *The Unmarried Mother and her Child* (1960) ch. 2; *Reform of the Grounds of Divorce: the Field of Choice* (1966 Cmnd. 3123) s. 33–7.
[29] A. E. Evans, 'Property interests arising from quasi-marital relations', 9 *Cornell LQ* (1923–4) 246 discusses their position.

think the marriage would spoil their relationship by making it too formal. They may refuse to marry because of the disadvantage from the point of view of income tax, especially tax on investment income.

Whatever the reason, and however stable the relation, sexual intercourse between an unmarried couple is 'unlawful', though it is not in general a crime. It is criminal in the case of incest, or when the girl is under 16 and in certain other cases which are discussed in Chapter 3. This section deals with cases where no crime is involved, but the sexual relation is unlawful in the sense of being outside marriage. A contract for which the whole or part of the consideration is sexual intercourse (or any other sexual relation) outside marriage is void,[30] as is a contract which tends to promote unlawful sexual intercourse. So, if Jack agrees to support Jill to whom he is not married on condition that she keeps house for him and that they have sexual intercourse, the whole agreement is void even if they mean it to be a legally binding one. It makes no difference that the agreement to have sex is understood rather than expressed.

So far as consideration is concerned, this rule depends on the sexual intercourse being in return for or partly in return for the promise. The support promised by Jack, or the domestic chores promised by Jill, must be *in return for*, or part of the return for, the unlawful sexual relations. Provided that Jack and Jill do not make their agreement in such a way as to induce unlawful sexual relations to begin or continue, they are free to make a binding contract about such matters as household expenses, their rights in the house or flat where they live, what is to happen if they part, and how the work is to be divided between them.[31] If, then, Jack and Jill have already decided to live together for three years, or while he has a job in Bradford, or until one of them tires of the relationship, they may be wise to do two things. First, any house or flat they buy should be put in their joint names, so that they hold the legal estate (i.e. the ownership) on trust for sale for the benefit of each of them equally unless a different division is agreed or implied. The same should be done

[30] A. L. Corbin on Contracts (1962) s. 1476; *Ayerst* v. *Jenkins* (1873) LR 16 Eq. 275; *Grant* v. *Butt* 17 SE 2d 689 (1942).

[31] *Lovinger* v. *Anglo-California National Bank of San Francisco* 243 P 2d 561 (1952); *Croslin* v. *Scott* 316 P 2d 755 (1957); *Hill* v. *Estate of Westbrook* 213 P 2d 727 (Cal. 1950).

if they rent accommodation; the lease should be in the name of both. Secondly, they should consider making a contract. It is true that while things go well between them no contract is really necessary. The point of making one is partly to save trouble and bitterness in case they break up. 'Breaking up is never easy, I know', but it can be made easier by a little advance planning. Thirdly, making a contract will help fix their minds on some practical details, for instance on the sharing of expenses and on what is to happen to the sharing arrangement if one or other loses his job. These, otherwise, may be overlooked.

The contract will not be a contract *of cohabitation* (which would certainly be void in law, since it would include a promise to have unlawful sexual intercourse), but a contract *between cohabitors*. It cannot unfortunately be asserted that the courts will uphold such a contract, since they may take the view that, even if the contract does not expressly or by implication provide for sexual relations, its mere existence has a tendency to persuade the parties to continue living together. But the contrary view—that once the parties have decided to live together the mere existence of a formal contract has no such tendency—is arguable. It is certainly worth while making a contract even in the present state of the law. In doing so (assuming it to be valid), cohabitors are freer than a married or engaged couple. Married people who are not separated cannot validly agree not to live together or not to have sexual intercourse.[32] They cannot exclude or whittle down the husband's duty to support the wife or the wife's duty to do the household chores and look after the children.[33] They cannot provide for future separation.[34] Nor can married people validly bargain for payment or property in return for doing these duties. A wife cannot bargain to be paid for cooking or even helping on the farm.[35] These duties and restrictions do not affect cohabitors. Jill does not have a duty to do Jack's washing or cook his meals. She is entitled to bargain to be paid for her services, if she wants to. Jack does not have a duty to support Jill.

[32] Above, ch. 1 n. 54f.
[33] *Youngberg* v. *Holstrom* 108 NW 2d 98 (1961 Iowa: farm wife cannot bargain for advantages under her husband's will in return for raising poultry and hogs and looking after a big garden); *Frame* 36 SW 2d 152 (Tex. 1931); *Oates* 33 SE 2d 457 (W Va 1945); *Haas* 80 NE 2d 337 (NY 1948).
[34] *Brodie* 1917 P. 271.
[35] Above, n. 33.

They may agree that she shall support him, and that he shall mind the house. They have no duty to continue living together, and so may properly agree about payments to be made and property to be shared when they part.

The only restrictions are that they cannot validly regulate their sexual relations (e.g. by agreeing that Jill is responsible for taking the contraceptive pill), or exclude the duty which the law places on both of them to support their children.[36] Nor can they agree to compensate one another for the break-up of the relation, since any damages or penalty to be paid by the cohabitor who brings the relation to an end will be void as an inducement to continue unlawful sexual relations.

Writing in California, Weitzman has made detailed suggestions about the form and contents of what she calls 'contracts within and contracts in lieu of marriage'.[37] These are well worth reading. But a warning is needed. In my opinion the whole contract will be void if it contains terms which provide for the sexual relations of the couple or terms which are meant or which have a tendency to induce them to come together or remain together in a meretricious relation, as it is called.[38] It should not be assumed that a court will be willing to sever the terms relating to (unlawful) sex from the others. On the other hand, the cases mentioned in the next section show that courts are now willing to give effect to implied agreements and trusts relating to accommodation shared by unmarried couples, at any rate once the relationship has come to an end.[38a]

Implied contracts and trusts

For the most part cohabitors do not make express contracts. These are only now coming into fashion and, even if they are upheld by the courts, most couples are not likely to be so formal. A good deal of importance therefore turns on the question whether the

[36] Ministry of Social Security Act 1966 s. 22; Affiliation Proceedings Act 1957 s. 1.

[37] L. J. Weitzman, 'Legal regulation of marriage: tradition and change', 62 Cal. LR (1974) 1122. Other suggestions in A. Coote and T. Gill, *Women's Rights: A Practical Guide* (1974) 335; (1973) 123 New LJ 591. But note warning.

[38] *Diwell* v. *Farnes* 1959 2 All ER 379, 388.

[38a] J. L. Dwyer, 'Immoral contracts', 93 LQR (1977) 386; *Andrews* v. *Parker* 1973 Queensland R 93.

courts will imply a contract between the couple, in particular
a contract about the ownership of, or rights in, the home.
Although the statute law about matrimonial homes does no apply
to unmarried couples, the courts, cautiously feeling their way, are
trying to give a remedy when justice requires it and when it can
be inferred that the couple meant to be legally bound. So, when
the woman gave up a rent-controlled tenancy in order to live in
a house that the man bought in his own name for her and their
twin daughters, it was held that the man was contracting that
she should be licensed to live in the house as long as the daughters were of school age and reasonably required the accommodation.[39] But, when a man kept a mistress for seventeen years
without his wife's knowing and bought a large house in Ken-
sington for her and their daughter in his own name, it was
held that she must vacate it when he died. Her lover, generous
as he was, and just because he was generous, could not be said
to have contracted that she should be allowed to stay for any
particular period.[40]

Apart from implied contract, the courts are sometimes able
to spell out an implied trust. This will be done when one party
—for example the man—acquires the ownership of land in such
a way as to induce the other to act to her detriment in the reasonable belief that she is thereby getting a beneficial interest in the
land.[41] 'Detriment' is to be taken broadly. When a man bought a
house in his own name for him and the woman cohabitor to live
with their daughter, and she did heavy work, including using a
14lb sledgehammer, to put it in condition, she was held entitled
to a quarter interest in the house under an implied trust. Here
it was understood that the house was to be in their joint names,
but the man used the excuse that she was under 21 for putting
it in his own; and the heavy building work fell outside the
domestic chores which a woman cohabitor can be expected to do
without reward unless she expressly contracts to be paid.[42]

When both have made a contribution towards buying or building a house or putting it in a good state, the court, in assessing
the beneficial interest to be allotted to the parties, takes account

---

[39] *Tanner* 1975 1 WLR 1246.
[40] *Horrocks* v. *Foray* 1976 1 All ER 737.
[41] *Gissing* 1971 AC 886, 905.
[42] *Eves* 1975 1 WLR 1338.

both of money contributions and of work done, rent saved and other broad considerations, as in the case of husband and wife. On this basis another sledgehammer-wielding woman, whose money contribution was only about one-twelfth of the price of the house, was held entitled to one-third of the proceeds of sale.[43] These rather vague principles only apply when there is no precise contract between the parties, and it may be that the courts will only treat them, in a broad way, as engaged in a joint effort if they intend to marry when that becomes possible. Yet from the point of view of their rights in the home there seems little difference between intending to marry (which may never happen if one of them is already married) and intending to live together indefinitely.

Statutory rights

Legislation is beginning to eat into the principle that a man and woman living together do not have the rights and duties of a married couple. It is not clear how far this process will go, since no one has so far thought out what the law is trying to achieve.

Under the Supplementary Benefits Act 1966[44] when two persons are cohabiting as husband and wife their requirements and resources are aggregated and treated as the man's. This means that if the man is in full-time work the woman is not entitled to supplementary benefit. The same applies to Family Income Supplement and Child Benefit.

To apply this rule the Supplementary Benefits Commission has to find out if the woman is living with a man. The Commission looks to three main points. Is there a sexual relation? Is the man supporting the woman? Do they have a joint household? Their inquiries, especially those concerning sex, cause resentment. The rule is defended on the ground that an unmarried woman living with a man should not be in a better position than a wife. But a wife has a right to be supported, whereas a woman who is living with a man without their being married has no right of support. It is true that most men in that position will support their woman partner or girl friend, but they are not bound to do

[43] *Cooke* v. *Head* 1972 2 All ER 38. Thirteen years earlier the Court of Appeal had said the analogy of husband and wife was not relevant: *Diwell* v. *Farnes* 1959 2 All ER 379.
[44] Ministry of Social Security Act 1966 s. 4 (2) and schedule 2 para 3(1).

so.[45] Strictly speaking, then, all that Supplementary Benefit should depend on is whether the woman is actually being supported by the man, not whether they are living or having sex together. There is no good reason for investigating their sexual relations, as opposed to whether the man is supporting the woman. It is important to respect the privacy of people who are badly off. They have little else to cling to.

Supplementary benefit law therefore treats the couple as married, though other parts of social security law—the law of pensions for example—do not. Under a 1975 Act a person who immediately before another dies was being maintained by the dead person in whole or part can apply for an order to the effect that the will or intestacy of the deceased does not make reasonable provision for her (or him).[46] Thus a woman living with and being maintained by a man who dies and who does not make a reasonable financial provision for her is put into a position almost (not quite) as favourable as that of a wife.

This is a surprising and, in the case of a woman who lived with a man for only a short time, unjustified provision. During the man's lifetime she has no right of support. Even if the couple, after living together, marry and then separate, the period spent living together before marriage does not count in reckoning what support the wife is entitled to from the husband on divorce,[47] though a period spent living together after divorce has been counted for this purpose.[48] An unmarried woman cannot obtain a maintenance order against the man she has been living with, even if he maintained her.

The principles that have been explained apply equally to couples of the same sex as to couples of opposite sex, except that since homosexuals cannot live together 'as man and wife' a court is not likely to imply a contract or trust in the sort of case in which it does for a man and woman who cohabit. Homosexual cohabitation is therefore not quite on a level legally with heterosexual cohabitation. But a homosexual couple may make a contract to settle their affairs subject to the same limits as a heterosexual couple, provided always that their relations are not against the criminal law—a matter dealt with in Chapter 4.

---

[45] Supplementary Benefits Administrative Paper 5 (1976).
[46] Inheritance (Provision for Family and Dependants) Act 1975 s. 1 (1)(e).
[47] *Campbell* 1976 Fam. 347.   [48] *Chaterjee* 1976 1 All ER 719.

3. THE REFORM OF MARRIAGE AND COHABITORS' CONTRACTS

Weitzman, in the article referred to, has argued that neither the contract of marriage nor the contracts of cohabitors, as the law now stands (and there is no great difference between US and English law on these matters), is flexible enough to keep in step with the facts of social life. Apart from the fact that many people live together without marrying, marriage does not always involve a lifelong commitment. In the US over 25 per cent of women now aged 35 may expect to be divorced by the time they are 50, and the average length of a marriage which ends in divorce is ten years.[49] The law of marriage assumes that we are dealing with a first marriage, and takes little account of the obligations arising from previous marriages. It assumes (though less than it used to) that the procreation of children is an essential part of the relationship. It assumes a strict division of labour between husband and wife, though it is now much commoner for wives to support husbands, at least for some years, and for both to contribute to household expenses. The rules of Jewish and Christian morality which forbid sexual relations except between husband and wife form the basis of marriage law, though nowadays many couples openly dissent from them.

Ought it therefore to be possible for both married and unmarried couples to contract freely about such matters as support, the division of labour and future separation? Ought they also to have the right to make valid contracts about sex? To agree how many children they shall have, and when? To settle whether contraceptives are to be used, and which of them is responsible for using them?

There is surely a difference between the terms of an agreement between domestic partners which concern sex and those which concern other matters like expenses or support. There is a strong objection to making promises which relate to sex directly or indirectly enforceable, for example by the award of damages. At most, agreements about sex might be taken into account when the partnership breaks up. Promises about money and chores are surely different. It is strange that men, women or a mixed group

[49] Weitzman 1202, 1204.

who set up house or share a flat together can make what contract they please about the domestic arrangements so long as no sex is involved, but that a similar contract between a couple who are having sex together runs a grave risk of being held void.

Even if the change has only a marginal effect on married and unmarried couples until a breakdown occurs, it should be made possible for them to contract validly about matters other than their sexual relations. In so far as they contract about sex, their agreements should be treated as unenforceable, not illegal.

As regards agreements to separate and to provide for maintenance on separation, the rule for married couples would be as at present, while the rule for unmarried couples would be that, whatever the agreement, either might bring the relation to an end when he or she wished. This freedom to break up is one of the main reasons for a couple not to marry. But if a partner did this without reasonable notice in a way which imposed financial hardship on the other, there would be a duty to compensate.

There may also be some room, as Weitzman thinks, for settling by arbitration some quarrels between couples who have not separated.

In the end, however, the most important contribution of the law is likely to consist not in allowing couples greater freedom to contract, nor in providing for arbitration. What is crucial is that courts and legislators should in their respective spheres give effect to the notion that both married and unmarried couples are domestic partners. Their partnership is not aimed at profit, but is a union for the sharing of living accommodation, furnishing, living expenses and the chores connected with running a home. If there are children it extends to supporting and bringing up the children. This is surely the basic idea which the couples themselves have in mind, and which the law should seek to give effect to if it is to fit the conditions of today. So long as marriage is the central institution of our society it will be necessary to have some differential between married and unmarried couples. But it need not be a wide one. Since marriage can now be dissolved more easily than a generation ago, being married as opposed to living together is often just a matter of form, or forms. What is important is whether a man and a woman are partners in fact, and this does not depend on pieces of paper.

3
Women as Victims

'You want to do me but I don't want to be done—O.K.?'
(Schuman/Mackay: *OK*)

I. MEN RULE?

One of the assumptions of present-day thinking is that women
have equal rights with men and so should be treated equally by
the law. The Sex Discrimination Act 1975 attempts to put this
idea into force in employment and some other parts of life. But
it does not do so in regard to sex. Many laws about sexual relations discriminate between men and women. They create offences
of which only men can be guilty, or of which only women can be
the victims. Thus, so far as the principal act is concerned, only
women can be raped and only men can be guilty of rape.[1] Only
men, who must be aged 14 or over, can be guilty of having sexual
intercourse with a girl under 16. Since the object of this law is to
protect girls against themselves, the girl is not guilty of this
offence.[2] Only men can in general commit buggery.[3] In many
other cases, set out in Chapter 4, sexual acts between males are
criminal but with few exceptions such acts between women are
not. To have intercourse with a woman by lies or threats is a
crime on the part of the man who does it, but it is no crime for a

[1] A woman can aid and abet: *Ram* (1893) 17 Cox CC 609.
[2] Not even aiding and abetting: *Tyrell* 1894 1 QB 710. It has never been
an offence for a woman to have sex with a boy under 16, though she may
easily commit an indecent assault in doing so.
[3] Sexual Offences Act (hereafter SOA) 1956 s. 12. A woman can commit
buggery with an animal: *Bourne* (1952) 36 CAR 125; *Packer* 1932 Victoria
LR 225.

woman to threaten or deceive a man into having sex.[4] It is an offence for a man to have intercourse with a woman mental defective, but not for a woman to have sex with a male defective.[5] In many circumstances it is criminal to abduct a woman for sexual purposes, but there are no similar crimes to penalise the abduction of men.[6] The law protects women more and penalises them less.

The laws assume that in matters of sex, if something goes wrong, the fault generally lies with the man. There must therefore be legal discrimination in favour of women. Equal treatment will lead to their being exploited by men. In the same way some argue that in matters of colour what is needed is not equality but discrimination in favour of coloured people. Similar arguments are advanced whenever it is desired that two groups should be equal, but one is in fact at present inferior in terms of physique, money or status. The reason why sex law favours women is partly explained by the physical facts. Only men, in general, can be guilty of rape or buggery, because for these crimes penetration is necessary. But that is not a complete explanation. One can imagine a world in which women dominated men and forced them to have sex when the women chose. In that world the most prominent sex crime would not be rape but something like 'badgering'. In our world, however, men are physically stronger than women and can force their attentions on women more easily than women can on men. So far as mental qualities are concerned there is some difference of view among experts. Clearly in society as it now is men are more aggressive, daring and violent than women.[7] They were in 1975 convicted of just under six times as many serious crimes of all sorts as women, twelve times as many violent offences against the person, and 184 times as many sex offences.[8] The law must be based on the needs of society as it now is, and not as ideally it might be. So it must take account of the male tendency to board and grapple.

Some women, however, especially those who think that women

[4] SOA 1956 s. 2, 3.
[5] SOA 1956 s. 7. But it may be an indecent assault: ibid s. 15(3).
[6] SOA 1956 s. 17, 18, 19, 21.
[7] S. Feshback, 'Aggression', in *Carmichael's manual of child psychology* (ed. P. Mussen 1970).
[8] Statistics for those found guilty on indictment from *Criminal Statistics England and Wales 1975* (Cmnd. 6566).

are oppressed by men and should be freer, put down the difference between the sexes largely to upbringing. Girls are taught to
play with dolls, boys with soldiers; and girls are discouraged
from playing with soldiers, boys with dolls. If education changed,
women and men would in time come to be equally enterprising,
or nearly so.

There is no doubt that at least part of the difference between
the sexes is the result of custom and pressure rather than physique
or heredity. Though twelve times as many men as women were
convicted of crimes of violence against the person, like assaults
and wounding, in 1975, only five years earlier, the proportion
was seventeen to one.[9] While men in 1975 were convicted of
just under six times as many serious crimes as women, fifteen
years before they were convicted of seven times as many.[10] Convictions for violence by women more than doubled between 1970
and 1975, from 1,305 to 2,748.[11] There is no reason to think that
women will not become more nearly the equals of men in crime.
There are clearly many aggressive women whose wish to break
rules has been held in check until recently by the fact that
they were brought up to behave in a feminine way, and many
men who are not prepared to tolerate their behaviour.

The sexes are more nearly alike in physical aggression than a
casual observer might think. But can the whole difference be
accounted for in this way? 'In the majority of species, and certainly mammalian ones, the male is more aggressive than the
female.'[12] In rats and monkeys females to whom male hormones
(androgens) are given become more aggressive and male rats who
are castrated at birth or when young become less aggressive.[13] It
seems likely that the extra ambition, drive and enterprise which
men now show has a physical basis. If it turns out that it does
not, and education changes in such a way that the sexes become

---

[9] *Criminal Statistics England and Wales 1970* (Cmnd. 3037). The figures
taken are for convictions on indictment for violent offences against the
person.

[10] *Criminal Statistics England and Wales 1960* (Cmnd. 1437). The figures
taken are for convictions on indictment.

[11] Above, nn. 8, 9.

[12] C. Hutt, *Males and Females* (1972) 108, citing N. E. Collias, 'Aggressive
behaviour among vertebrate animals', *Physiol. Zool.* 17 (1944) 83–123.

[13] C. Hutt 110–12.

equal or nearly equal in these respects, the law about sex will have to be drastically revised.

At present the criminal law is mainly directed against male aggression. This slant is reflected in ordinary language, including obscene words, which conceive of sex as something men do to women, something that is done to women, rather than as something that women do to men or that men and women do together. Dick screwed Jane, Jane did not screw Dick, nor did they screw one another.[14] Not only are women thought of as passive in sex, but language suggests that what happens to them is degrading. To be fucked is to be a victim.

That women must be protected against marauding males is, therefore, a social need, as matters now stand, and perhaps a need that could not be altered except by genetic or hormone techniques of a sort which are not acceptable. In particular, women are exposed to men who use violence against them for sexual purposes (rape, indecent assault) and who seduce them when they are immature. Something must be said of the social background to both these forms of wrongdoing before the law on the subject is set out.

Rape (and to a lesser extent indecent assault) is a crime of violence, not just in the technical sense that some force must generally be used against the victim without her consent, but in the more important sense that it is mostly committed by men who are inclined to use force to obtain what they want. A careful study of rape in Philadelphia in 1958 and 1960 yields results which can with due caution be applied to England, where the amount of rape is generally lower than in the US.[15] In this study Amir found that more than half the known offenders had taken part in multiple rape.[16] It seems that a young man who is in the company of another often feels that he must show that he is as tough and virile as his mate. Not surprisingly, more than half the rapes took place between Friday evening and Saturday night,[17] at the times when young men expect to have sex. The offenders were mostly under 24;[18] their victims were slightly

---

[14] R. Baker. ' "Pricks" and "Chicks" : a plea for persons', *Philosophy and Sex* (ed. R. Baker and F. Elliston 1975) 45, 58–9.

[15] M. Amir, *Patterns in Forcible Rape* (1971).

[16] Amir 200.

[17] Amir 339.

[18] Amir 51.

younger.[19] The rapists are not usually repressed or sexually inadequate people. Most of the incidents were planned in advance.[20] In a little more than half the cases the man and woman knew one another, though not necessarily well: in the rest (42 per cent) they were strangers.[21] Twelve times as many black men were convicted of rape as white in proportion to their numbers.[22] This is a sign that rape goes with a tendency among a certain group (sometimes called a subculture) to resort to violence: there is a great deal more violence among the black than the white community in Philadelphia. The rapes committed by black men were committed mainly against black women,[23] thus within the group in which violence was common. Most of the offenders were poor, or relatively poor.[24] In about 19 per cent of the cases the woman could, according to the police, be said at least to some extent to have led the man on:[25] she agreed to sexual intercourse but later withdrew her consent; she did not react strongly enough when the man insisted on sex or by her words and gestures encouraged him to press ahead. (These figures for cases in which the victim is partly at fault are contested by supporters of the woman's point of view.)[26]

The way in which the rape occurs obviously varies according to whether the parties know one another. A stranger may rape a woman by waylaying her in a dark alley on her way home or giving her a lift in his car and stopping in a secluded spot, though rape in the full view of strangers is not unknown. When the man and woman know one another it is often found that they have been drinking before the rape incident. Each may misread the other's intentions, or to be so dulled that he does not care.

On the man's side, then, rape is mainly a crime of young people who are used to violence and who wish either to make clear to themselves or their peers that they are men or just to enjoy themselves. What of the victim? There are those who have

[19] Amir 51.
[20] Amir 172.
[21] Amir 234.
[22] Amir 44.
[23] Amir 43.
[24] Amir 72.
[25] Amir 266.
[26] Below, n. 31.

argued that women secretly wish to be raped.[27] It is certainly part of the chase, and makes it more exciting, not to be caught too easily, but it is another matter to suppose that when Jill makes clear that she does not want Jack to have sexual intercourse with her she does not know her own mind. It is not true, as male myth has it, that a woman cannot be made to have intercourse against her will, but only that she cannot be made to unless the man is prepared to use or threaten to use a dangerous amount of force : a knife, a stranglehold, a severe beating. Faced with threats of this sort many women, quite reasonably, resist no more strongly than men resist a mugging. Nor is there any real evidence that women or girls are specially prone to imagining that they have been raped when they have not. The danger is rather that, when a couple has broken up, the woman will seek revenge by inventing an incident of rape or indecent assault and using it to lay a charge against the man.

Because men are more aggressive and more interested in sex than all but a minority of women,[28] the male and female points of view about rape are bound to differ. Susan Brownmiller has composed a powerful attack on the institution of rape as a device, or part of a series of devices, for oppressing women.[29] 'Rape is to women what lynching was to blacks (viz. in the US), the ultimate physical threat by which all men keep all women in a state of . . . intimidation.'[30] It is not just randy men but institutions dominated by men, like the police and the lawyers, language with a male slant and theories invented by male professors which combine to keep women down. In one study of New York rape it was found that when police*men* investigated the charges laid by women 15 per cent were thought to be false, but when *women* did the investigation only 2 per cent was considered false.[31] According to some women, when they complain of rape in England the police and doctors conduct the inquiry in such a humiliating way that, quite apart from the questions they may be asked in court proceedings, women victims of rape

[27] L. Eidelberg, *The Dark Urge* (1961) ch. 1.
[28] M. Schofield, *The Sexual Behaviour of Young People* (1968 ed.) 80–1, 220, 230–1; *Promiscuity* (1976) 46f.; Tripp, *The Homosexual Matrix* (1975) 153–4.
[29] *Against Our Will: Men, Women and Rape* (1975).
[30] Brownmiller 229.
[31] Brownmiller 387.

will do better to keep away from the police.[32] The police and police doctors strongly deny this.

Rape is a battlefield between men and women. The protection of young girls and women who are in some way incapable against seduction by men is equally important, though it does not attract so much passion.

Schofield's *The Sexual Behaviour of Young People*[33] gives a good picture of the sex life and attitudes of teenage boys and girls (between 15 and 19) in England in the sixties. He found that 11 per cent of the younger teenage boys (under $17\frac{1}{2}$) had had sexual intercourse, and 30 per cent of the older boys. For girls the figures were 6 and 16 per cent for younger and older, respectively.[34] This does not seem particularly high, and it connects with the fact that over a third of the boys and nearly two-thirds of the girls thought that sexual intercourse before marriage was wrong.[35] Both sexes tend to pass through something of a cycle. It begins with dating and kissing, including deep kissing, which more than half of both boys and girls try at least once. It goes on to various forms of petting, including feeling a girl's breasts over and under her clothes, touching a girl's sex organs and letting her fondle the boy's (twice as common among the older as among the younger teenagers). The final stage of petting is something called 'genital apposition', which involves contact, short of a proper fuck, between the boy's and girl's sex organs. This usually happens when the couple are at least partly undressed and could have full intercourse if they wanted. They prefer not to, in order to avoid pregnancy or disease.[36] The final stage, reached (as explained) by about a third of the boys and a sixth of the girls (according to what they told the researchers) by 19, is sexual intercourse. It is quite likely, of course, that the boys exaggerated their sexual experience a bit, while the girls concealed some of theirs. Otherwise one must suppose that there was a small number of girls who were very promiscuous.[37]

These figures should probably be increased to take account of

---

[32] Brownmiller 15.

[33] M. Schofield, *The Sexual Behaviour of Young People* (1968 ed.).

[34] Schofield *Young People* 45–6, 224.

[35] Schofield, *Young People* 258.

[36] Schofield, *Young People* 50–1.

[37] Schofield, *Young People* 220 (not altogether convincing. Why were promiscuous girls not included in his sample?).

the change in society between 1965 and now. Nevertheless, it is in point to note that in Schofield's sample only about 5 per cent of girls (against 12 or 13 per cent of boys) had had sexual intercourse by the age of 16.[38] This is relevant to the question of the age of consent, which is at present 16.

2. CRIMES AGAINST WOMEN

The law tries to guard women against sexual relations which are thought to involve exploitation, by making the men who have sex with them guilty of a crime if they do so in certain conditions : in particular if the woman does not freely consent, or if the man is in a position of authority over her, or if the woman is a young girl or a mental defective. These crimes, together with the rarer cases in which men are protected against sexual advances by women, are dealt with in the present chapter. Prostitution, which may also involve the exploitation of women, is reserved for Chapter 5. The protection of men, including boys, against the advances of other men comes in Chapter 4.

The various sex crimes against women overlap. They may, however, conveniently be divided into those which turn on (a) the woman's lack of consent, (b) abuse of authority, (c) the exploitation of children, and (d) the exploitation of defectives.

(a) *Lack of consent: violence, deception, drugging*

A number of offences mainly protect women (including girls) against those who have sex with them or attempt to do so against their will by force, fraud or drugs. These include (i) rape, (ii) indecent assault, (iii) procuring sex by threats, (iv) procuring sex by false pretences, (v) administering drugs for sexual purposes, (vi) forcible abduction, (vii) fraudulent abduction. What is common to these crimes is that the guilty person (usually a man) makes use of improper methods in order to have sexual intercourse himself or to enable some other man to do so.

(i) *Rape*
Rape is committed by a man who has unlawful sexual intercourse

---

[38] Schofield, *Young People* 49–50.

with a woman who at the time of the intercourse does not consent to it.[39] In this and the other crimes to be discussed later in this chapter unlawful sexual intercourse means intercourse outside marriage.[39a] The man must be 14 or over.[40] He must either know that the woman does not consent at the time of intercourse or be reckless (i.e. not care) whether she consents.[41] The maximum penalty is life imprisonment.[42]

Sexual intercourse involves penetration of the woman by the man : his penis must, no matter how little, have been within her labia.[43] For purposes of rape and other sexual offences no emission of semen is necessary,[44] nor need the penetration be deep or prolonged, nor need the woman's hymen, if still intact, be broken. The offence consists in the violation of the woman, not the satisfaction of the man.

A boy under 14 cannot be guilty of rape or any offence involving sexual intercourse.[45] This strange rule comes by an indirect route from Roman law in which 14 was the age of puberty and majority, and it was thought indecent to inquire whether a boy under that age had in fact attained puberty.[46] The age of majority and marriage having been raised, the reason for the rule has long since disappeared, but it lingers on in the English criminal law. Nor, probably, can a boy under 14 be convicted of attempted rape. He can, however, be convicted of indecent assault, or ordinary assault, if he does what would in an older man amount to rape,[47] but, illogically, not of assault with intent to commit rape.[48] He can be guilty of helping or advising another man to

[39] Sexual Offences (Amendment) Act 1976 s. 1(1)(a).
[39a] For rape by husbands, see ch. 1 nn. 71–4.
[40] *Waite* 1892 2 QB 600; *Tatam* (1921) 15 CAR 132.
[41] SOAA 1976 s. 1(1)(b).
[42] SOA 1965 s. 1 and 2nd schedule 3.
[43] *Lines* (1844) 1 C. and K. 393.
[44] SOA 1956 s. 44.
[45] Above, n. 40.
[46] Justinian *Institutes* 1.22.pr. According to the New South Wales court such inquiry would encourage 'those particular statements of indecent things which wear away the nice sense of the refined, placed by the Maker in the human mind as one of the protections of its virtue': *R. v. Willis* 4 SCR (1865) 59, rejecting the argument that the rule did not apply in the Australian climate.
[47] *Waite* 1892 2 QB 600; *Williams* 1893 1 QB 320.
[48] *Philips* (1839) 8 C. & P. 736. The rule is illogical because it does not follow from the supposed fact that the boy cannot penetrate that he cannot intend to.

commit or attempt rape (viz. of aiding, abetting, counselling or procuring).[49] A woman can also be an accessory,[50] and so can the husband of the victim.[51]

The intercourse must be without the woman's consent. Though in the first half of the nineteenth century it used to be said that the man must act with force or against the woman's will,[52] this did not cater for the case of the man who has intercourse with a sleeping woman. So this positive way of putting it has now given way to the negative requirement that she must not consent. In most cases of course a man who does not secure the woman's consent will indeed have to resort to violence or threats of violence to overcome the woman's resistance. The woman is not necessarily expected to put up a fight. If the man hits her or threatens her with a knife, she need not run the risk of serious injury to save herself from being violated. If in those circumstances she submits, she has not consented, for the consent required by the law is not one wrung from her by the prospect of injury.[53] Nor is there consent if a young child submits to the advance of an older man out of deference to authority, or because she is too backward or too young to understand that she is being invited to have sexual intercourse.[54]

Respect for freedom has the consequence that a woman, including a prostitute, who has sex with many men, does not lose her right to choose her partners. Nor does a woman who has a regular boy-friend, or is living with a man, consent to intercourse with him on any and every occasion. In those cases the woman's way of life and her relation to the man are no more than factors to be taken into account in deciding whether she agreed to sexual intercourse on this occasion. A wife is an exception. As explained in Chapter 1, she is taken by a fiction to have consented, when she married, to intercourse with her husband no matter when and where, apart from the exceptions there noted.[55]

Not all cases of rape involve violence. Sometimes a man

[49] *Eldershaw* (1828) 3 C. and P. 396.

[50] *Ram and Ram* (1893) 17 Cox CC 609.

[51] Hale 1 *Pleas of the Crown* 629; *Cogan* 1976 QB 217.

[52] J. C. Smith and B. Hogan, *Criminal Law* (3rd ed. 1973) 326.

[53] K. H. Koh, 'Consent and responsibility in sexual cases', 1968 Crim. LR 81; *Burles* 1947 Victorian LR 392.

[54] *Day* (1841) 9 C. and P. 722; *Fletcher* (1859) Bell CC 63; *Lambert* 1919 Victorian LR 205.

[55] Ch. 1 nn. 71–4.

deceives the woman about his identity or about the nature of the sex act in such a way that she does not really consent to intercourse with him, though she may appear to do so. One example, specially mentioned in the Sexual Offences Act,[56] is when a man induces a married woman to have sexual intercourse with him by impersonating her husband. The consent is not a real one in this case because the married woman makes a mistake as to the man who is having sex with her. Does the law on this point depend on the fact that sexual intercourse is lawful with the supposed partner, the husband, and unlawful with the real one? Presumably not. Sex is such a personal matter that in all cases of mistaken identity, whether the woman is married, living with another man, or single, her consent should be excluded unless it can be shown, as would often (not always) be the case with a prostitute, that she would have consented even had she known.

A mistake as to the nature of the sex act will also exclude the woman's consent. When in 1876 a quack doctor told a girl of 19 that he was doing a surgical operation to cure her fits and she believed this, it was held that she did not consent to sex with him.[57] It would be different if at the present day an analyst told a woman that her psychological difficulties could be helped by allowing him to have sexual intercourse with her. In this case the woman would consent to the sex act, though she might be mistaken about its effect on her mind. The same is true of other lies and deceptions which do not go to the identity of the man or the nature of the act. Hence for John to say that he will marry Jill, or pay her £100, when he intends nothing of the sort, or David that he is well-off and unmarried when he is really supporting a wife on the dole, or Michael that he loves Jill when he is in fact indifferent to her, will not make the intercourse rape, even if Jill believes what is said and consents as a result.[58] In some of these cases, however, strange as it may seem, an offence is committed, namely that of procuring a woman by false pretences

---

[56] SOA 1956 s. 1(2). This reverses a line of decisions (e.g. *Jackson* (1838) 8 C. & P. 286; Smith and Hogan, 3rd ed. 1973 p. 328 n. 14) but should be thought of as declaring the common law position.

[57] *Flattery* (1877) 2 QBD 410; cf. *Williams* 1923 1 KB 340; *Morgan* 1970 Victorian LR 337. *Harms* 1944 2 DLR 61 (Canada) goes too far.

[58] *Papadimitropoulos* (1957) 98 CLR 249 (Australia: belief that she was married to the man in question); *Clarence* (1888) 22 QBD 23.

to have unlawful sexual intercourse in any part of the world.[59] A false pretence does not include a statement about what the speaker intends to do,[60] so that David and Michael are guilty of a crime for which the maximum punishment is two years in prison, but John is not. This is one of those offences which thousands of men commit but which almost never lead to prosecution.

A woman who is asleep does not consent to sexual intercourse (unless she has given consent in advance) and one who is drunk or drugged may not have done so, depending on the facts.[61] That a woman in drink or on a drug trip does not object to a man's advances need not mean that she consents, since she may be in no state to decide one way or the other.

The man must know that the woman does not consent, or not know, and not care, whether she does. This was decided by the House of Lords in *Morgan*[62] and confirmed by the Sexual Offences (Amendment) Act 1976.[63] Consequently if a husband invites another man to come to his house and have sex with his wife and tells him to disregard any show of reluctance on her part, since she will only be pretending, the man is not guilty of rape if he believes what he is told and has intercourse with the wife, despite her protests, in that belief. In *Morgan*[64] itself the evidence of the other men to this effect was not believed, and they were held rightly convicted, but that does not alter the general principle.[64a]

Many people criticised the decision in *Morgan*, and (like the author)[65] thought that the man should be acquitted only if he had reasonable grounds to believe that the woman consented. As a sop to this point of view, Parliament in the 1976 Act laid down that on a trial for a rape offence (which includes not just rape but attempted rape, aiding and abetting rape, counselling and

[59] SOA 1956 s. 3.

[60] *Dent* 1955 2 All ER 806, though not about a sexual offence, is wide enough to cover the case.

[61] *Camplin* (1845) 1 Den 89; *Young* (1878) 14 Cox CC 114; *Commonwealth* v. *Burke* 105 Mass. 376 (1870).

[62] 1976 AC 182.

[63] SOAA 1976 s. 1(2).

[64] 1976 AC 182.

[64a] Applied in *Cogan* 1976 QB 217.

[65] See below, pp. 77–8.

procuring rape and incitement to commit rape)[66] the presence or absence of reasonable grounds for believing that the woman consented is something which the jury must have regard to in deciding whether she did consent, along with other relevant matters.[67] This is just to say that they must use their common sense, which, fortunately, juries do anyhow.

The 1976 Act has introduced some special rules of procedure for the trial of rape offences (which as stated include attempted rape, being an accessory to rape or attempted rape, and inciting rape).[68] In a rape trial and in the Magistrates' Court inquiry into a rape offence the woman alleged to be the victim cannot now be asked questions about her sexual experience with anyone except the man being tried, unless the judge gives permission.[69] This he must do only if he is satisfied that to refuse would be unfair to the man.[70] This is an important reform, which makes it clear that a woman is free to have sex outside marriage with Tom and Dick while refusing it to Harry and that her sex with Tom and Dick is no evidence that she consented to Harry's advances. But, though prostitutes can also choose their clients, a judge might be inclined to let in evidence that the woman was a prostitute.

Another change in the law deals with publicity in rape cases. Publicity can be humiliating for the woman and damning for the man. Under the new provision, once someone is accused of a rape offence nothing can be published or broadcast in England or Wales which is likely to identify the woman complainant.[71] The judge may lift the ban if he is satisfied that this is necessary to induce witnesses to come forward at the trial, or that the ban is likely to cause substantial prejudice to the defence.[72] He may also in the public interest do so to the extent that he is satisfied that the ban imposes substantial and unreasonable restrictions on the reporing of the trial proceedings.[73] Men accused of a rape offence are also given the cloak of anonymity, with exceptions like

[66] SOAA 1976 s. 7(2).
[67] SOAA 1976 s. 1(2).
[68] SOAA 1976 s. 7(2).
[69] SOAA 1976 s. 2,3.
[70] SOAA 1976 s. 2(2).
[71] SOAA 1976 s. 4(1) cf. Michigan Crim. Cod. s. 520J(2); J. A. Scutt in 50 Aust. LJ (1976) 615, 620–2.
[72] SOAA 1976 s. 4(2).
[73] SOAA 1976 s. 4(3).

those which apply to the woman. But while the woman is protected against publicity even after the trial and appeal (if any), the man's protection ends if he is convicted.[74] Those who publish or broadcast matters contrary to this new law, which is meant to protect the victims of rape and those charged with rape from publicity, are liable to a fine of up to £500.[75]

(ii) *Indecent assault*

Anyone who indecently assaults a woman is punishable with up to two years' imprisonment. Indecent assaults on males are dealt with in Chapter 4, but the same principles apply, and only the punishment is different. Unlike in the case of rape, the principal offender may be a boy under 14 or a woman.[76]

It is an assault to use force against someone without his or her consent or to threaten to use force here and now, immediately. Hence 'I'll strangle you if you won't let me sleep with you after the party' is not an assault, but 'I'll strangle you if you don't open your legs before I count ten' is.

It is not necessary that the force used should be great, or indeed that it should be anything which the ordinary person would call force. Touching without consent (technically battery) is enough. It is therefore an assault for a man to put out his hand so that he brushes against a woman he passes, or still more, to kiss or cuddle her against her will. To touch against the will of the person touched is an assault. The suggestion that the action must be 'hostile'[77] is a misleading way of making a valid point.[78] A woman (or, if it comes to that, a man) does not usually want to be touched in a way that has sexual overtones, whether it is her sex organs or some other part of her body that is felt. If therefore the touching or feeling is of this sort, and hence 'indecent', it need not be shown to be hostile. The act is an assault, though the man who touches her is trying to be intimate, not hostile. The same is true if the person touched consents in fact to an indecent

[74] SOAA 1976 s. 6.
[75] SOAA 1976 s. 4(5).
[76] SOA 1956 s. 14, 15 cf. *Hare* 1934 1 KB 354 (woman on boy of 12).
[77] *Burrows* 1952 1 All ER 58 n.; *DPP* v. *Rogers* (1953) 37 CAR 137, but the actual decisions are right, as there was no indecent touching by the accused.
[78] As explained in *Sutton, The Times* 4 May 1977: photographing naked boys is not an assault, even if some (non-sexual) touching took place.

touching but cannot consent in law. The touching must then be an assault.[78a] But if the touching does not have sexual overtones it cannot always be assumed that the woman objects to it. In many circles, for instance, it is usual to kiss the hostess when arriving at a party. In such a case the touching or feeling must be shown to be hostile in order that it should count as an assault, or there must be some reason to think that she does not consent. To give a friendly pat, even if not actually welcome, is not a crime.

To threaten to touch a woman here and now is an assault : so it was an assault for a man on a train to expose his penis to a woman in the compartment and move towards her asking her to have intercourse, even if he did not touch her.[79] But it is different if the man makes it clear that he does not intend to take the initiative but rather wants her to touch him.[80] That is not an assault, though if the invitation to touch the sexual parts is made to a child under 14 it will amount to the crime of indecency with children.[81]

The assault must be indecent : that is, it must be accompanied by circumstances of indecency towards the woman assaulted. If the act is in itself decent, like touching a woman's hand, an indecent motive will not make it indecent.[82] Three sorts of action may be distinguished. Some are indecent unless explained; some are on the face of it capable of being either decent or indecent; some are presumed not to be indecent. If a man touches or threatens to touch a woman's sex organs without her consent this, unless explained by some proper purpose (such as medical examination),[83] is an indecent assault. So is it if, while assaulting her, he exposes himself to her and so makes his sexual purpose clear.[84] If he does an act which is commonly, but not always, the first stage in sexual relations, such as kissing her, against her will,

---

[78a] This point was misunderstood in *Mason* (1968) 53 CAR 12 where, it was alleged, a 39-year-old woman had intercourse with six boys of 14 to 16 and touched their private parts during the preliminaries : Veale J. directed that this would not be indecent assault. The direction would be correct only if she remained totally passive.

[79] *Rolfe* (1952) 36 CAR 4.

[80] *Fairclough* v. *Whipp* 1951 2 All ER 834.

[81] Indecency with Children Act 1960 s. 1(1).

[82] *Kilbourne* 1972 AC 729.

[83] *Armstrong* (1885) 49 JP 745.

[84] *Beal* v. *Kelley* 1951 2 All ER 763 (assault on boy).

the assault is indecent if he makes clear his wish then and there to have sex with her, for example by saying so.[85] If he does, or threatens something from which he gets sexual pleasure but which is not ordinarily a stage in having sexual relations, for example by removing her shoe,[86] this is not an indecent assault unless, perhaps, both are kinky enough to regard it as a stage towards sexual intercourse.

The law as to consent is the same as for rape,[87] except that a girl under 16, whose consent is a defence to a charge of rape if she understands what sexual intercourse is, cannot in law consent to indecent assault.[88] This means that even if she in fact consents a crime is committed, as when a man put his finger in the vagina of a 15-year-old girl with her consent.[89]

One difficult issue regarding consent is more likely to arise in indecent assault than in rape cases. A sadist may get sexual pleasure from beating a woman or in some way making her feel pain. In *Donovan*[90] a man caned a girl of 17. His conviction for indecent assault was quashed because the jury was wrongly directed, but the court expressed the view that no one can validly consent to the infliction on himself of such violence as it likely to cause more than trifling bodily harm. Whether or not it is any longer a crime to maim oneself,[91] in view of the fact that suicide is now lawful,[92] it seems that it is still an offence to maim another or to inflict grievous bodily harm on another even with his or her consent.

But this can only be true when there is no good reason, or just cause, for the maiming. A man may have himself sterilised, and the surgeon who does the operation is not guilty of any crime, at

---

[85] *Leeson* (1968) 52 CAR 185.

[86] *George* 1956 Crim. L.R. 52.

[87] *Bolduc and Bird* (1967) 63 DLR 2d 82 (Canada—fraud).

[88] SOA 1956 s. 14(2).

[89] *McCormack* 1969 2 QB 442.

[90] 1934 2 KB 498. Swift J. contrasted the case with one of 'manly diversions', such as 'cudgels, foils and wrestling.' Ibid. p. 508. L. H. Leigh. 'Sado-masochism, consent and the reform of the criminal law', 39 MLR (1976) 130.

[91] *Wright* (1604) 1 Coke Inst. 127 a–b reports that a 'young, strong and lustie rogue' was convicted of maim for causing his companion to strike off his left hand to improve his chances as a beggar.

[92] Suicide Act 1961 s. 1. In Roman law even slaves had a natural right to maim themselves. Justinian, *Digest* 15.1.9.7 (Ulpian 29 ed.).

least if there is a good medical or social reason for it.[93] Generally speaking sadistic or masochistic sexual practices are not likely to involve any injury serious enough to count as maiming. If they do (and a caning is hardly in this class), the person inflicting them, if he knows this, is in my view guilty of assault, since, though it is good to give sexual pleasure to others, the prospect of doing so cannot be a just cause for maiming them.

As with rape, the man must know that the woman does not consent to his touching her in the way he does or threatens to do, or else not care whether she consents. But when the woman would be held to have consented if she had not been under 16 or a defective, it need not be shown that the man knew this. He acts at his risk, so far as these specially protected women are concerned.[94]

(iii) *Sex by threats*

It is an offence to procure a woman by threats or intimidation to have unlawful sexual intercourse in any part of the world. Corroboration is necessary.[95]

The wording and history of the offence suggest that what the legislator had in mind was the conduct of agents who use threats to recruit prostitutes, generally young, often for brothels abroad. A woman may be guilty. But clearly the crime covers the more obvious case of the man who uses threats to induce a woman to have intercourse with himself. To do so may not amount to rape, because the threats may not exclude the woman's consent. He may threaten something which does not involve violence, such as the loss of her flat or job, or some future violence which the jury finds consistent with her present consent.

(iv) *Sex by false pretences*

It is also an offence to procure a woman by false pretences or false representations to have unlawful sexual intercourse in any part of the world. Again, corroboration is needed.[96] The same

---

[93] *Bravery* 1954 3 All ER 59, 67–8 (Denning LJ dissenting); National Health Service (Family Planning) Administration Act 1972 s. 1 (local authority may provide for sterilisation by vasectomy).

[94] Arguing from *Prince* (1875) LR 2 CCR 154 (abduction) but see n. 134.

[95] SOA 1956 s. 2.

[96] SOA 1956 s. 3.

comments apply to this as to obtaining sex by threats. The deception has to be about a present fact and not about the man's future intentions.[97] Hence the married man who persuades a woman to give way by saying he is not married commits a crime, but a man who succeeds by promising to marry the woman is not guilty even if he does not carry out the promise. Not many women are likely to bring a charge in this type of case.[98]

(v) *Drugging for sexual purposes*

It is an offence for anyone to apply or administer to a woman any drug, or anything intended to stupefy or overpower her, so as to enable a man to have sexual intercourse with her. It is also an offence to cause anything of the sort to be taken by her for that purpose. Corroboration is needed.[98a] The maximum penalty is two years' imprisonment.

A woman may be guilty of this crime. Jill may ply Doris with drink, drugs or medicines so that Tom can have intercourse with Doris. But again the more usual case is that in which the man who wishes to have sex with the woman himself administers the drugs. He does not 'cause' the drug to be taken if she knows what she is taking and freely agrees to take it, even if he hopes that as a result she will be willing to have sexual intercourse. The words 'apply', 'administer' and 'cause to be taken' all imply something done against the woman's will, to which she does not consent with a full knowledge of what she is taking.

Hence it is not an offence for a man to take a woman to a pub in the hope that she will, after she has drunk a certain amount of alcohol, agree to sex, provided that he does not force her to drink or deceive her as to what she is drinking. But if she actually becomes stupefied by drink she will be incapable of consenting to sexual intercourse, and it will be rape for him to take advantage of her while in that condition.[99]

(vi) *Forcible abduction for sexual purposes*

It is a crime for a person to take away (abduct) or detain a

[97] Smith and Hogan, 331 argue for a wider meaning, which would include false promises.

[98] But cf. *Welham, News of the World* 8 May 1977 (alleged pretence that accused were policemen arresting prostitute for soliciting, so that she agreed to have sex with them free).

[98a] SOA 1956 s. 4.

[99] *Camplin* (1845) 1 Den 89.

woman of any age against her will with the intention that she shall marry the abductor or someone else, or have sexual intercourse with them.[100] The abductor must use force or must abduct her for the sake of her property or expectations of property. This crime has an old-fashioned sound so far as property is concerned, but it can apply to cases far removed from the kidnapping of a wealthy heiress. If a man locks a woman in a room until she agrees to intercourse with him, or drags her into his car so that he may have sex with her in a country lane, he is guilty of a crime the maximum penalty for which is fourteen years in prison. She need not be in the possession of a parent or guardian.

(vii) *Fraudulent abduction for sexual purposes*

It is also a crime which carries a maximum of fourteen years' imprisonment to take or detain a woman under 21 out of the possession of her parent or guardian against his or her will by fraud and with the intention that she shall marry the abductor or another or have sexual intercourse with them.[101] But this is a crime only if the girl has property or expectations of property from her next-of-kin. Still, a record-player is presumably sufficient.

The reference to 21 is misleading, since a child now comes of age at 18[102] and is not after that in the possession of her parent or guardian even if she was before.

(b) *Abuse of authority: incest*

There are cases in which a girl or woman consents to sexual intercourse with a man but the man, in getting her consent, has abused his position as a father, teacher or other person in authority over her.

It can happen, though less often, that a boy or man consents to sexual intercourse with a woman who abuses her position as a mother, teacher or the like. These two possibilities are dealt with in this section. A third type of case in which a man in authority takes sexual advantage of a boy or man in his charge is dealt with in the next chapter.

[100] SOA 1956 s. 17.
[101] SOA 1956 s. 18.
[102] Family Law Reform Act 1969 s. 1.

Certain cases of abuse of authority are covered by the crime of incest, but incest ranges a good deal further. It is an offence for a man over 14 to have sexual intercourse with his daughter, granddaughter, sister or mother, provided that he knows of the relationship at the time.[103] It is also a crime for a woman over 16 to permit her father, grandfather brother or son to have sexual intercourse with her by her consent, provided again that she knows of the relationship.[104] Because a girl under 16 commits no crime by permitting incest, her father etc. committed no crime at common law by inciting her to have sexual intercourse with him.[104a] But by statute such incitement now carries a maximum of two years imprisonment.[104b] In all these cases illegitimate relationships count, and a half-brother or sister is included.[105]

People cannot marry if sexual relations between them would amount to the crime of incest. But neither can a man marry his aunt or niece or, in case anyone should think of doing so, his grandmother, not to mention his father's, son's, grandfather's or grandson's wife, and his wife's mother, daughter, grandmother or granddaughter.[106] Yet he can have sex with any or all of these relatives without running foul of the criminal law.

The maximum punishment for incest is seven years in prison unless a man is charged with committing it on a girl under 13, in which case he is liable to life imprisonment.[107] Attempts are punishable by up to two years' imprisonment, or seven when the victim is a girl under 13.[108] A father or grandfather convicted of incest with a girl under 21 can be divested by the court of his authority over her and, if he is her guardian, removed from the guardianship.[109]

There are other crimes specially directed against those who, to have sexual relations, abuse their authority. A person who is responsible for a girl under 16 is liable to up to two years' imprisonment if he causes or encourages her to be a prostitute or

[103] SOA 1956 s. 10(1).
[104] SOA 1956 s. 11(1).
[104a] *Whitehouse*, 1977 3 All ER 377.
[104b] Criminal Law Act 1977 s. 54(1).
[105] SOA 1956 s. 10(2), 11(2).
[106] Marriage Act 1949 Schedule 1 as amended. S. 78(1) extends this to half-blood and illegitimate relatives.
[107] SOA 1956 2nd Schedule 14(a).
[108] SOA 1956 2nd Schedule 14(b).
[109] SOA 1956 s. 38.

causes or encourages someone to have unlawful sexual intercourse with her or to commit an indecent assault on her.[110] The
person responsible for her is her parent or legal guardian or the
person who has actual control or charge of her,[111] such as a school-
teacher. The person responsible for her is held to have caused
or encouraged the girl to have sex if he knowingly allowed her to
consort with or be employed by or continue to be employed by a
prostitute or 'person of known immoral character'[112] such as a
pimp. Is a business man who is known to have sex with as many
of the typists and secretaries as will let him a 'person of known
immoral character'? Why not?

(c) *The exploitation of children*

Even though she consents to intercourse, and even apart from
incest or prostitution, a girl needs protection up to a certain age.
To secure this the law makes it a crime for a man to have sexual
intercourse with her under the prescribed age. The law differs
according to whether the girl is under 13, 14, 16 or 21, and
according to whether the man has sexual intercourse or commits
some other sexual act with her, or abducts her from her parent or
guardian for sexual purposes.

For a man to have unlawful sexual intercourse with a girl
under 13 is a crime for which the maximum penalty is life
imprisonment.[113] The intercourse could only be lawful in a most
unusual case such as that of a marriage valid under that age
according to a foreign system of law.[114] Consent is no defence.
Life imprisonment can also be imposed on the owner or occupier
of premises who induces a girl under 13 to resort to or be on the
premises for unlawful sexual intercourse with a man or men, or
knowingly allows her to do so. The same penalty falls on anyone
who acts or assists in the management or control of the premises
in these circumstances.[115]

It is an offence, created in 1960, to commit an act of gross
indecency with or towards a child under 14, or to incite a child

[110] SOA 1956 s. 28(1).
[111] SOA 1956 s. 28(3).
[112] SOA 1956 s. 28(2).
[113] SOA 1956 s. 5.
[114] *Mohamed* v. *Knott* 1969 1 QB 1 (wife of 13).
[115] SOA 1956 s. 25.

under that age to an act of gross indecency with the person
inciting or another. The maximum penalty is two years'
imprisonment.[116]

This offence can be committed by a man or woman against
a girl or boy. As explained in Chapter 4, an act of gross indecency
must be a sexual act. Such an act usually involves contact with
the sex organs of another or masturbation in the presence of
another. A mere kiss, even if passionate, is probably not an act of
gross indecency.[117]

The crime, which was created by the Indecency with Children
Act 1960, fills a gap in the law by protecting a young girl (or
boy) when the man neither has sexual intercourse with her nor
assaults her, but invites her to have some sexual contact with him,
or performs some sexual act in her presence. An example is when
a man exposes his penis to a girl under 14 and asks her to touch
it.[118] Whether she does so or not this is not an assault, since the
man does not touch her. But it is an act of gross indecency.
Indeed a man who stays passive when a young girl puts her
hand over his penis may thereby commit an act of gross indecency, since he may in effect be inviting her to continue.[118a] The
age chosen is arbitrary. Clearly the age of consent to sexual intercourse, at present 16, should also be the age of consent to other
sexual acts, at least with adults.

Unlawful intercourse with a girl under 16 is also an offence.[119]
Sixteen is the age of consent to sexual intercourse. The maximum
penalty is two years in prison. The prosecution must be begun
within a year of the alleged offence. It is quite common (and
proper) for the police not to prosecute teenage boys for this
offence.[120] A man who marries a girl under 16, the minimum age
for marriage,[121] is not guilty if he has sex with her under age
when he reasonably believes her to be his wife, for example
because he thinks she is older.[122] Nor is a man under 24 guilty
if he has not before been charged with sexual intercourse or

[116] Indecency with Children Act 1960.
[117] Ch. 4 n. 24.
[118] *Fairclough* v. *Whipp* 1951 2 AER 834.
[118a] *Speck* 1977 2 All ER 859.
[119] SOA 1956 s. 6(1).
[120] *Commissioner of Police of the Metropolis ex p. Blackburn*, 1968
2 QB 118, 139.
[121] Marriage Act 1949 s. 2.
[122] SOA 1956 s. 6(2).

attempted sexual intercourse with a girl under 16, and if on the occasion for which he is now charged he reasonably thought she was 16 or over.[123] From this arbitrary rule it may be inferred that it is no defence to a man of 24 or over, or who has been charged before, that he reasonably thought the girl was 16 or over. Indeed it seems that in these offences which depend on the girl being under a certain age it is no defence that the man believes, however reasonably, that she is over the age.[124] The law about mistake as to age is therefore quite different from the law about mistake as to consent. There is in my opinion a good reason for the difference. A man cannot ask a girl for her birth certificate before deciding whether to have sex with her. It is often very difficult to tell a girl's age. Hence the law could not protect girls under a certain age if it merely required the man to take reasonable steps to discover their age. The reasonable steps would in practice be confined to judging from her appearance and asking her, neither of which would necessarily reveal the truth. The risk is therefore put on the man. If he has been misled by lies or appearance he will not be severely punished. But it is much easier for a man to discover whether a woman consents to sexual intercourse than to find out her age, and if she has reached the age of consent she should be capable of making her attitude clear. For this reason the law holds the man guilty only if he knows that the woman does not consent, or is indifferent. This may go too far, but clearly the man should not be made liable in such a case unless, at the least, he is at fault in not realising that she does not consent.

The same maximum penalty of two years is laid down for the owner or occupier of premises, or anyone concerned in their management or control who induces a girl under 16 to resort to or be in them for unlawful sexual intercourse with a man or men.[125]

Once a girl has reached 16 it is generally speaking no offence, short of the use of force, deception, or drugs, for a man to persuade a woman to have sexual relations with himself. But he must not take an unmarried girl under 18 out of the possession of her parent or guardian against their will with the intention

[123] SOA 1956 s. 6(3).

[124] Arguing from *Prince* (1875) LR 2 CCR 154, together with SOA 1956 s. 6(3), 7(2), 9(2), 14(4), 27(2). This runs counter to the general trend in modern criminal law: *Sweet* v. *Parsley* 1970 AC 132.

[125] SOA 1956 s. 26.

that she shall have sexual intercourse with a man or men, for example with the abductor.[126] It is a defence that he believes on reasonable grounds that she is 18 or over.[127] Two years in prison is the maximum penalty. Nor may a man (or a woman) procure a woman under 21 to have unlawful sexual intercourse anywhere in the world with a third person.[128] Thus, even if Jack and Jill are married, Jack must not induce Jill to take part in a wife-swapping party or swinging group until Jill is 21. The maximum penalty is two years in prison. 'Procure' implies persuasion or inducement. If Jill, being under 21, suggests to Jack that she would like to have sex with David, Jack commits no offence by agreeing. The wording of the law suggests that the original object of this law was to stop the recruitment of prostitutes, but the effect is much wider.

(d) *The exploitation of defectives*

There are five offences meant to protect women defectives, that is those who suffer from 'severe subnormality' so that they cannot look after themselves. A man who has unlawful sexual intercourse with a defective is guilty of an offence.[129] So is anyone who procures a woman defective to have unlawful sexual intercourse anywhere in the world.[130] Likewise, anyone who takes a woman defective out of the possession of her parent or guardian (i.e the person who has lawful care or charge of her) with the intention that she should have unlawful sexual intercourse with a man or men.[131]

The owner or occupier of premises or anyone who acts or assists in their management or control is guilty of a crime if he induces a woman defective to resort to them or to be on them for unlawful sexual intercourse with a man or men.[132] Anyone who causes or encourages the prostitution anywhere in the world of a woman defective is likewise guilty of an offence.[133] In all these instances the maximum penalty is two years' imprisonment.

[126] SOA 1956 s. 19(1).
[127] SOA 1956 s. 19(2).
[128] SOA 1956 s. 23.
[129] SOA 1956 s. 7(1).
[130] SOA 1956 s. 9(1).
[131] SOA 1956 s. 21(1).
[132] SOA 1956 s. 27(1).
[133] SOA 1956 s. 29(1).

But in none of these five cases is an offence committed if the accused person did not know that the woman was a defective and had no reason to suspect it.[134] It has been held that the test is not whether, on the known facts, any ordinary person would know or have reason to suppose that the woman was a defective, but whether he himself knew or had reason to suspect this.[135] To call this, as the court did, a 'subjective approach' rests on a confusion. Whether the accused person *knew* that she was a defective is a question about his state of mind. Whether he had *reason to suspect* this is only partly a question about his state of mind. The answer depends on whether he knew facts from which an ordinary person would conclude (though he himself did not) that she was defective.

The statutes call the defence that the man was ignorant an 'exception' and lay down that the accused must prove that he comes within it, viz. on a balance of probabilities, not beyond reasonable doubt.[136] The drafting of these provisions is shoddy. They mean but fail to say that the sexual intercourse with the defective woman is unlawful but that the defendant is excused because of his mistake.

In the upshot there is no way in which a man can have sexual intercourse with a woman defective, unless he is married to her, without committing a crime. Even if he is willing to look after and provide for her he is not excused. This can be hard on the woman whom it is meant to take care of.

3. THE REFORM OF THE CRIMINAL LAW

We can assume that in the near future at least the law will continue to be based on the notion that men are more aggressive than women, but will take into account that the sexes are drawing closer together in this as in other respects. It will therefore continue to protect women against the sexual assaults and advances of men when they are not in a position to fend for themselves.

The room for change is therefore quite small. But in three

[134] SOA 1956 s. 7(2), 9(2), 21(2), 27(2), 29(2).
[135] *Hudson* 1965 1 All ER 721.
[136] Above, n. 84 and SOA 1956 s. 47: *Carr-Braint* 1943 2 All ER 156; *Dunbar* 1957 2 All ER 737.

areas in particular one can reasonably ask whether the present law protects women too little, too much or just enough. I am referring to the problems of consent in the law of rape; incest; and the age of consent to sexual intercourse with girls.

Rape

For a number of reasons it is difficult to frame a satisfactory law of consent to sexual intercourse and other sexual acts. Because he is usually more daring a man is apt to think that a woman will allow him to go further than she really intends. A woman, being more cautious, is apt not to realise how far a man wants and intends to go. Each misreads the other's mind. Negotiations for having sex are not, apart from prostitution, carried on like those for the rent of a house. There is often no definite stage at which it can be said that the two have agreed to sexual intercourse. They proceed by touching, feeling, fumbling, by signs and words which are not generally in the form of a Roman stipulation: 'May I kiss you?', 'You may'; 'May I feel your breasts?', 'You may'—and so on. The man judges the woman's response rather from her expression (the dilation of the eye pupils is said to be important), her bodily movements, her words and from past experience, if any. It is easy to be wrong.

It would be wise, though less romantic, and less likely to lead to a criminal charge, if men made their intentions clearer, and if women who were not willing to allow sexual intercourse, or some form of petting short of intercourse, said so at an earlier stage. The law must, however, deal with people as they are, and English people in particular are inclined to say too little rather than too much. In this state of affairs the courts and legislature have decided that if a man honestly believes that the woman consents to sexual intercourse at the time of the alleged rape offence he is not guilty of the offence. The decision in *Morgan*,[137] which laid this down, was solidly based on earlier cases which go back for a century at least.[138] From a technical point of view it cannot be faulted.

It is not, however, obvious that the risk of mistake should fall on the woman rather than the man. She has a right that her body

[137] 1976 AC 182; E. M. Curley, 'Excusing rape', 5 *Philosophy and Public Affairs* (1976) 325.
[138] *Lloyd* (1836) 7 C. & P. 318, 319 is the earliest.

should not be violated, and in practice recourse to the criminal law is the only way in which, unless she is a karate expert, she can vindicate that right. So she has an interest in the proceedings which is to be balanced against that of the man. The best way to balance them is to hold, as did the minority of the House of Lords in *Morgan*,[139] that only a reasonable mistake as to consent is a defence to a rape charge. The objection of the Heilbron Committee, that it would be too difficult to fix a standard of reasonable conduct in relation to a rape charge, is not convincing.[140] The man has a duty to find out whether the woman is willing to have sexual intercourse with him and it is perfectly sensible that a jury should be asked whether he took reasonable steps to find out.

It is true that if this were the position the law about rape would diverge from the law about, for example, theft. A person is not a thief if, honestly but without good reason, he believes that he has a right to the property taken.[141] But bodies deserve better protection than goods. The fact that the man was impatient rather than callous can and should be taken into account in fixing sentence. It is true that if the man is acquitted the woman will not in future generally be exposed to the humiliation of being known to the world as a woman who has brought a rape charge against a man without success. But though the ban on publicity is an important step forward, it does not alter the fact that a rape case is far more a contest between the woman and the man than between the state and the man. In that contest it is important, without unfairness to the man, to strike as even a balance as possible. After all, an accused person who kills or wounds in self-defence or the defence of another must show that he acted reasonably,[142] and while sexual intercourse without consent is not wounding, it is, in the eyes of many women, not far removed from it.

It may be said that if a man believes, though not reasonably, that a woman consents to sex his behaviour should not be called rape. If so, the offence might be termed 'unlawful sexual inter-

[139] 1976 AC 182, 221 (Lord Simon of Glaisdale); cf. *Sperotto* 1970 1 New South Wales Rep. 502.

[140] *Home Office Report of the Advisory Committee on the Law of Rape* (1975), Cmnd. 6352 10.

[141] Theft Act 1968 s. 2(1).

[142] *McInnes* 1971 3 All ER 295. Criminal Law Act 1967 s. 3(1).

course' and there might be a rule that on a rape charge the jury can find the accused guilty of having unlawful sexual intercourse if they think that the man believed, though without good reason, that the woman consented.

Incest

In the section on the criminal law incest came under the heading of sexual abuse of authority. The existing law of incest, however, covers cases such as incest between brother and sister, which need have no such element about them. The fact is that the objects of the present law of incest are rather mysterious.

Incest was an offence only in the church courts until in 1908 Parliament made it an ordinary crime.[143] It arouses strong feelings, and must be tried by a High Court judge unless the presiding judge on the circuit decides otherwise.[144] Heavy sentences are sometimes imposed : even in recent years there have been some of between four and seven years in prison.[145]

In nearly all societies whether primitive or advanced there seems to be some restraint on sex between people who are conceived of as close relatives. The practical effect of these bans varies enormously, since the word, for example, which we translate 'sister' may refer to anything between what we would call a sister (a sibling), on the one hand, and all the women belonging to your group, on the other. Hence a rule which says you may not marry your 'sister' may force you to seek a partner outside your own group or clan. The words which we translate as 'incest' are also very varied. Some of them, such as our word, mean 'unchaste' but others refer to blood-shame, disruption of order or behaviour that is out of place.[146] There is always some restriction, but not all societies have a horror of incest.[147] Relations within the narrow 'nuclear' family are prohibited in most societies; some

[143] Punishment of Incest Act 1908. Lord Halsbury opposed the bill on the ground that the discussion of such matters in court would be worse than the acts themselves.

[144] Cross and Jones, *Introduction to Criminal Law* (7th ed. 1972) 414.

[145] In 1973, when 129 people were convicted of incest, thirteen fathers were sentenced to four years or more in prison.

[146] R. Needham, *Remarks and Inventions: Skeptical Essays about Kinship* (1974) 61, 68.

[147] Needham 68.

further restrictions are common, but who they extend to varies a great deal from one people to another.[148]

Hence, though our rules of incest are historically derived from the Bible, it is not easy to be clear about their present social purposes. Three possible aims are worth mentioning. There is evidence that the children of close relatives are more likely than the average to suffer from genetic defects and that the chances increase rapidly if the union is between relatives in the first degree, such as brother and sister, mother and son, father and daughter.[149] Secondly, studies of kibbutzim in Israel seem to show that children who grow up together in a close-knit unit, unless separated by the age of 6, seldom look for marriage partners within their own group.[150] Westermarck argued that, just as husbands and wives find one another less attractive after a long period of married life, so, for example, a brother and sister who are brought up together will not be sexually drawn to one another. The royal brothers and sisters who in Egypt were expected to marry were separated in childhood just in order to stimulate attraction.[151]

Finally, sex within a small 'nuclear' family, especially between different generations is likely to be disturbing, and to introduce jealousies and tensions which should be absent from the calm of the close family circle.

The genetic dangers to the children of close relatives are serious, but since we do not in general forbid people to marry because of genetic defects this would not be enough by itself to justify the crime of incest or the ban on marriage within the prohibited degrees. The fact that we tend to look for sexual partners outside those who grew up with us in the same house or institution is, again, a reason why most of us do not want to have sex with or to marry our sisters rather than a reason for imposing rules which forbid it. The third reason—family tension—is the most weighty. It would justify not a law directed against incest as such but one forbidding parents and other persons in authority in the home,

[148] G. R. Leslie, *The Family in Social Context* (3rd ed. 1976) 62.

[149] 59 *Eugenics Review* (1967) 76.

[150] J. Shepher, 'Mate selection among second generation kibbutz adolescents and adults', *Archives of Sexual Behaviour* (1971) 1. 293–307.

[151] E. Westermarck, *The History of Human Marriage* (1922) 2. 36: Leslie 67.

such as guardians, from having sexual relations with children under the age of majority, viz. under 18. The main problem of course concerns fathers and teenage daughters. On the other hand, there seems no compelling reason why sexual experiments between brothers and sisters, though hardly to be encouraged, should lead to criminal proceedings. The law of criminal incest might therefore be abolished as such, and replaced by a law of sexual abuse of authority, which would extend not merely to parents and guardians, but also to teachers and other persons in charge of children under 18. There are indeed already countries, such as France[152] and Belgium,[153] in which incest is not a crime but abuse of authority is punishable.

If this policy were accepted, it would not necessarily lead to any change in the law about the prohibited degrees of marriage. There are, it seems to me, good reasons why a man should not marry his aunt or niece,[154] even if sexual relations between them are lawful, as they already are. The point of the ban is to keep the sort of relaxed family tie which we have with our aunts, uncles, nephews and nieces : subtly different from that with parents and grandparents, children and grandchildren, yet adding greatly to the strength of family feeling and to the security of those who enjoy it.

The age of consent
The age at which a girl can, by consenting to sexual intercourse with a man, make it lawful in the sense of not criminal for him to have intercourse with her is generally called the age of consent. The age of consent has been 16 for nearly a hundred years. Should it now be lowered?

Before 1885 it was not an offence to have sexual intercourse with a girl with her consent, though naturally her age had a bearing on whether she was capable of consenting to sex. In that year, as a result of scandals in connection with child prostitution, and the light sentence passed on Mary Jeffries after her conviction for keeping a brothel, public opinion was aroused.[155] A Criminal Law Amendment Act was carried through Parliament which

---

[152] Penal Code art. 333.
[153] Penal Code art. 377.
[154] Marriage Act 1949 Schedule 1 as amended.
[155] M. Pearson, *The Age of Consent* (1972).

made it a crime to have sexual intercourse with a girl under 16, subject to a limited defence if the man is under 24,[156] and a more serious offence to have intercourse with a girl under 13.[157] At that time the age of marriage was 12, so that the age of consent was four years above the age of marriage until 1929, when the Marriage Act raised it to 16 also.[158]

In 1972 the school-leaving age was raised from 15 to 16,[159] so that the school-leaving age, the age of consent to sex and the age of marriage are now the same. This is the result of a historical accident, but accidents are the cloth of which society is woven. The fact that 16 is the age of consent is well known to most people, and they have become used to a limit which was originally designed simply to prevent the prostitution of young girls. It would be awkward for both parents and teachers if the age of consent to sexual intercourse were below the school-leaving age. There is also a certain good sense in the idea that when it is possible to have sexual intercourse it should also be possible for the girl to marry if she bears a child, subject of course to her parents' consent.

For these reasons, and because 16 is the age of consent in the neighbouring EEC countries apart from France and Denmark,[160] the age of consent should remain at 16. Those who seek to reduce it argue that many girls under 16 now have sexual intercourse and that, in any case, there is little point in prosecuting the boys who have sex with them. In 1860 the average age of a girl's first periods was between 16 and 17. Now it is between 12 and 13,[161] and the age of consent, they say, should be as close as possible to that of physical maturity.

If sexual intercourse becomes usual for girls of 13 to 15 the law will have to be changed. That has not happened yet. Schofield's 1965 study showed that at that time only some 5 per

---

[156] CLAA 1885 s. 5.

[157] CLAA 1885 s. 4.

[158] Now Marriage Act 1949 s. 2.

[159] Raising of the School Leaving Age Order No. 444 of 1972, under the Education Act 1944 s. 35.

[160] West German penal code art. 182; Italian penal code art. 530; Belgian penal code art. 372(1); Swiss penal code art. 191(1); Netherlands penal code arts. 245, 247, but French penal code art. 333(1); Danish penal code art. 222(1) fifteen.

[161] M. Schofield, *Promiscuity* (1976) 13.

cent of girls under 16 had had intercourse.[162] Since then the percentage has probably increased, but not to the point at which sex under 16 has become standard for a girl of that age. Though 5 per cent of girls under 16 is, over the whole of England, a large number, one must not fall into the trap which affects many practising lawyers, social workers and psychologists who meet many problem types and few ordinary people. Having little idea of figures, they misjudge the extent to which the sample of people they encounter represents the rest of society. They think the pattern can be deduced from those in care, in approved schools or in consulting rooms.

It is of course the boy or man, not the girl, who is liable to prosecution. Here the law should, in my view, be altered so that a boy under the age of majority is not liable to be prosecuted for having sexual intercourse with a girl of 13 or over but under 16, at least if she is not more than a year or two younger. The age of 18, having been chosen as the age of majority, should mark a dividing line. Under it sex with girls who have reached the age of puberty should count as a teenage experiment. Over it there should be full responsibility. Here again, some neighbouring countries have given a lead.[163] At present in England a man under 24 has, on a first charge, the defence that he reasonably believed the girl to be over age.[164] Some would want to extend this so that men of any age would have a similar defence of reasonable mistake as to age. For the reasons given above[165] this is to be resisted. The area is one in which for the law to protect girls effectively the man must be held to act at his own risk, since in practice he can do no more than go by the girl's appearance and what she says about her age. The rule of guilty mind or *mens rea* does not require that we should know all the elements of an offence before we are found guilty. It requires rather that we should know when we are entering an area of risk. But of course it is in point in sentencing to know whether the girl appeared to be over age, and whether she was sexually experienced, indeed a prostitute : she may belong to the minority of women who are highly promiscuous, indeed obsessed with sex.

[162] M. Schofield, *The Sexual Behaviour of Young People* (1968 ed.) 50.
[163] Belgium penal code art. 372 bis.
[164] SOA 1965 s. 6(3).
[165] Above, nn. 124–5.

4

Liking Your Own Sex

'Girls will be boys and boys will be girls.
It's a mixed up world'

(The Kinks, *Lola*)

I. HOMOSEXUALS

This chapter deals with the legal position of men who have sexual relations with other men, and women who have sex with other women. Such people are called homosexual[1] (and in the case of women also 'lesbians'), as opposed to those men and women who have sexual relations with one another and who are called heterosexual. Marriage between members of the same sex, however, is dealt with in Chapter 2, male prostitution in Chapter 5 and sex with boys under the age of puberty (paedophilia) in Chapter 3.

Most men prefer sex with women and most women prefer sex with men. This is what people are taught and what, in general, society expects. The majority conform not merely through fear of what others will say, but because they are attracted to the opposite sex. A minority, however, do not conform at all, or not all the time or in all circumstances.

Since in most countries, including England, homosexual relations between women are generally not criminal, and since most of the studies concern sex between men, what follows is mainly about men. On Kinsey's figures for white US males about 4 per cent of men have sex only with other men throughout their

---

[1] I use the term to refer to those who *practice* sexual relations with their own sex. It is sometimes used for those who are *attracted to* their own sex even if they do not have sex with them, or those who *consider themselves* homosexual, whatever their practice may be.

lives.[2] The percentage of women who have sex only with other women is lower. Though Kinsey's methods can be criticised in certain respects, his results as regards homosexuality are not likely to be far wrong, since people who are not homosexual are not likely to say that they are. The figure of 4 per cent seems to be confirmed by a more recent survey in Sweden[3] and can be accepted as a rough guide to the number of homosexuals in Western countries, including England.

Most homosexuals conceal the fact. A minority, however, admit it, at least within certain circles. These form the core, though by no means the whole of the homosexual group or 'subculture', the gay scene. This has its pubs and its clubs, its language and its baths, its favoured professions like interior decorating and dancing.[4]

Homosexual men are more promiscuous than homosexual women or heterosexual men, perhaps because men are in general more inclined to seek variety in sex than all but a small percentage of women.[5] It is no surprise, then, that though some form long-term attachments, and even think of themselves as 'married', the relations between men and men are usually not as stable as those between men and women or between women. They are offgoing rather than ongoing.

Men who prefer their own sex tend to contact them, obviously, in the places where they concentrate (gay bars, clubs, baths, and the like), through advertisements in contact magazines or friends who are known to be homosexual. As will be seen in a later section, whether a man who contacts another for sexual purposes in one of these ways commits a crime depends on the circumstances. Those men, on the other hand, who make contacts in public toilets are nearly always in breach of the criminal law.

Most of what has been said about men who are exclusively homosexual applies to some extent to those who are partly so. Kinsey found that apart from the 4 per cent hard-core male

[2] A. C. Kinsey and others, *Sexual Behaviour in the Human Male* (1948) 623; cf. *Report of the Committee on Homosexual Offences and Prostitution* ('Wolfenden' Cmnd. 247, 1957) s. 38; W. Barnett, *Sexual Freedom and the Constitution* (1973) 192 n. 156; M. Schofield, *Sociological Aspects of Homosexuality* (1965) 157, 206.

[3] Barnett 258–9.

[4] C. A. Tripp, *The Homosexual Matrix* (1977) 276–7.

[5] M. Schofield, *The Sexual Behaviour of Young People* (1968 ed.) 80–1, 220, 230–1; *Promiscuity* (1976) 46f.; Tripp 153–4.

homosexuals about 6 per cent of men confine their sexual interests to other men for at least three years after they have reached adolescence. Another 27 per cent have some sexual experience with other men after reaching that age.[6] In all, then, some 37 per cent of men were found to have some homosexual experience between puberty and old age. But these figures must be kept in perspective. In the case of 31 per cent out of 37 the men's experience was confined to their youth, and occurred at the age of puberty or when they were adolescent.[7]

Though these figures refer to the USA of thirty years ago they probably give some clue to the extent of homosexuality in the England of today. If this is so, something like a third of the men in our society, though not exclusively homosexual, have sex with other men, even after they are grown up, at least at a certain stage of their life or in certain circumstances. They may do so because they like variety, because they are cut off from their wives or from other women, because they are drunk or high or otherwise uninhibited, because they have a need for deep relations with members of both sexes, or just to please a friend. A careful study of sex in public toilets in an American city showed that most of the men who wank (masturbate) or suck one another in these places, and who one might think were the most lonely and twisted of homosexuals, are married men who in general prefer, or say that they prefer, sex with women.[8]

There is a difference between the practices of the men who have sex with both women and men (sometimes called bisexuals) and their attitudes. In practice every sort of mix is to be found, from the man who goes with another man only when he has had too much to drink to the one who has a wife or mistress and also a regular boy-friend, the promiscuous male who chases 'anything that moves', and the man who will settle for a woman only when no other man is to be had. Attitudes are less varied. Of the men who are not in practice exclusively homosexual only a few actually think of themselves as homosexual. Some of these fit into the gay scene. The majority deny, sometimes with vehemence, that they are homosexual. Many can persuade themselves that to be

[6] Kinsey and others (above, n. 2) 623, 650–6.
[7] Barnett 192. Gagnon, *Int. Ency. of Social Sciences* 14(1968) 219 concludes that 85 per cent of those who have homosexual experience (viz. 31 per cent of the total) do so during puberty or adolescence.
[8] L. Humphreys, *Tearoom Trade* (1970) 112–13.

active rather than passive is not queer, or that a man is not a homosexual if he does not kiss another man, or that an occasional man on the side does not count.[9] Indeed they may refuse to call themselves bisexual. In a sense they may be right, for this word can be taken to refer not only to the practice of having sex with both women and men, but to the rarer attitude of those who have serious relationships with both sexes, and perhaps find a different sort of happiness or satisfaction in each.

What has been said of men can be applied with caution to women. The number of homosexual women—lesbians—is probably lower than for men and the percentage of bisexual women also seems to be lower. The lesbian subculture is less prominent than the male gay scene,[10] and is sometimes just a part of it, as in the case of gay clubs which are open to both sexes. But with the present vigour of the movement for women's liberation the position may soon change.

The causes of homosexual attraction, if 'cause' is the right word to use, are unknown.[10a] No one has managed to show that it is inborn, that a genetic factor is involved.[11] On the other hand it has been argued that there are physical differences between homosexuals and heterosexuals. It is said that homosexuals are sexually precocious, come to puberty earlier and have on the average a larger penis.[12] But most evidence suggests that sexual attitudes are learned, and that the learning is spread over a period. This applies equally to liking the opposite sex and liking one's own. Experiments with monkeys, which may be a pointer to the human condition, show that if they are separated from one another in childhood and cannot play with monkeys of the opposite sex before they mature, they do not learn to have sex in the normal way after maturity.[13] If one can argue from monkeys to human beings, we are most likely to have good relations with the opposite sex if we grow up together and play together before puberty and after. This is an argument for mixed education.

Freud and many psychoanalysts thought that people's sexual

---

[9] Humphreys 111–17.   [10] B. Magee, *One in Twenty* (1968 ed.) 152f.

[10a] D. J. West. *Homosexuality Re-examined* (1977) 7.

[11] Barnett 138–43; Money, 'Sexual dimorphism and homosexual gender identity', 74 *Psychological Bull.* (1970) 428.

[12] Tripp, 83–4.

[13] H. Harlow, 'Sexual behaviour of the rhesus monkey', in F. A. Beach, *Sex and Behaviour* (1968).

attitudes become fixed in early childhood. Freud gave some far-fetched explanations of how, in his view, this happened, including, for example, the fear of castration.[14] Even if these are rejected it remains possible, though not proved by any statistical study, that attitudes to sex become settled in early childhood. Other writers think that a process like imprinting takes place, by which, at a crucial stage of growth, a child's attitude to his own and the opposite sex is fixed by some experience he or she goes through.[15] On this view the seduction of a child before or near puberty, or some adventure at the time of puberty, may determine what he or she prefers. Some medical studies, however, deny that seduction of a child is likely to have lasting effects. According to these, parents are apt to be unnecessarily alarmed about the seduction of their children.[16]

It is a popular belief that homosexuals often have possessive mothers and that their fathers are frequently absent or, if present, ineffective. At any rate, homosexuals seem more inclined than heterosexuals to describe their parents in this way.[17] But whether a close relation between mother and son is a cause or effect of his being homosexual is not clear.[18] Certainly some homosexuals are searching for a father figure, and others seem to be driven by a high ideal of male prowess, perhaps under the influence of their mates and peers, which takes on a sexual tinge.[19] Others, again, may simply lack the self-confidence to take on the normal male role with girls.

In the end nothing but an informed guess is possible, but it seems most likely that sexual attitudes are not inborn but have to be learned. They are complicated and depend to some extent on how a child imitates its parents and peers. As with any process of learning there are various ways in which the process of learning to be heterosexual can go wrong. A boy may take his mother rather than his father as a model of behaviour at a certain stage of his development, or a girl her father rather than her mother.

[14] Tripp 77–80.

[15] Barnett 167, 204–11; cf. on imprinting, K. Z. Lorenz, *King Solomon's Ring* (1952).

[16] Schofield, *Homosexuality* 154–5; *Wolfenden Report* (above, n. 1), s. 98; Barnett 165.

[17] Barnett, 151–4, 156–9, 180 and 72; Schofield, *Homosexuality*, 105; Ploscowe 212.

[18] Tripp 79–80.

[19] Tripp 74f.

Rather than take a man or boy whom he admires as a model to imitate a boy may become emotionally attached to him to an extent which excludes emotional attachment to the opposite sex; and a girl may become attached to a woman or another girl in a similar way. No doubt there are many other ways in which people fail to fit the expected mould, just as there are many ways in which a child may fail to conform at school or in the home. Having a lone-wolf, off-beat outlook on life may be one factor in encouraging a non-conformist attitude to sex.

If this is the right way to look at the matter homosexuality is not simply a matter of taste, like a preference for gin-and-tonic rather than bitter. Nor is it a matter of deviance, like shoplifting rather than paying for a pair of jeans. It is not primarily a matter of breaking rules but of dissenting attitudes. It resembles political or religious dissent, being an atheist in Catholic Ireland or a dissident in Soviet Russia. In such cases the dissenter differs from those around him or her by failing to acquire, or rejecting, a whole set of feelings which together make up the orthodox and conformist way of life.

If the reason why some children do not conform in sex has to do with the personality of their parents there is little that can be done about the matter. Possessive mothers and ineffective fathers have plenty of heterosexual children and they cannot anyhow be stopped from marrying and having children. In sex as in other spheres of life there will always be a non-conforming minority.

2. THE LAW

The law is not concerned with homosexual attitudes, but with acts. From a social point of view these acts are generally disapproved whether they are done between men or between women. The law, however, distinguishes. In most modern societies homosexual acts between men are forbidden altogether or allowed only between consenting adults in private. Otherwise they are criminal offences. Such acts between lesbians, on the other hand, are either not criminal or, if they are, are seldom prosecuted. In England homosexual acts between men have since 1967 in general not been criminal if they take place between those over 21 in private.[20] Between women such acts are generally lawful if both parties are over 16. But in both cases there are exceptions, as we shall see.

Since the laws are mainly directed against men I shall deal with male homosexual acts first. The acts to be considered are: first, intercourse in which a man's penis penetrates the anus of another. Colloquially called 'fucking' or 'bumming', the technical name in English for this form of sex is 'sodomy', a term which also applies to intercourse of the same sort with a woman. 'Buggery' is a wider conception which covers not merely sodomy but intercourse with an animal.[21] Such is the English usage. In the USA 'sodomy' is in many states used in a very wide sense to mean any homosexual act, including those listed below.[22] Indeed it sometimes extends to any act other than normal heterosexual intercourse. This wide interpretation can be explained by the desire of courts in some American states to see that homosexual acts other than buggery are punishable even if there is no statute specially referring to them.

Apart from buggery the main homosexual acts are sucking another's penis (fellation), masturbating another and making contact with the whole of another's body including his genitals (sometimes called genital apposition). Any of these, and any other act which involves contact with the genitals of another man (unless it can be justified by some good reason such as medical examination) counts in English law as an act of gross indecency,[23] a term which also applies to the act of masturbating in the presence of another, even without contact.

The phrase 'gross indecency' suggests a contrast with ordinary indecency. Perhaps it would be an act of ordinary but not gross indecency for a man to kiss another man with sexual intentions or in a way that had sexual overtones.[24]

In England, then, a homosexual act between males may be criminal if it is either an act of buggery or one of gross indecency. But not all such acts are criminal.

[20] Sexual Offences Act (hereafter SOA) 1967 s. 1(1).
[21] *Cozins* (1834) 6 C. & P. 351; *Brown* (1889) 24 QBD 357 (CCR).
[22] *State* v. *Philips* 430 P. 2d 139 (19 Ariz. 1967); R. M. Perkins, *Criminal Law* (1967) 389.
[23] SOA 1956 s. 13.
[24] Smith and Hogan, *Criminal Law* (3rd ed. 1973) 360.

When homosexual acts by men are not criminal
By the Sexual Offences Act 1967 it is provided that a homosexual act in private is not an offence against the criminal law
if the parties consent to it and have reached the age of 21.[25] There
are a number of exceptions to this, which will be set out below.
But before we come to the exceptions something must be said
of the requirements of consent, age and privacy.

Consent here means what it means in other areas of sex law.
So a man who induces another to have homosexual relations by
force or threat of force is not protected. Nor is one who stupefies
another with drink or drugs and takes advantage of him in that
state, or who impersonates the other's regular boy-friend, and so
hoodwinks him into having sex. What of a threat of exposure?
If one man induces another to have sex with him by threatening
to expose him as homosexual, and the latter agrees as a result of
the threat, has he genuinely consented? It seems that he has,
though under pressure. There is a gap in the law here. It is an
offence to procure a woman by threats, intimidation, false pretences or false representations to have sexual intercourse in any
part of the world, including sex with the person who makes the
threat, etc.[26] There is no similar law against procuring a man to
have sex with another man by threats or fraud. But a man who
misleads another as to the nature of the act, for example by
pretending that he is giving medical treatment, would be acting
without the patient's consent, unless he made it clear that the
'treatment' consisted in a homosexual act.

There is a special rule about those who are mentally defective.
A man who suffers from 'severe subnormality' cannot consent so
as to prevent a homosexual act from being an offence. If, however, his partner proves that he did not know and had no reason
to suspect that the man was suffering from 'severe subnormality',
this is a defence if otherwise the man in question would be held
to have consented.[27] The Act does not say that the mentally subnormal man cannot be charged. In practice he would not be,
but technically he is guilty because though the mentally normal
partner has consented the subnormal man has not, and the Act
requires that *both* should consent in order to exclude criminal

[25] SOA 1967 s. 1(1).
[26] SOA 1956 s. 2, 3.
[27] SOA 1967 s. 1(3).

responsibility.[28] This is still clearer if both partners are suffering from severe mental subnormality. Clearly such subnormal persons should be exempted from criminal responsibility for their sexual acts. They may not be so subnormal that they do not understand the nature of their acts, and they should not, even technically, be denied the possibility of having sex.

Apart from cases of 'severe subnormality', if the man charged genuinely believes, though without good reason, that the other has consented, he is, as the law now stands, not guilty if the parties are of the right age and acting in private.[29]

A person attains 21 at the first moment of the day before his twenty-first birthday.[30] It is to be noted that the 1967 Act adopted the age of 21, not that of majority, as the age of consent. Hence, though majority has been reduced to 18, the age of consent to homosexual acts remains at 21.

In regard to homosexual, as to heterosexual, offences the question arises whether a reasonable mistake as to the partner's age should be a defence. At the moment it is probably not. The decision in *Prince*,[31] which has stood for a long time, concerned the abduction of a girl (which is not a sexual offence), and it could be argued that it does not apply in view of the later decision in *Morgan*,[32] which concerned the defence of mistake as to the woman's consent on a charge of rape. But the wording of the 1967 Act probably implies that reasonable mistake as to age would only be a defence if Parliament expressly said so.[32a] It has not done this, and it is best to assume that the risk of making a mistake about his partner's age falls on the man who has sex with him. As in the case of girls under 16, it would be difficult to protect those whom Parliament wants to protect unless this were the rule.

A homosexual act takes place in private if it is not committed in public. It is in public if it is in a place where more than one member of the public could see that it was being committed, whether or not anyone actually saw it.[33] But this refers to the

[28] SOA 1967 s. 1(1).

[29] Arguing from *Morgan* v. *DPP* 1976 AC 182.

[30] *Re Shurey* 1918 1 Ch. 263.

[31] *Prince* (1875) LR 2 CCR 154.

[32] *Morgan* v. *DPP* 1976 AC 182; Cross, *Law Quarterly Rev.* 91 (1975) 540.

[32a] SOA 1967 s. 1(3): mistake as to severe subnormality of partner.

[33] Arguing from cases on indecent exposure: *Bunyan* (1844) 1 Cox 74; *Thallman* (1863) 9 Cox. 388.

act being seen by persons who do not make a special effort to spy. The act is not public merely because one or more persons look through a chink in a curtain or a key-hole. In the ordinary way, then, a homosexual act in which three men take part in the bedroom of a house or a hotel room would be done in private. The 1967 Act lays down nevertheless that, however private the place, the act is not to be treated as done in private if more than two people take part.[34] The same is true if two take part while a third is present but does not take part. Finally, the 1967 Act has a special provision about public lavatories. If a homosexual act is committed in a public toilet, even in a locked cubicle which cannot be seen into, the homosexual act is not treated as taking place in private. The public lavatory is for this purpose one to which the public have or are permitted to have access, whether they pay or not.[35] Hence the toilet of a public house or garage is included.

It is for the prosecution to prove that a homosexual act was done without the consent of the parties or that they have not attained 21 or that it was not performed in private.[36]

There are some exceptional cases in which homosexual acts between consenting persons over 21 in private are still criminal. They are criminal in Scotland and Northern Ireland; even in England and Wales certain disciplinary offences and certain forms of abuse of authority remain criminal. Thus, persons over 21 in the armed forces may be charged with homosexual offences under the Army, Air Force and Naval Discipline Acts even in respect of consensual acts committed in private.[37] The same is true of men on the staff of a mental hospital, or with responsibility for mental patients, who have homosexual relations with their patients.[38] Finally, a man who is the member of the crew of a United Kingdom merchant ship may be charged with a homosexual offence with another member of the crew of that, or any other, UK merchant ship, even if the consenting parties are over 21, and act in private.[39]

Homosexual acts under the 1967 Act which are not criminal

[34] SOA 1967 s. 1(2)(a).
[35] SOA 1967 s. 1(2)(b).
[36] SOA 1967 s. 1(6).
[37] SOA 1967 s. 1(5).
[38] SOA 1967 s. 1(4).
[39] SOA 1967 s. 2(1).

are not fully lawful either, even for the purposes of the criminal law. On the contrary, they are regarded, rather like prostitution (which is not in itself a crime), as being undesirable from the point of view of public policy, 'contrary to public morals'. This has the consequence, as we shall see, that it is criminal for two people to agree or 'conspire' to promote or further homosexual acts between consenting adults (one at least of whom is a third party) in private, even though the acts they promote are not criminal.[40]

When homosexual behaviour is criminal
In cases (some of which have just been mentioned) which are not within the protection of section 1 of the 1967 Act, male homosexual behaviour may be criminal either because the person charged performed a homosexual act or because he did some other act with the intention that he or another should perform a homosexual act. This last sort of act may be called a preliminary homosexual act—that is, an act preliminary to a homosexual act. There are also crimes connected with male prostitution. These are left for the next chapter. I here deal with the first two sorts of crime.

(a) *Homosexual acts.* These are divided into acts of buggery between males and acts of gross indecency (apart from buggery). Buggery has been defined. For it to be committed the penis of one man must penetrate the anus of the other.[41] The penetration need not be complete; the slightest penetration suffices, and emission or orgasm is not necessary. If penetration takes place both partners, active and passive, are guilty of buggery.[42] Unless the parties are over 21 and acting in private, consent is no defence, though it is relevant to the sentence.[43] The maximum sentence varies according to the circumstances. If the accused committed the act with a boy under 16 the maximum is life imprisonment, if with a youth between 16 and 21 with his consent five years (provided that the accused is over 21), two years if the accused is under 21.

[40] *Knuller v. DPP* 1973 AC 435; cf. *Bishop* 1975 2 QB 274 (imputation of homosexuality is attack on prosecutor's character).
[41] *Reekspear* (1832) 1 Moody 342; *State v. Massey* 58 NM 115, 266 P. 2d (1954).
[42] *People v. Bond* 136 Cal App. 2d 572, 289 P. 2d 44 (1955).
[43] SOA 1967 s. 3(1).

If committed with a person over 21 with his consent the maximum is also two years. If with a man of 16 or more without consent the upper limit is ten years.[44] To be convicted the accused must be at least 14, and this seems to be the law whether he penetrates his partner or his partner penetrates him.[45] There is, however, no good reason to extend the presumption that boys under 14 cannot have sexual intercourse to the case of passive buggery. Indeed there is no good reason for keeping the presumption at all. According to a more rational decision, a boy under this age can aid and abet buggery by standing watch.[46]

The scale of penalties for buggery is strange : for instance, a youth of 18 who commits buggery with a boy of 15 is technically liable to life imprisonment.

Apart from acts between consenting adults in private it is an offence for a man to commit an act of gross indecency with another man whether in public or private.[47] The acts other than buggery which fall within the description 'gross indecency' have already been described. Most of the acts described involve bodily contact between the two men, But this is not essential. If, for example, one masturbates in sight of another he is committing an act of gross indecency. Whether he can be said to commit it *with* the other man has given rise to much doubt over the last thirty years. It has now been decided in *Preece*[48] that he can be, but only if the two are co-operating. If, with the consent of both men, which may be tacit, one performs a sexual act which is directed towards the other he is guilty of committing an act of gross indecency with the other. This may involve contact, as when one man touches the other's penis, or may not, as when one man masturbates in order to excite the other. 'With' therefore means 'in co-operation with', not 'in the presence of' or 'directed towards'.[49] It has been so decided because, if one man could be convicted of committing an act of gross indecency with another without the consent of the other, this would reflect on the second

[44] SOA 1967 s. 3 amending SOA 1956 Schedule 2 Para. 3.
[45] *Tatam* (1921) 15 CAR 132; Smith and Hogan 358; Williams 1964 Crim. LR 686.
[46] *Cratchly* (1913) 9 CAR 232.
[47] SOA 1956 s. 13.
[48] *Preece* 1977 1 QB 370 (CA) following *Hornby and Peaple* 1946 2 All ER 487; *Hunt* 1950 2 All ER 291.
[49] *Hall* 1964 1 QB 273.

man, though the second man could not himself be convicted. Hence to touch another man's penis without his consent will simply be an indecent assault, and to masturbate in his presence with a view to arousing him will be an attempt to commit an act of gross indecency if the other does not cooperate. If he does consent the full crime is committed.

There is one complication. As *Preece* accepts, it is possible for John to be convicted of committing an act of gross indecency with James though James is acquitted of committing a similar act with John.[50] This is because the prosecution must prove its case separately against each.

It is also an offence to be a party to an act of gross indecency,[51] for example by helping the men concerned, as when one man stands watch for the police while two others have sex together. The maximum punishment for committing or being a party to gross indecency is ordinarily two years' imprisonment. This is increased to five if the person convicted is over and the partner under 21.[52] There is no technical reason why a boy under 14 should not be guilty of an act of gross indecency. In practice, of course, a prosecution would be most unlikely, even in the case of a very young prostitute.

(b) *Preliminary homosexual acts.* We have dealt with homosexual acts in the full sense. Now let us turn to those criminal acts which prepare the ground for, or are steps towards, the commission of a homosexual act either by the person charged or by another. These preliminary acts consist of (i) attempts to commit buggery or gross indecency, or (ii) inciting, or (iii) procuring someone to commit these acts, or (iv) assault with the intention of committing buggery, or (v) indecent assault by a man on another man, or (vi) soliciting by a man for homosexual purposes, or (vii) indecent exposure with such purposes in mind, or (viii) conspiring to corrupt public morals by facilitating homosexual acts.

(i) An attempt to commit buggery or gross indecency where the completed offence would be criminal (like other attempts) carries the same maximum punishment as the completed crime, except that for buggery of a boy under the age of 16 the maxi-

---

[50] *Pearce* 1951 1 All ER 493; *Preece* 1977 1 QB 370.
[51] SOA 1956 s. 13.　　　[52] SOA 1967 s. 3(2).

mum sentence is ten years' imprisonment.[53] The attempt must, in this type of case, be an act which comes close to the completed offence.

A Canadian court upheld a conviction for attempted sodomy when the man charged took a boy into a stable, proposed sodomy, spread a blanket on the floor, took down his trousers and took hold of the boy just as the police arrived.[54]

(ii) To incite, i.e. to influence or try to influence, another to commit a homosexual act, where the completed act would be criminal, is an offence punishable, if tried on indictment, with imprisonment at the court's discretion,[55] but in practice the penalty is not likely to exceed that for the completed offence. The same is true of attempt to incite another to commit a homosexual act.

(iii) Even if the completed act is not criminal, it is an offence to procure a man to commit an act of buggery with a third man, that is to say, to take steps to see to it that they do so.[56] If John persuades George to commit buggery with Robin in private, and they do so, both George and Robin being over 21 and consenting, John is guilty of a crime created by the 1967 Act and is liable to two years' imprisonment. But if John got George to commit buggery with himself (John) he would, if over 21 and in private, commit no offence.

The same is true of gross indecency. If John persuades George to commit gross indecency with Robin. John will be guilty of a crime even if George and Robin are not. The punishment is the same as for gross indecency. But if John persuaded George to commit gross indecency with himself (John) in private and both were over 21 no crime would be committed.[57]

In cases of procuring the offence is complete when the buggery or gross indecency is committed with the third man. If the homosexual act is not committed, the person who seeks to procure it may nevertheless be convicted of an attempt, as when a man, with a view to sex, wrote a letter to a boy which, though apparently innocent, would have conveyed to him an invitation to

[53] SOA 1956 2nd schedule 3 and SOA 1967 s. 3(1).
[54] *Delip Singh* (1918) 26 BCR 390.
[55] Smith and Hogan 173.
[56] SOA 1967 s. 4(1).
[57] SOA 1956 s. 16 read with SOA 1967 s. 4(3).

meet him for sex, though the boy's mother intercepted the letter.[58]

The fact that it is criminal to procure or attempt to procure another person to do a homosexual act which is not in itself an offence marks a difference between the way in which the law treats homosexual and heterosexual acts, for there is no corresponding crime of procuring heterosexual acts.

(iv) There is a special offence, punishable with a maximum of ten years' imprisonment, of assault with intent to commit buggery.[59] It seems unnecessary to have such a special crime; an assault of this sort will almost certainly amount to an act of gross indecency or an attempt to commit a homosexual act.

(v) Indecent assault on a man is a crime punishable with a maximum of ten years' imprisonment.[60] It need not be a homosexual offence, since a woman can indecently assault a man. Generally, however, it, like other sexual offences, is committed by a man. Consent is of course a defence, but not in the case of an assault on a boy under 16, who is treated (by a legal fiction) as incapable of consent. Consent by a mental defective suffering from 'severe subnormality' is also treated as invalid in law. Where, however, the mental defective actually consents, the accused is guilty only if he knew or had reason to suspect that the other was a defective.[61]

Even when the consent of the partner is ineffective there must be an assault. The accused is not guilty of an indecent assault unless he does a positive physical act by which he touches or threatens to touch the other man. In *Burrows*[62] it was said that the act must be 'hostile', but this is surely a mistake, for if it were true, there would be few convictions for indecent assault. For a man to invite another, for example, to touch his penis, is not an assault, not because it is not 'hostile' but because it is not a positive act involving contact. The positive act must also be indecent. This means that it must involve the sex organs, or must be done with a view to immediate sexual activity. It would not be enough merely for the accused to pull someone into his car

---

[58] *Cope* (1921) 16 CAR 77 cf. *Miskell* 1954 1 All ER 137. (C-M.A.C.) contrast *Woods* (1930) 143 LTR 311 (CCA: apparently heterosexual letter).
[59] SOA 1967 s. 16.
[60] SOA 1956 s. 15(1).
[61] SOA 1956 s. 15(2), (3).
[62] *Burrows* 1952 1 All ER 58 n.; 35 CAR 180 (CCA).

with a view to stopping for sex later on. This would only be an ordinary assault accompanied by an indecent, i.e. sexual, intention. But if the accused threatens here and now to have sex against the victim's will, this will amount to an indecent assault, since the threat of present force is in itself an assault.[63]

But an act which does not amount to an indecent assault because, for example, the accused merely asks to be touched, may lead to a charge of gross indecency, if the partner does what is asked. If he refuses, a charge of attempt to procure an act of gross indecency will lie. If a man commits such an act with a boy under 14 he can also, since 1960, be charged with the special offence of committing an act of gross indecency with or towards a child under 14, or inciting a child under 14 to commit an act of gross indecency with him or a third person.[64] This adds nothing to the criminal law so far as assaults on boys under 14 are concerned; it is different as regards girls. The law in this area is messy, since a child under 16 cannot consent to an indecent assault,[65] whereas if he is between 14 and 16 and masturbates a man at his request no offence is committed.

The maximum punishment for indecent assault on a girl or woman is two years' imprisonment (or five if she is under 13) against ten for an assault on a boy or man.[66] The contrast is too sharp, especially as regards paedophiles, who seek to have sex with children under puberty, often without regard to the child's sex. A uniform maximum of, say, five years, would allow the court to take account of the special features of each case.

(vi) It is a crime for a man persistently to solicit or importune in a public place for immoral purposes.[67] For the soliciting to be persistent it must be addressed to more than one person, or to the same person on more than one occasion, or must last for a reasonable length of time.[68] The maximum punishment on indictment is two years' imprisonment. Though

[63] Smith and Hogan 340, preferring the Canadian approach (*Quinton* 1947 SCR 234) to the South African (*Abrahams* 1918 CPD 593), Australian (*Nisbett* 1953 VLR 298) and New Zealand (*Turner* (1900) 18 NZLR 874).

[64] Indecency with Children Act 1960, s. 1(1).

[65] SOA 1956 s. 14(2), 15(2).

[66] SOA 1956 2nd schedule 17.

[67] SOA 1956 s. 32.

[68] *Dale* v. *Smith* 1967 2 All ER 1133; cf. *Burge* v. *DPP* 1962 1 All ER 666 n.

not originally so intended, this crime is generally charged against men who solicit in a public place—that is, one to which the public has access—for homosexual purposes.

(vii) Indecent exposure, and similar acts which outrage public decency, may be committed by a man for homosexual purposes. Provided the act could have been seen by more than one member of the public, no intention to annoy them need be shown, nor need they have felt disgust.[69]

(viii) To agree with someone to provide facilities for homosexual acts in which a third person will take part, amounts to the crime of conspiracy to corrupt public morals even if it falls short of *procuring* a homosexual act. It does not matter that the acts would be between consenting adults and in private. Hence if two or more people agree to publish homosexual advertisements in a magazine, they are guilty of conspiracy and are liable to a fine or imprisonment at the discretion of the court. But an agreement or publication of this sort does not in itself amount to a conspiracy to outrage public decency, or to an actual outrage (vii above), since an outrage to public decency is an assault on the senses, especially the sense of sight, rather than the mind.[70]

Lesbian homosexual acts

There is nothing to show that homosexual acts between women have ever been regarded as crimes at common law; even between men, only buggery was a common law crime. It may have been different in the church courts. So far as women are concerned, therefore, homosexual acts are criminal in England only[71] if performed by one woman on another without her consent or in a case in which the other girl or woman is not legally capable of consenting. The law of indecent assault naturally applies to an assault by one woman on another, provided that some positive act of a sexual character is committed. Though consent is in general a defence, a consent by a girl under 16 is ineffective in law to prevent the act being an assault.[71a] A woman defective suffering

---

[69] *Crunden* (1809) 2 Camp. 89; *Bunyan* (1844) 1 Cox. 74; *Maylin* 1963 2 QB 717 (CCA).

[70] *Knuller* v. *DPP* 1973 A.C. 435. This decision is not affected by the Criminal Law Act 1977 which abolishes most of the common law of conspiracy: see s. 5(3).

[71] They are criminal e.g. in Georgia, USA: Barnett, 18.

[71a] SOA 1956 s. 14(2).

from severe subnormality cannot effectively consent either.[72] A woman who commits an act of gross indecency with or towards a child, including a girl, under the age of 14, or who incites a child under 14 to an act of gross indecency with herself or another is liable, on indictment, to imprisonment for a maximum of two years.[73]

Acts of gross indecency between women are mainly of three sorts.[74] One is masturbation, including mutual masturbation. The second is the act by which one woman licks the private parts of the other (*cunnilingus*). Thirdly, one woman may lie on top of the other and move as in heterosexual intercourse so as to stimulate the clitoris of each (tribadism). Other similar acts which involve sexual contact, or where the women are acting in concert, may also count as acts of gross indecency, but not, it is thought, mere kissing.

Though in civil law it can be libel or slander to say of a woman that she is a lesbian,[74a] in criminal law homosexual acts between women are treated much more lightly than those between men, The merits of this state of the law are discussed later.

3. OBJECTIONS TO, AND DEFENCES OF, HOMOSEXUALITY

In Britain and other Western countries homosexuality is generally disapproved. It is true that people are more tolerant of it than they were thirty years ago. In particular, a small majority have come to think that homosexual acts between consenting adult men should not be crimes.[75] But there is a great difference between thinking that something should not be a crime and treating it as socially acceptable, still less approving it.

In this section the reasons given for objecting to homosexuality are discussed, together with the reasons given for approving or defending it. The objections come down to three: that it tends to reduce the population or to prevent its increase, that it undermines the position of women and the institution of marriage, and that it is unnatural and disgusting. Some of these objections apply more to sex between men than between women.

[72] SOA 1956 s. 14(2), (4).
[73] Indecency with Children Act 1960 s. 1(1).
[74] Magee, 118; C. Wolff, *Love Between Women* (1971).
[74a] *Kerr* v. *Kennedy* 1942 1 KB 409.
[75] Below, ch. 7 nn. 11–12.

If men have sex with other men they are less likely to have sex with women and so are less likely to produce children. Hence the population will not be as great as it would be if male homosexuals married. The same applies to a lesser extent to lesbians, but it is often assumed that women who prefer women are more likely than men who prefer men to marry and have children. The objection is therefore less strong in their case. It may indeed be easier for a woman who does not care for men to adopt a passive sex role than for a man who does not care for women to adopt an active one. This would partly account for the different way in which they are treated in law.

The population argument, of course, assumes that society needs to multiply, perhaps for defence or for economic reasons. Indeed, if one considers societies in which homosexuality has been tolerated or encouraged, like ancient Greece,[76] or some Islamic and Buddhist countries, it seems that one feature of these societies is that they have too many, rather than too few, people. There was, for instance, in ancient Greece, seldom enough food to go round and, as a result, a good deal of emigration. But in other societies, for example Catholic Ireland, the answer to excess population has been seen as late marriage. From this point of view homosexuality is simply one method of birth control.

The Israelites of the Bible, whose traditions were partly received by Christianity, set great store on increasing numbers.[77] So they condemned not just homosexuality but sex with animals, withdrawal (*coitus interruptus*), perhaps also masturbation. Any form of sex other than normal intercourse between man and woman was a threat, even if a minor one, to a sound population policy. These forms of sex, but especially homosexuality, could be thought of in political and religious, not just in moral, terms. They amounted to treason or blasphemy. Those who did such acts were siding with the enemies of Israel, or with the gods which the enemies worshipped, and not with their own country and God.[78] So there was a connection between political, religious and sexual dissent. It is important to understand this connection if we are to understand the law relating to homosexuality and other forms

---

[76] H. Licht, *Sexual Life in Ancient Greece* (1953) 411.

[77] Exodus 22.19; Leviticus 18. 22, 23; 20. 13, 15; Deut. 27. 21.

[78] Canaanites: Leviticus 20. 23; 1 Kings 14. 24, 15. 12, 22. 46; Westermarck, *Moral Ideas* 2.486.

of contraception or sex which cannot lead to conception. Nor is it just a historical connection. There really is a link, in my opinion, between these various forms of dissent. It is not for nothing that the term 'bugger' was originally the word for a religious heresy, supposedly of Bulgarian origin.[79] Even at the present day, there are those who see a connection between immorality and treason.[80]

If we forbid homosexual acts to ensure that the population increases or does not decrease, our reasons are stronger or weaker according to the needs of the society we are living in. Nowadays, especially in Britain, most people would like the population to decline, or at least to increase only slowly. The same is true in many, but not all, parts of the world. In general, the argument against homosexuality based on population is less strong than it once was.

A second argument concerns the position of women. Homosexual men are less likely to marry and to support wives. Hence, even apart from the argument about population, homosexuality tends to undermine the economic position of women, most of whom look for support to husbands. But the converse is not true. Sex between women does not undermine the economic position of men. Hence the objection on this ground to lesbians is less strong than the objection to male homosexuals. This may be part of the explanation why social opinion and the law treats the two sorts of homosexuality differently. When women are in an inferior position socially as well as economically, male homosexuality is tolerated; this was the case in the Greek, Islamic and Buddhist societies already mentioned.[81] But when women, though dependent on men for their living, are treated from a social and religious point of view as equals or nearly equals, they are likely to oppose homosexuality. On the other hand, with more women earning their own living, their opposition to homosexuality is likely to lessen. There are some signs that this is happening.

The money argument is not confined to the womanly point of view. To other men a man who does not marry and raise a family escapes his proper responsibilities. It is clear that many

[79] J. C. S. Runciman, *The Medieval Manichee* (1947) 176.
[80] P. Devlin, *The Enforcement of Morals* (1959) 14.
[81] R. Patai, *Sex and Family in the Bible and the Middle East* (1959) 168.

homosexuals do not marry and in that case they are better off than their married colleagues.[82]

The idea that men should support women, and that it is wrong for them to adopt a way of life which makes this difficult or less likely, is connected with the previous point about population. It assumes that women will mostly bring up children rather than work in industry or on the land. Its force is therefore weakened in those societies in which it is no longer urgently necessary to increase the population and where women are freer to support themselves.

The two arguments against homosexuality so far discussed may sound rather over-simple, even to those to whom it is important to maintain the population, the institution of marriage and the economic security of women. Of course it is not true that *no* homosexuals marry or have children. Indeed, since the marriage rate has risen to 95 per cent or more of the population of Britain it is obvious that many homosexuals do marry. Does it follow that homosexuals should be approved by the critics who are concerned with population or the support of women, provided they marry and have children? Or that bachelors should be condemned even if they are not homosexuals? It does not. For one thing, married homosexuals are likely to be unfaithful to their wives and, in general, to find themselves in a false position. But, even apart from this, moral attitudes are not strictly limited by the purposes they ultimately serve. We condemn theft in order to uphold respect for property and continue to do so even if in a particular case the owner of the stolen property is not likely to miss it or to suffer from its loss. At most this is thought of as a mitigation of the offence. So in the case of sexual tendencies, homosexuality is condemned because it tends *in general* to frustrate population increase and the support of women in marriage. The fact that in a particular case it may not do so because the homosexual in question marries and has a family is thought of as no more than a mitigation, if indeed it does not make matters worse.

There is indeed a reason why the moral rules relating to sex should be, if anything, stronger than the moral rules relating to property or violence, in the sense of allowing of fewer or no exceptions. This is that sexual urges are particularly strong, and

[82] Magee 94.

are not likely to be held in check by anything short of clear, unconditional rules and attitudes.

The third argument against homosexuality is that it is unnatural and disgusting. The word 'natural' has many meanings.[83] To a homosexual his or her acts are 'natural', in the sense that they conform to *his* or *her* nature or makeup; he or she would feel uncomfortable acting differently. But in another sense homosexual acts, and any form of sex other than normal intercourse between man and woman, are unnatural. They are unnatural in that there is no advantage from the point of view of the survival of the human species in these forms of sex, whereas in normal sex between man and woman there is. It would be begging many questions to speak of a design set by God or nature, but clearly the normal act tends to the survival of human kind and the others do not.

Another, connected sense in which the normal sex act between man and woman is natural and the others not is that the genital organs are so made that in normal intercourse the man's (for the most part) fits the woman's fairly easily. This is not true of intercourse between men. Buggery is therefore especially 'unnatural'. It is also for many people disgusting, by virtue of its association with excretion. Furthermore the passive role in buggery is like the role of a woman in normal intercourse and so is thought unmanly.

All these points (apart from the one about disgust and excretion) are connected. They rest on the fact that most people's moral and emotional outlook is based on the idea that men should ensure the survival of the human race and its increase, take the initiative in sexual relations with women and support them economically, so that women can devote their time to bearing children and raising families. Despite the greater freedom of women and the over-population of many parts of the world it is clear that most men must continue to perform these traditional roles. But plainly the need to increase the population, if it exists at all, is less than it used to be and so is the need to ensure that women are supported by men. A minority of homosexuals are no threat to the rest of society, though they cannot expect to be as highly regarded as those who bear the main burden of raising families and supporting women.

It is therefore worth while looking briefly at the arguments advanced in defence of homosexuality. The main one is of course

[83] R. T. Atkinson, *Sexual Morality* (1965), discusses some of them.

the liberal argument in favour of allowing adults to do their own thing. Sex is so intimate and compelling a part of life that it is specially harsh not to allow a man or woman to express his or her sexual bent in the way that seems to him or her most natural, however it may appear to others. Besides this, various advantages are urged for homosexuality. Some of these are not borne out by careful scrutiny, but others are real enough. Homosexuals are not more intelligent, artistic, original or creative than the rest of society. Some famous generals, writers and artists have been homosexual, but no more than in proportion to the rest of the population. Nor, on the other hand, are they more given to crime (apart from homosexual crimes) or mental illness than others. Schofield's careful study demonstrated how closely they resemble the rest of the population.[84] Those in jail are like other prisoners, those who consult psychiatrists are like other visitors to psychiatrists, while those who keep out of jail and the consultant's chair are like the rest of the people who manage to avoid both. At most they are subject to some stresses which others avoid, since they generally conceal their sexual bent. This may account for the widespread impression that homosexuals are often bitchy.

The real advantage of the gay life is that it tends to be freer, better off, less class-conscious and less restricted than some of its heterosexual rivals. It acts to some extent as a criticism of marriage and cohabitation and helps us to see how these might be improved. Homosexuals do not form long-term relationships so readily as heterosexuals, and this is an advantage in some professions which entail long absences or varied emotional responses.[85] This does not mean that children should be told that they have a choice between being heterosexual and homosexual. On the contrary, they should be guided, as at present, towards the heterosexual way of life. This is not just because homosexuals are less likely to be happy, as society now stands, than heterosexuals. A more important reason is that parents and teachers should teach children what they themselves believe to be right. If they are democrats they should teach children to accept democracy, not dictatorship, as the natural arrangement. The same is true of sex. But though it may be agonising for parent, child or both, not all will be able to conform.

[84] M. Schofield, *Sociological Aspects of Homosexuality* (1965) ch. 9.
[85] Tripp 277.

4. THE REFORM OF THE LAW

Protestant countries have been slower than Catholic countries to recognise the fact of male homosexuality, perhaps because in them the Old Testament has had more influence and the sacrament of confession less. In recent years, however, many of them have come to terms with it by changing their laws so that male homosexual acts between consenting adults in private are no longer punishable. Illinois took this step in 1961,[86] England in 1967. Other protestant states, such as Scotland, Northern Ireland and many states of the USA still treat acts of this sort as crimes.[86] If, as I believe, the former course and the one long followed in Catholic countries, is the right one, the lawyer's task is to work out the consequences in detail of that general policy.

If there is a right of sexual freedom (and the question is briefly discussed in Chapter 7), the right to be homosexual is simply an aspect of it. The role of the law is then to give effect to that right and to protect those who are not mature enough to exercise it. The two main issues to be considered concern the age of consent to homosexual acts and the restrictions which are now imposed on homosexual expression by those who have reached the age of consent.

As to the first issue, it is now permissible for a man to have sex with another man in private with his consent if both have reached the age of 21. In 1967, when this limit was fixed, 21 was the age of majority. The age of majority has since been reduced to 18[88] and it seems clear that the age of majority for sexual, including homosexual, purposes, should not be higher than it is for other purposes. A man who can decide for himself whom to marry can decide for himself whether he prefers women or men. So the age of (homosexual) majority should not be above 18 in present-day England. Nor should it be below the age at which it is permissible for a man to have sexual intercourse with a girl, which is now 16. There are arguments for both 18 and 16. The lower age would tend to make the law for men and women similar, which is in general a good thing. The higher age would cater for the fact

---

[86] Illinois Criminal Code (1961) s. 11.
[87] Examples in Barnett 316–24.
[88] Family Law Reform Act 1969 s. 1.

that we do not really know when sexual attitudes become fixed, so that if heterosexuality is to be encouraged, the law should postpone the age of sexual majority as long as it reasonably can.

Our neighbours are divided. France,[89] Denmark,[90] Belgium[91] and West Germany[92] opt for 18, the Netherlands for 16.[93] Numbers and caution suggest that we should prefer 18. But sexual experiments by teenagers are in a special class. While it should continue to be a crime for a man over 18 to have homosexual relations with a man under that age, it should not be a crime for a boy under 18 to have relations with a boy (or girl) over, say, 14, at least of they are not separated in age by more than a year or two. Belgian[94] and West German[95] law give a lead in this direction.

While there is a good case for having a higher age for male homosexual than for heterosexual majority it is not sensible, once that higher age is reached, to place special limits on homosexual activity which do not apply to sex between men and women. A number of limits of this sort exist in English law at the moment :

(i) Acts between adult men in private are criminal if more than two people (of whatever sex) are present. Whatever is to be said for and against group sex applies equally to sex between men and between men and women, or to group sex which includes both.

(ii) It is a crime to procure homosexual acts between adult men in private but not between an adult man and a woman over 21. So far as prostitutes are concerned the problems are discussed in the next chapter. As regards what may be called purely 'social' procuring (as when someone gives a party at which he encourages his guests to have sex together if they wish) there is surely no ground for making a distinction.

(iii) According to *DPP* v. *Knuller*[96] it is open to a jury to find that advertisements in a magazine inviting homosexual acts,

[89] Penal Code s. 331(3) read with Law of 5 July 1974.
[90] Penal Code of 15 August 1967 s. 225(2).
[91] Penal Code s. 372 *bis* as inserted by Law of 8 April 1965 s. 87.
[92] Penal Code s. 175 (Law of 25 November 1973).
[93] Penal Code s. 247 (art. 248 *bis* was repealed by Law of 8 April 1971 s. 212.
[94] Penal Code s. 372 *bis* (by person over 18 with person under 18).
[95] Penal Code s. 175 (same).
[96] *Knuller (Publishing, Printing and Promotions) Ltd* v. *DPP* 1973 AC 435. Not in Utah : *State* v. *Musser* 118 Ut. 537, 223 P. 2d 193 (1956).

even if confined (as in that case they were not) to acts between consenting adults in private, amount to a conspiracy between the advertisers and the owners or editors of the journal to corrupt public morals. The motives for this decision, so far as it did not merely follow the earlier decision in *Shaw* v. *DPP*,[97] are high-minded but wrong-headed. Under a law of adult consent the public interest is served by allowing homosexuals of the proper age to advertise for partners of the same age. So long as the laws about obscenity and public decency are not broken, it is a positive advantage that homosexuals should make contact in this way rather than in public toilets or parks. The chance of doing so is likely at least in some instances to lead to a stable partnership. Since *Knuller* is a decision of the House of Lords, however, only legislation can now change the law in the sense suggested.

(iv) The adult consent principle does not apply to the armed forces or the merchant navy, in which male buggery and gross indecency continue as offences even between those over 21.[98] The problem of abuse of authority in certain institutions (not only those mentioned but also, for example, prisons) is best met by disciplinary regulations and domestic proceedings in the institution itself. Apart from this the general law should apply. In particular it is wrong that the sailor, prisoner or airman whose superior takes advantage of the fact that he is entitled to give him orders should be even technically guilty of a crime. Nor should there be a difference, so far as the problem of discipline is concerned, between heterosexual and homosexual conduct.

Another point concerns the language of the law. In England 'buggery' and 'gross indecency' are used to describe homosexual acts, in the USA 'sodomy' and a variety of other terms such as 'unnatural offence', 'crime against nature' and the like. Legislation should be clear and economical. 'Unnatural' is too vague, and the concept, even if it were clear, is too debatable for a legislator : people are not agreed on what is contrary to nature. Legislators should aim at sobriety and moderation. 'Gross indecency' is too emotive a term for the statute book. Finally, there is no need for the legislator to have separate penalties for

[97] *Shaw* v. *DPP* 1962 AC 220.
[98] SOA 1967 s. 1(5), 2.

buggery and other forms of homosexual act. Any moral difference there may be between buggery and other acts can be taken into account when the court fixes the punishment. It is, however, not easy to see what moral difference there can be, unless the buggery causes physical harm. But in that case it is the physical harm and not the way it comes about that makes the offence more serious.

In the upshot one step in a rational reform of the law will consist in substituting 'sexual act' for the traditional expressions. This has been done, for example, in West Germany.[99]

To give effect to what has been suggested, we should need a law of indecent assault together with two consensual offences. The first, replacing the present law of male buggery and gross indecency, would be the offence by a male of committing a sexual act with or in the presence of a male under 18 or inviting him to commit a sexual act with or in the presence of the person inviting or a third person. This offence could only be committed by a man of 18 or over.

The second offence would be that of sexual abuse of authority. This offence would be of similar content but could be committed only by a parent, guardian, teacher or other person in charge or control of a man under 18. While the maximum penalty for the first offence would be moderate—perhaps two years' imprisonment—the maximum for the latter would be higher.

Like our present laws those suggested here offend against the claim for equal treatment of men and women. This is unfortunate, but should be accepted. The sexes are very different in their attitudes to sex. Men are far more adventurous.[100] There are more male than female homosexuals. The ways of women arouse less feeling than those of men. The objections to homosexuality apply more strongly to men than to women. It is a bad legislative policy to create new offences unless they are absolutely necessary in the interests of the peace of society. Most societies manage without making lesbian conduct criminal. If this is thought to make life too easy for lesbians, it should be remembered that from a social point of view they are often in a worse situation than homosexual men.[101] It is less easy for them than for men to meet one another in pubs, clubs and other places where they will feel at home.

[99] Law of 23 Nov. 1973 (BGB1. 1973.1.1725).
[100] C. Hutt, *Males & Females* (1972) 108–17.   [101] Magee, 118–73.

5

Sex for a Living

'It is selling your soul not selling a service'
(Kate Millett, *The Prostitution Papers* 36)

I. PROSTITUTION

There are a number of ways in which people can make a living
out of sex. The best known is that by which a prostitute provides
sexual services in return for a payment in money. A prostitute
is sometimes said to sell herself or her body, but this is inaccurate.
She makes with her client a contract for services, like that between
a dentist, repairer or cinema owner and their customers. But
whereas the contracts of the dentist and the others are generally
valid and can be enforced, the prostitute's contract is 'illegal'—
not criminal, but also not enforceable. So she cannot sue her
client for the money and, if he pays, he cannot claim its return
even if she fails to provide the sexual service she promised.

Prostitution shades into the relation between a man and the
girl-friend (or boy-friend) he supports in return for sexual services
Here the girl-friend earns her keep by sex (and perhaps other
services also) but is not a prostitute if she has sex only with her
lover.

The agreement by which the man supports her in return for
sexual services outside marriage is, like the prostitute's, 'illegal'.
So she cannot sue if he does not buy her a fur coat as promised
and he cannot sue if, after he has bought it, she goes off with
another man.

Are we to view marriage also as an exchange of sex for money?
Some people think of marriage as an arrangement by which a
woman provides for a man's sexual wants in return for support.

To Kant it was a lease of the wife's sex organs. Even if this analysis is right, there is a difference between marriage and prostitution. A married woman is not paid for each act of sex. She relies for support on the general law which makes husbands support wives, and the general law applies even if the couple do not have sex together. A prostitute on the other hand is specifically paid for each sexual act, or for sexual intimacy which is to last a definite period, such as half an hour or a night.

The present chapter deals with sex for a living in the sense in which some people make a profession and others an occasional practice of supporting themselves in whole or in part from earnings which are the reward of particular sexual acts. These people are prostitutes or, at any rate, find themselves from time to time 'on the game'.

The definition of a prostitute is not altogether straightforward. A prostitute may (apart from legal quirks) be of either sex. She (or he) must work for money or other reward. She must be willing when 'on the game' to accept those clients who fulfil the necessary conditions. She must be willing to perform some sexual act with them.[1]

There are male as well as female prostitutes. The women, however, greatly outnumber the men, perhaps by more than ten to one. This is not surprising since the number of wholly heterosexual men seems to be about fifteen times the number of wholly homosexual men. So it is convenient to speak as if prostitutes were women, and to allow 'her' to include 'him', reversing the presumption in statutes that 'words importing the masculine gender shall include females'.[2]

A woman who is willing to have sex with all and sundry but who does not demand to be paid in money or kind is sometimes called a prostitute. Most people, however, would nowadays simply think of her as promiscuous—a nymphomaniac perhaps, not a professional. But the reward need not be in money. Food, lodging, travel and other services will do, provided that it is agreed that they are a return for sex.

It is sometimes said that a woman is a prostitute only if she is willing to have sex with any man who wants it. If this were

---

[1] Cf. the French decree of 5 Nov. 1947: 'any person who agrees habitually to sexual relations with an indeterminate number of persons for reward.'
[2] Interpretation Act 1889 s. 1(1)(a).

true there would not be many prostitutes. For one thing she is
not on duty twenty-four hours a day, seven days a week. She has
her day or afternoon off, and, when working, often a quota of,
say, three or four clients ('tricks') an evening. If she is lucky
enough to get through these quickly she may take some time off.
Apart from prostitutes living in the most desperate conditions or
(not of course in the UK) in official brothels there is some room
for being choosey. Some white prostitutes, for instance, do not
take black clients; they give this as a reason against having
official brothels, where they would not be allowed to discriminate.

A prostitute is really no more indiscriminate than a dentist or
garage owner, although she is called a 'common' prostitute and
he is not called a common dentist or garage owner. She is indiscriminate in the sense that she is willing to have sexual relations with anyone who fulfils minimum conditions as to payment,
health, colour, age and the like, at least when she is on duty.[3]
The client must be able to pay. Some prostitutes will only go with
a man who has a car or flat, or whose looks they like. The better
her condition in life the greater the chance for the prostitute to
be selective. It is a delicate question where the line is to be drawn
between prostitution and having a number of lovers. What is one
to say of the 'afternoon prostitute' who works at home, perhaps
with her husband's approval, and reaches clients through contact magazines? She is a prostitute provided she is willing to take
those clients who apply, if they can pay and if her quota is not
full.

A prostitute is usually willing to allow ordinary sexual intercourse, but not all do. Some, for instance in massage parlours,
will only masturbate clients. Others confine themselves to sucking the man's penis (fellation). Some make a point of allowing
sex only in ways different from those they use with their regular
boy-friend or pimp.[4] This may be important in helping them to
turn off, so that they do not become emotionally involved in
their work. There is often a demand from the client for kinky
forms of sex, including whipping and other sadistic or masochistic
practices which rouse the man by giving or receiving pain. Some
prostitutes cater for these. But provided a woman is willing to

---

[3] Gebhard, 'Misconceptions about female prostitution', *Medical Aspects of
Human Sexuality* 3 (1969) 24.
[4] C. H. Rolph, *Women of the Streets* (1955) 59–60.

allow some form of sex act, she can be a prostitute even if she excludes other forms.

So much for the definition of a prostitute. She works either for herself or for a pimp or manager, or partly for herself and partly for a pimp. She earns money or kind by agreeing with her client the amount to be paid. Payment is usually, though not always, in advance of the sexual act. Sometimes the agreement is by a tout or agent acting for the prostitute or pimp, and sometimes payment is made direct to the pimp (ponce), if she has one.

The clients of prostitutes, both female and male, are nearly all men, but there are a few women who go to brothels and rather more who support men in return for sex. Pimps and touts, who live on the earnings of prostitution, are generally men, but a woman may manage a brothel (like the traditional madame) or run a call-girl service.

Prostitution is often said to be the oldest profession. It seems to be as old as life in towns, and may have existed where roads cross even before there was town life. In many societies it has been the only, or the easiest, way for a woman to earn a living. In the Roman world, for instance, a free woman who was not supported from her own property or by her husband or family could hardly earn a living except as a prostitute. In other societies prostitution has—at least for some prostitutes—been approved and given religious significance : temple prostitution was once common. Recently, with growing wealth, prostitution in industrial countries has declined,[5] and Marxist states try to eliminate it. A hundred years ago optimists (from their own point of view) foresaw its end. Amos thought he was writing the history of a dying profession.

In the world of affluence and inflation we are not so naive. Sheer poverty is not such a spur, but some women (and men) take to earning money from sex on the side to keep up their standard of living. In the UK there are perhaps 50,000 prostitutes, in addition to part-timers, of whom nine-tenths or more are women, mostly in big cities.[6]

There are several different sorts of prostitution, depending on

[5] 'Prostitution and fornication must, even under the most despairing view of the future of society, be looked upon as constantly diminishing evils' : S. Amos, *Laws in force for the prohibition, regulation and licensing of vice in England and other countries* (1877) 229.

[6] Guesses in Sicot, *La Prostitution dans le monde* (1964) 38, 48, 52.

how the contacts are made and where the sexual acts take place.
A woman may simply solicit in the street, taking the risk of a fine,
or in a pub or hotel. She may build up a set of clients who contact her personally by telephone or letter or by going to her
favourite resort. The contact may be through a tout (though the
Street Offences Act of 1959 made this more dangerous) or by
an agent who arranges for the prostitute to come to an agreed
place when the client is waiting. This is the system used for call-
girls, who are summoned by telephone when needed. Or she may
have a job which on the face of it is not connected with prostitution, for instance in a massage parlour where the masseuses are
expected or allowed to masturbate the customers, or in an escort
agency where the escorts are expected or allowed to go to bed
with the men they escort. In that case the contacts are made
through the business. Another method, used by part-time prostitutes who are also housewives or who have another job, is to make
contacts through a magazine in which the notices are not on the
face of them advertisements for prostitution, but for 'swinging
partners' and the like.

The places where the sexual acts take place vary according to
the system of contact and to what is available. At its simplest
prostitution can be carried on in an alley or on the grass. Usually
a prostitute tries to provide at least a simple room, either her
own, or her ponce or friend's. But as there are legal and practical
difficulties about doing this, prostitutes must often settle for sex
in a car, or in the man's flat or at a hotel which is not fussy about
letting a room for an hour or so. A hotel of this sort shades into
a brothel proper, which may be managed by a pimp or madame.
Prostitution which is accessory to massage takes place, of course,
in the massage parlour and the escort agency girl may well end
the evening in her companion's hotel bedroom. The part-time
prostitute who is also working or running a home will use her
own house or flat. New forms of prostitution are being invented
all the time.

Why have greater wealth, better education and more permissive sexual morals not stopped prostitution? A number of studies
have shown that most prostitutes, at least in industrial societies,
are on the game because they prefer it, not because of poverty or
the cunning designs of pimps. They prefer it to work in an office
or factory, either because it is better paid, or because it allows a

freer, more irregular, more exciting way of life.[7] It brings them into contact with men from different walks of life. Occasionally it leads to a really good catch, ending in marriage and middle-class status. So, despite the routine of sex, the long hours walking the street or the fact that the earnings are siphoned off to pimps, there are women who stay in prostitution until they can no longer earn. Though they would not like their sisters or daughters to follow the trade, they prefer it for themselves. In this their attitude is not unlike that of married homosexuals, if for 'sons' we read 'daughters'.[8]

There are some observers who think that with the freer attitudes of affluent society towards sex men will stop resorting to prostitutes. Certainly the apparent decline in their numbers stems from less demand. It has become rarer for a man to have his first sexual experience with a prostitute.[9] But the client will not disappear. Many men like variety and excitement. Some want kinky forms of sex which their wives or girl-friends will not provide. Some are away from home for long periods. There are foreign workers, visitors, men who are constantly on the move. Short of world-wide Marxist repression, a core of prostitutes and their clients will remain.

Is the profession well paid? In the UK at least the range of earnings seems enormous. The poorer will go with a man for £5 or less often in very sordid conditions, in a dark doorway or a tawdry room. A high-class prostitute may charge £50 or more a night, operate from a luxury flat, and earn several hundred pounds a week. One afternoon prostitute, working at home with her husband near at hand, charges £12 for a two- or three-hour session which includes tea and sympathy.[10] Except for a very few, it is no goldmine, but the money or other perquisites are in practice free of tax. The prostitute who can manage without a pimp or agent is in money terms better off than her sister. But

[7] G. Geis, *Not The Law's Business* (1972) 176; *Wolfenden Report* s. 223. Far-fetched explanations from C. Lombroso and E. G. Ferreo, *La Donna Delinquente* (1893) to E. Glover, *The Psychopathology of Prostitution* (1969). These range from excessive love of animals to frigidity.

[8] Geis 26.

[9] Geis 182.

[10] S. Yeger, 'Whoring on the side', *New Society* 24 June 1976. Geis (1972) for the US speaks of three ten-dollar tricks a day, 5,000 to 6,000 dollars net a year. Sicot 28, 38 gives prices for France in the same range, as does P. le Moal, *Etude sur la prostitution des mineurs* (1965) 53.

to go it alone can be dangerous, especially for young women working the streets. The overheads can be heavy, since landlords overcharge. The work is exhausting. Many prostitutes look haggard, yet soldier on.

Most prostitutes spend freely and seldom have cash to spare. Though an increasing number are independent, many pay a large part of what they earn to a pimp. The role of pimps in the game can easily be misunderstood. A woman prostitute takes great risks : murders are not infrequent. Her clients are older, at times unscrupulous, men. She moves in criminal circles or on the fringes of the underworld. She may well need a protector. Besides, a prostitute makes friends and falls in love. Her ponce may be a man whom in the first place she liked and did not charge for sex.[11] Pimps often exploit whores, but they often fill a professional or personal need, and act as an insurance against risks which are by no means fanciful.

2.   THE LAW

The definition of a prostitute has been considered already. In Rome a promiscuous woman was treated as a prostitute even if she took no reward; the same has been held in Utah.[12] But in English law a 'common prostitute' must be a woman and must offer her body for 'common lewdness', that is for sexual acts with an indefinite number of clients, in return for money or other reward.[13] Since the sexual acts need not amount to intercourse it is enough if she sucks or masturbates men, or they lick her. Hence even a virgin may be a prostitute.[14]

The laws relating to prostitution are either directed to prostitutes themselves or to those who help them and profit from their trade. These types of law will be considered in turn, first for women, then for male prostitutes. A final section deals with contracts by prostitutes.

[11] *Wolfenden Report* s. 301; C. H. Rolph 115. C. and R. Milner, *Black Players* (1973), has a good account of a pimp's point of view. Le Moal 54 found that in Paris two-thirds of prostitutes had pimps.

[12] *Salt Lake City* v. *Allred* 19 Utah 2d 254, 430 P 2d 371 (1967); *Bayouth* v. *State* 294 P 2d 856 (Okla. 1956). Cf. *People* v. *Brandt* 306 P 2d (Cal. 1956) 1069, 1070.

[13] *de Munck* 1918 1 KB 635, 637; *Webb* 1964 1 QB 357, 366.

[14] *de Munck* 1918 1 KB 635; *Webb* 1964 1 QB 357.

(a) *Laws directed to women prostitutes*

Prostitution is not in itself criminal in England or in the EEC countries.[15] In the US, however, to be a common prostitute is a crime, generally of a minor sort, under vagrancy legislation of a kind similar to the English Vagrancy Act of 1824.[16] This legislation was originally directed against those who refuse to maintain themselves or their families, unlicensed pedlars, beggars and the like. Though the English version does not make prostitution as such a crime it penalises a common prostitute who wanders in the public strees or public highways or in any place of public resort and *behaves in a riotous or indecent manner.*[17] The maximum penalty is a month's imprisonment or a fine of £20.

Mere soliciting does not amount to 'riotous or indecent behaviour'.[18] There must be an element of indecency, and it is a question of fact whether that is present.[19] The riotous or indecent behaviour must occur in a public place. So when a man in a car picked up two prostitutes and drove them to some waste land in Sheffield where he had sex with them in the car, it was held that they could not be convicted of this crime as the indecent behaviour did not take place in the street.[20]

Such was the care of the nineteenth-century Parliament for young men of the upper classes that the Universities Act 1825 lays down that a prostitute found within the precincts of Oxford or Cambridge University may be dealt with as an *idle or disorderly person.*[21]

More important than these is the crime of *loitering or soliciting for purposes of prostitution.* Many prostitutes, especially poorer ones, cannot make a living without soliciting in the street. Under the Street Offences Act 1959, which replaces and updates nineteenth-century legislation, it is an offence for a common prosti-

[15] Smith and Hogan 345; *Encyclopédie Dalloz*, Droit pénal III s.v.
[16] Perkins, *Criminal Law* 393; *People* v. *Brandt* 306 P 2d 1069 (Cal. 1956); American Law Institute, *Model Penal Code* (1962) s. 251. 1; Ploscowe 285 (source of too much disease, crime, disorder and wasted lives for the law to tolerate).
[17] Vagrancy Act 1824 s. 3.
[18] *Bonner* v. *Lushington* (1893) 57 JP 168, 169.
[19] *de Ruiter* (1880) 44 JP 90.
[20] *Carnill* v. *Edwards* 1953 1 All ER 282.
[21] Universities Act 1825 s. 3. In *Hopkins* (1882) 56 JP 262 it was held that 'walking with an undergraduate' is not a crime triable in the Vice-Chancellor's court.

tute to loiter or solicit in a street or public place for the purpose
of prostitution.[22] This summary offence can attract a fine of up
to £10 for a first offence, £25 for a second offence and three
months in prison, with or as an alternative to a fine of up to £25,
for a third or further offence.[23] A policeman may arrest without
warrant a prostitute whom he reasonably suspects of committing
this offence.[24]

The new law was enacted as a result of the report of the
Wolfenden Committee[25] which recommended that an attempt
should be made to drive prostitutes from the streets. Under the
previous law this was difficult. The prosecution had to prove
annoyance, the fine even for a repeated offence was only £2
and the law only applied in towns. In practice the new law is not
always as severe as it might seem. When it came into force the
Home Office instructed the police to work in twos and, if they
see a woman loitering or soliciting who has not been convicted for
it before, to tell her what they have seen and caution her. The
caution is recorded at the police station and in a central register.
The woman must, if willing, be put in touch with a welfare
organisation or probation officer. A woman police officer deals
with the arrangements for this. If the prostitute is seen loitering
or soliciting again she is given a second warning. On the third
occasion she may be arrested.[25]

A 'common prostitute' is simply a female prostitute. 'Common'
merely indicates that she is willing to have sex with all those
clients who satisfy her conditions. But the adjective adds nothing
and could be dispensed with. 'Loitering' is not a word much used
in ordinary speech. The idea is that of lingering, repeatedly slow-
ing down or making frequent pauses. Though a Scottish judge
has taken the contrary view,[26] it seems clear that one can loiter
when driving a car or vehicle, for instance by tailing another
vehicle and stopping whenever it stops.[27]

Loitering for the purpose of prostitution is an offence even
though the prostitute does not actively solicit customers. If she

[22] Street Offences Act 1959 s. 1(1).
[23] Street Offences Act 1959 s. 1(2).
[24] Street Offences Act 1959 s. 1(3).
[25] Home Office Circular 109/1959, giving effect to street Offences Act
1959 s. 2.
[26] *Williamson* v. *Wright* 1924 SC(J) 57, 60–1 per Lord Hunter.
[27] *Bridge* v. *Campbell* 1947 WN 223.

loiters, it is enough that she intends them to approach her. Soliciting, on the other hand, is actively inviting prospective customers to have sexual relations. A prostitute may solicit by words, as with the traditional 'How about a good time, dearie?', by gestures, such as smiles or wriggles,[28] by taking a man's arm or by any other method which is intended to attract his attention. The offence must be committed in a street or public place. For purposes of the Act 'street' includes lanes, alleys, subways and the like, open for the time being to the public. Doorways and entrances of premises abutting on a street and ground adjoining and open to a street are also treated as part of the street.[29] A public place is one to which the public go in fact, even though they may not do so as of right, and even though some sorts of people may be excluded.[30] Hence a pub, when open to the public,[31] or a dance hall, during a public dance, may be public places.[32]

It has been held that a prostitute can be guilty of soliciting though the client does not realise she is soliciting him.[33] This seems wrong, for soliciting is like asking or inviting, and it is surely impossible to invite someone to a party if he does not receive the invitation. The correct view is rather that taken in the later case of *Smith* v. *Hughes*.[34] Once the prospective client notices the words or signal, whether or not he responds, the soliciting is complete. Before that there is at most an attempt to solicit. If the invitation is indirect, as when a tout solicits for her in the street,[35] or a tobacconist puts an advertisement for her in his shop window,[36] the prostitute, if not herself present, cannot be held to have solicited in the street or public place. The Act is aimed at preventing people from being molested or accosted by prostitutes who are physically present. The tout, however, is guilty of an offence of soliciting and the tobacconist is guilty of conspiracy to

[28] *Horton* v. *Mead* 1913 1 KB 154 (a case on male soliciting).
[29] Street Offences Act 1959 s. 1(4).
[30] *Waters* (1963) Crim. LR 437 (CCA) a case on the Road Traffic Act 1960 s. 6.
[31] *Mapstone* 1963 3 All ER 930, a case of affray.
[32] *Williams* v. *Boyle* 1963 Crim. LR 204 (QB), a case on the Road Traffic Act 1960 s. 6.
[33] *Horton* v. *Mead* 1913 1 KB 154.
[34] *Smith* v. *Hughes* 1960 2 All ER 859 (QB).
[35] *Smith* v. *Hughes* above at p. 861.
[36] *Weisz* v. *Monahan* 1962 1 All ER 664.

corrupt public morals and, if he makes a charge for the advertisement, of living on the earnings of prostitution.[37] Finally, the
prostitute herself, if she appears in the window in such a way as
to invite men, even silently, in the street to have sex with her is
guilty of soliciting in the street : if she is close at hand, and the
message reaches the public place, that is enough.[38]

(b) *Laws directed against those who help or profit from female
prostitution*
These laws are aimed partly at those who encourage others
to become or remain prostitutes, partly at those who manage
prostitutes or the business of prostitution, partly at those who
provide other forms of help (e.g. premises or publicity) for it to be
carried on, partly at those who make a profit from it by living
on the earnings of prostitution. Some laws fall into more than
one of these classes. Both criminal and civil laws come into play.

(i) *Encouraging prostitution.* To prevent young girls from being
induced to take up prostitution it is made an offence for anyone
to cause or encourage the prostitution of a girl under 16 for
whom he is responsible. It is equally a crime to cause or encourage anyone to have unlawful sexual intercourse with her, or
to commit an indecent assault on her. The maximum penalty is
two years' imprisonment. A person who knowingly allows the
girl to consort with a prostitute or person of known immoral
character, or to enter or continue in their employment, is deemed
to have caused or encouraged the prostitution, etc. if the girl
actually becomes a prostitute, or has sexual intercourse or suffers
an indecent assault.[39] Apart from rare cases which can for present purposes be neglected, all sexual intercourse by a girl under
16 is unlawful and any sexual act with her whether amounting
to intercouse or not will be an indecent assault, since she cannot
consent to it.[40]

The persons responsible for the girl are her parent, her legal
guardian, the person who has her in his possession or custody
(eg. an aunt with whom she lives) and anyone into whose charge

[37] Sexual Offences Act 1956 s. 32; *Shaw* v. *DPP* 1962 AC 220.
[38] *Behrendt* v. *Burridge* 1976 3 All El 285.
[101] SOA 1956 s. 18.
[40] SOA 1956 s. 14(2).

one of these commits her (e.g. the head of her school, the person in charge of the holiday camp she is at).[41] A girl who looks to the court to have been under 16 at the time of the alleged offence is taken to have been under 16 unless the contrary is shown.[42]

The person responsible for the girl may be held to have encouraged unlawful sexual intercourse if he does not prevent her sleeping in the same bed with a man, when he could do so, even though there is an elder girl (the man's fiancée) between them in the bed.[43] Much depends on the case. If a young girl who has a nightmare is allowed to sleep in the same bed as her grandfather, her parents are hardly encouraging unlawful sexual intercourse.

So much for the under-16s. It is also an offence for anyone to procure a girl under 21 to have unlawful sexual intercourse in any part of the world with a third person. This also carries two years' imprisonment.[44] It would naturally apply to recruiting a girl for prostitution or arranging for customers for her.

The protection of women from prostitution does not end at the age of 21. Provisions directed against what used to be called the white slave trade, and backed again by a maximum penalty of two years in prison, make it a crime for anyone to procure a woman to become a common prostitute in any part of the world.[45] It is also a crime to procure a woman to leave the UK if the accused intends that she should become an inmate of or frequent a brothel elsewhere, or to leave her usual residence in the UK if he intends her to become an inmate of or to frequent a brothel anywhere for the purposes of prostitution.[46] 'Procuring' involves an element of persuasion and implies that apart from the persuasion the woman would not have done what she did.[47] But the persuasion can consist in the lure of money. A woman employed for massage in a massage parlour is procured by her employer for prostitution if she is told that she can earn extra by masturbating the clients.[48] If, however, she has already decided to take up prostitution or leave for the brothel, the would-be persuader has not

---

[41] SOA 1956 s. 28(3), (4).
[42] SOA 1956 s. 28(5).
[43] *Ralphs* (1913) 9 CAR 86; cf. *Moon* 1920 1 KB 818, 824.
[44] SOA 1956 s. 23 and 2nd schedule 24(a).
[45] SOA 1956 s. 22(1)(a).
[46] SOA 1956 s. 22(1)(b), (c).
[47] *Christian* (1913) 78 JP 112.
[48] *Broadfoot* 1976 3 All ER 753.

'procured' her, unless perhaps he persuades her not to change her mind. Otherwise he has at most attempted to procure her.

A husband who persuades his reluctant wife to take up after-noon prostitution in order to keep up their standard of living will be guilty of procuring, not to mention living on the earnings of prostitution.

'Causing or encouraging' is perhaps wider than 'procuring', since it may cover cases in which the woman has decided to become a prostitute or has become one and the accused merely lends her his support or help. If this is so then there is point in the existence of a separate offence, with the same penalty, of causing or encouraging the prostitution in any part of the world of a woman defective suffering from severe subnormality. The accused is not guilty of this offence if he does not know and has no reason to suspect that the woman is a mental defective.[49]

A prostitute may wish to leave the profession or to leave the brothel where she is working. To prevent obstacles being put in her path it is made an offence to detain a woman against her will on any premises with the intention that she shall have un-lawful sexual intercourse with a man.[50] It is also an offence to detain her against her will in a brothel.[51] Anyone who withholds her clothes or other property or threatens legal proceedings if she takes away the clothes he provides is deemed to detain her if he does this with the intention of inducing her to remain in the brothel or premises.[52] But there is no general offence of dissuad-ing a woman from giving up prostitution.

The offences we have so far discussed do not apply to male prostitution. They all carry a maximum punishment of two years in prison.

(ii) *Managing prostitutes and brothels.* Certain laws strike at those who manage prostitutes or brothels. It is an offence punish-able with seven years' imprisonment on indictment for a woman to exercise control, direction or influence over a prostitute's move-ments for gain and in a way which shows she is aiding, abetting or compelling her prostitution.[53] This offence is directed against

[49] SOA 1956 s. 29(1) and (2).
[50] SOA 1956 s. 24(1).
[51] SOA 1956 s. 24(1).
[52] SOA 1956 s. 24(2).
[53] SOA 1956 s. 31.

the madame who, though she may not keep or manage a brothel, controls prostitutes by procuring customers for them, whether she makes the arrangements by telephone (as in the case of call-girls) or in some other way. She must act for gain. The exercise of control in itself is not a crime. Nor is it a crime for a woman to live on the earnings of prostitution unless she controls the prostitute or unless the prostitute is male.[54] If the prostitute is a woman only a woman can be guilty of controlling her for gain and only a man of living on her earnings. The law in this area is messy.

On the other hand either sex can be guilty of keeping or managing a brothel, or of assisting or acting in the management of a brothel, a summary offence carrying a maximum of three or, on reconviction, six months' imprisonment.[55] A brothel is at common law a place to which both sexes resort for sexual acts outside marriage.[56] This definition has been extended by the 1967 Act so that, for present purposes, it now includes a place to which people resort for lewd homosexual practices (which just means homosexual acts) if resorting to it for heterosexual acts would have led to its being treated as a brothel.[57] There can be a brothel without prostitutes. Provided that men and women (and now also men and men, or women and women) go to it for sex outside marriage it does not matter whether they pay for sex or whether they are simply couples who find it a convenient place to resort to where, for example, they may rent a room for an hour. But generally a brothel contains prostitutes, and evidence that the women visiting the premises are prostitutes is admitted in order to show that it is a brothel.[58]

One prostitute (or amateur) does not make a brothel, whether she is the tenant of the premises or not.[59] There must be at least two.[60] If there are, the premises can be a brothel even if one prostitute is a tenant and the other not,[61] or if both are non-tenants. A great deal turns on whether the premises in question

[54] SOA 1967 s. 5(1).
[55] SOA 1956 s. 33.
[56] *Justices of Parts of Holland, Lincolnshire* (1882) 46 JP 312, 313; *Winter* v. *Woolfe* 1 KB 549.
[57] SOA 1967 s. 6.
[58] *Korie* 1966 1 All ER 50 (Liverpool Crown Court).
[59] *Caldwell* v. *Leech* (1913) 109 LTR 188.
[60] *Singleton* v. *Ellison* 1895 1 QB 607; *Strath* v. *Foxon* 1955 3 All ER 398.
[61] *Gorman* v. *Standen* 1964 1 QB 294.

are to be considered a single unit. If separate flats, rooms or floors are let separately to different prostitutes they prima facie constitute separate premises, not a single brothel.[62] But if the activities of the prostitutes are coordinated, either by the landlord or by themselves or a third person, they may amount to a brothel, provided that they are close enough to constitute a 'nest of prostitutes'.[63] In other words there must, besides more than one prostitute, be physical proximity and an element of common management.

To manage a brothel is to take an active part in running it, not merely to do menial tasks like answering the door or sweeping the floor, necessary though these may be.[64] The manager, for example, may fix appointments with customers. To assist in the management is to help him in this, in collecting money from clients, in keeping out undesirables or in other ways. A prostitute working for a man or woman who manages the brothel may herself be assisting in the management if she has a say in what goes on.[65]

(iii) *Helping in other ways: use of premises.* Apart from management the most important offences connected with helping prostitution are based on allowing premises to be used for prostitution. A lessor or landlord who lets the whole or part of any premises knowing that they are to be used in whole or part as a brothel is liable to three months' imprisonment, rising to six on reconviction. A similar crime is committed by an agent who knowingly lets such premises. When the brothel already exists, the landlord, lessor or agent commits an offence if he is wilfully a party to their use as a brothel continuing.[66] It has been held that even though individual rooms were let under separate tenancies the premises as a whole might be let for use as a brothel.[67] But the landlord commits no offence if the lettings are genuinely separate lettings to individual prostitutes.[68] The dividing line is a thin one.

[62] *Strath* v. *Foxon* 1955 3 All ER 398.

[63] *Durose* v. *Wilson* (1907) 96 LT 645; *Donovan* v. *Gavin* 1965 2 QB 648.

[64] *Abbott* v. *Smith* 1964 3 All ER 762 (Liverpool Crown Court).

[65] *Gorman* v. *Standen* 1964 1 QB 294.

[66] SOA 1956 s. 34.

[67] *Donovan* v. *Gavin* 1965 2 QB 648.

[68] *Mattison* v. *Johnson* (1916) 85 LJKB 741.

The tenant, occupier or person in charge of premises commits a summary offence with the same maximum punishment if he permits the whole or part to be used as a brothel. If the tenant or occupier is convicted, the lessor or landlord may require him to assign the lease or other contract by which the premises are held to some other approved person. The lessor or landlord's approval must not be unreasonably withheld. If the tenant fails to assign the lease within three months the lessor or landlord may bring it to an end and the court by which the tenant was convicted may make a summary order for delivery of possession of the premises to the lessor or landlord.[69] It is a summary offence also for a tenant or occupier (for example of a public house) knowingly to permit them, or part of them, to be used for the purposes of habitual prostitution.[70]

To summarise the position so far as premises are concerned : a prostitute acting on her own may ply her trade on her own premises or those of which she is the tenant without fear from the criminal law. A landlord may let premises to her knowing she intends to practise prostitution in them, so long as he does not then or later (by virtue, for example, of other lettings of adjacent rooms) make the premises let part of a brothel. Provided that he avoids creating a brothel he can let a number of rooms or flats to tenants whom he knows will use them (separately) for prostitution. That is the criminal law. But in civil law the neighbours of the landlord may complain of a nuisance if the enjoyment of their property is spoiled by the comings and goings of the prostitutes and their clients and the decline in value which goes with having property near what the layman (but not the lawyer) would call a brothel.[71] They may sue the landlord for an injunction and damages. The prostitutes, if worth suing, are jointly liable. The level of damages will of course depend, among other factors, on how select is the area in which the prostitutes are operating.

Premises in which to work are not the prostitute's only need. Just like any other woman, she needs food, living quarters for herself (as opposed to her trade), ordinary clothes and medical care. Those who supply her with these things, provided they do not overcharge just because she is a prostitute, commit no crime

---

[69] SOA 1956 s. 35(1), and 1st schedule.
[70] SOA 1956 s. 36.
[71] *Thompson–Schwab* v. *Costacki* 1956 1 All ER 652.

and can enforce their contracts against her as they could against
any other customer. As for goods and services which she needs or
wants specifically as a prostitute—special equipment, whips,
erotic books, advertisements for her trade—those who supply
these for gain knowing their purpose are, as we shall see, living
on the earnings of prostitution. The contracts which they make
with her are 'illegal' in civil law and they will be unable to sue
her if she fails to pay. Even if they give her goods or help her
free of charge, for instance because she is their mother or sister,
they may be guilty of conspiring to corrupt public morals; a
crime for which the punishment lies in the discretion of the
court.

This crime was analysed by the House of Lords, in relation to
prostitution, in *Shaw* v. *DPP*.[72] The accused persons published
the 'Ladies Directory', in which prostitutes advertised their
names, addresses, photographs and in some cases the forms of sex,
kinky or otherwise, they were willing to practise. The advertisements were published for payment, so that the publishers were
living on the earnings of prostitution. But even had they charged
nothing, it is clear that the House of Lords would have upheld
their conviction, as it in fact did, for conspiracy to corrupt public
morals. The exact limits of this crime are difficult to define. It has
since been held to include agreement to advertise for homosexual
acts between adult males in private after these acts ceased in 1967
to be criminal.[73] On one reading of *Shaw* the jury may properly
find that any agreement to promote sex outside marriage is a
conspiracy to corrupt public morals, which are rooted in marriage
and the family.[74] On the other hand one could take the House of
Lords to be saying that they may do so in the case only of unnatural forms of sex whether between men and women or
between men and men. In that case advertisements for normal
sexual intercourse with a prostitute would not raise a charge of
conspiracy. This second opinion gives more force to the word
'corrupt' which, as Lord Simon of Glaisdale said, is a strong
word.[75]

---

[72] 1962 AC 220.
[73] *Knuller* v. *DPP* 1973 AC 435. See above, p. 100 n. 70.
[74] *Shaw* v. *DPP* 1962 AC 220, 268 per Lord Simonds ('provoking libidi-
nous desires').
[75] *Knuller* v. *DPP* 1973 AC 435, 491.

(iv) *Profiting from prostitution.* It is a serious offence—the most serious in the law of prostitution—knowingly to live wholly or in part on the earnings of prostitution.[76] Only a man can be charged with the crime if the prostitute is a woman. A woman who does the same as a male pimp must instead be charged not with living on the earnings of prostitution but with controlling prostitutes for gain.[77]

A man who lives with, or is habitually in the company of, a prostitute is presumed to be knowingly living on the earnings of prostitution unless he proves the contrary. The same is true of a man who exercises control, direction or influence over a prostitute's movements in a way which shows he is aiding, abetting or compelling her prostitution with others.[78] But of course these methods of proof are not exhaustive. The prosecution can show by other evidence that the man is living on the earnings of prostitution.[79] On a summary charge six months in prison is the maximum sentence, but on indictment this rises to seven years.[80] Before 1959 the maximum was two years' imprisonment.

One must distinguish between the earnings of a prostitute and the earnings of prostitution. To let a room to a prostitute, even a known prostitute, at the ordinary rate is not to live on the earnings of prostitution, since she must live somewhere. Prostitution is not a crime, and the law is not to be used to stamp it out by creating a void round the prostitute in which no one can deal with her. The lessor may be living on the earnings of a prostitute, but he is not living on the earnings of prostitution.

To live on the earnings of prostitution takes one of three forms. In the first the man receives the very money earned by the prostitute, which is paid directly to him by the client, or else is paid by the client to the prostitute and then by the prostitute to the man. It makes no difference whether the payment to the man is regarded by the prostitute as a gift, a payment made under pressure or a return for unspecified services in connection with her profession. Whichever is the case she is in effect supporting him, or partly supporting him, and he is her pimp, ponce or souteneur.

[76] SOA 1956 s. 30(1).
[77] SOA 1956 s. 31.
[78] SOA 1956 s. 30(2).
[79] *Clarke* 1976 2 All ER 696.
[80] SOA 1956 2nd schedule 30.

In the other forms the man need not be a pimp though he often is. The second form of living on the earnings of prostitution is when for reward a man provides a prostitute or her client with goods or services which are needed for purposes of prostitution. Examples are special clothes for the prostitute, transport for her or her client to a secluded spot, and advertisements of her trade. We have come across an example of advertising in *Shaw*.[81] So far as transport is concerned, it has been held that a man who parked his car outside a pub frequented by prostitutes and charged for allowing it to be used there for prostitution was living on the earnings of prostitution. So was he when he charged for driving the prostitute with her client to a secluded spot and either waited until they had had sex or returned to fetch them the next morning. So again when he charged servicemen, who could have returned to their base free, for hiring a car to take them back with a stop for sex on the way.[82]

The third form of living on the earnings of prostitution occurs when a person provides a prostitute with goods or services (which may or may not be used for prostitution) at a higher charge than the normal, knowing that the prostitute can pay only out of the proceeds of her trade. An example is the landlord who lets a room to a prostitute not for purposes of prostitution but for her own living accommodation at a higher rent than he would charge a tenant who was not a prostitute.[83] In this case the landlord is living on the earnings of prostitution, since not merely is he paid out of them (as he would be even if he charged the prostitute a normal rent) but he makes extra money simply because his tenant is a prostitute.

Hence the law about living on the earnings of prostitution goes a good deal beyond the relation of prostitute and pimp, or parasite, at least in principle. A contractor or decorator who charges a prostitute more for cleaning or decorating her room because she is a prostitute is living on the earnings of prostitution. But it is not enough to take a fee without the consent or knowledge of the prostitute for introducing clients to them. To take such a fee is not to take the earnings of or to control prostitutes.[84]

[81] 1962 AC 220.
[82] *Calvert* v. *Mayes* 1954 1 QB 342.
[83] *Thomas* 1957 2 All ER 181; 41 CAR 117.
[84] *Ansell* 1975 QB 215.

Male prostitution

Like the prostitution of women, male prostitution is an ancient profession. The law of England, however, has until recently taken the view that a prostitute must be a woman. This view underlies the Sexual Offences Act 1956[85] and the Street Offences Act 1959.[86] Only since the 1967 Act which removed homosexual acts between consenting adults in private (in most cases) from the reach of the criminal law has any attention been paid in English legislation to male prostitution.

As a result, the criminal laws about male prostitutes, while they achieve the same broad effect as those about women, differ from them in detail. The statutes may conveniently be divided once more into those directed against the prostitutes themselves and those against people who help or profit from prostitution.

(a) *Laws directed to male prostitutes*

A man cannot be a 'common prostitute' and so cannot be charged with loitering or soliciting in a public place for the purpose of prostitution. But a male prostitute can be charged with persistently soliciting or importuning in a public place for immoral purposes, which carries the same maximum penalty of two years' imprisonment.[87] 'Immoral purposes' include, besides touting for custom for a woman prostitute, homosexual purposes.[88]

But in any case male prostitution is criminal for any prostitute under 21 because a man under 21 who has sex with another man is guilty of buggery or gross indecency, even if the other man is adult and the act is committed in private.[89] Since it is the young who do best in the trade, this does not stop the prostitution of men under 21.

(b) *Laws directed against those who help or profit from male prostitution*

The criminal laws about encouraging prostitution are all confined

[85] SOA 1956 s. 22, 28, 29, 30, 31, all of which require or assume that the prostitute is a woman.

[86] Street Offences Act 1959 s. 1, 2.

[87] SOA 1956 s. 32.

[88] *Horton* v. *Mead* 1913 1 KB 154; *Crook* v. *Edmondson* 1966 1 All ER 233 (kerb crawling to solicit women prostitutes not an offence).

[89] C.4 p. 94.

to women prostitutes. But since it is a crime to procure a man to commit buggery or gross indecency with a third man (not the procurer), anyone who procures a man to become a male prostitute or finds clients for a male prostitute must be committing a crime, difficult though it may be to prove.

Brothel-keeping and letting or permitting premises to be used as a brothel apply since 1967 to male brothels, and the 1967 Act also created the crime of living on the earnings of male prostitution, which carries with it on indictment a maximum term of seven years in prison.[90] The differences between the laws against male and female prostitution are therefore matters of detail and history rather than principle.

The contracts of prostitutes

The contract of a prostitute with her client is 'illegal'. This means that she cannot sue for the agreed price and that he cannot recover his money if she fails to perform the sexual act promised or does it badly. Since it is a crime to live on the earnings of prostitution or to control prostitutes, a pimp or manager cannot sue a prostitute for an agreed share of the earnings of prostitution. But it is more doubtful whether the prostitute, if she has handed over the money, may claim it back in this case. The law in this case is arguably intended not merely to penalise the pimp but to protect her, and she is claiming not the reward of prostitution but the return of money paid without good cause. The law is probably, however, more limited: she can recover the payment only if she can prove coercion or undue influence.[91]

Those who supply prostitutes with the necessities of life at the ordinary charge can sue for their money.[92] If they overcharge her because she is a prostitute the whole contract is made illegal, since it is directed towards enabling the supplier to live on the earnings of prostitution. They cannot, in my view, sue for the normal price or rent in this case. When the goods or services supplied can be used either for an innocent purpose or for prostitution, the supplier can recover unless the agreement specifies the

---

[90] SOA 1967 s. 5.
[91] On which see G. Treitel, *The Law of Contract* (4th ed. 1975) 270.
[92] *Lloyd* v. *Johnson* (1798) 1 Bos & Pull 340; 126 ER 939; *Appleton* v. *Campbell* (1826) 2 C. & P. 347–8.

use to be made of them (which is unlikely). But if the only use in the circumstances is for prostitution, and the supplier knows that his client is a prostitute, he cannot recover, even though it is not a term of the contract that the goods or services should be used for prostituti: n or that the payment for them should be made out of the proceeds of prostitution.[93] Hence according to nineteenth-century cases which have not been overruled, a launderer who washed smart clothes for a known prostitute was entitled to recover the laundry charge,[94] but those who hired an expensive carriage to a known prostitute could not recover the hire.[95] In the nineteenth century even a poor woman needed clean linen but, unless she was a prostitute, she did not travel in an ornate carriage.

3. PROS AND CONS

Prostitution is not usually classed as a positive good. The Wolfenden Report calls it 'an evil of which any society which claims to be civilised should seek to rid itself'.[96] The United Nations Convention of December 1949 says that prostitution and its accompanying evils—trade in human beings—are incompatible with the dignity and value of the human person and endanger the well-being of the individual, family and community.[97]

This adverse view is fairly modern. For many centuries, though prostitutes had a low status in society, the profession was thought to fill a need and only a rare feminist thought it could be suppressed. Such an early feminist was the empress Theodora, who tried to redeem prostitutes by housing them away from temptation on the far shore of the Bosphorus in a convent from which, it is said, some of them, bored with their idle life, jumped at night. Whatever its truth, this story is typical in one respect, in that it shows men and prostitutes on one side, respectable (or in the case of Theodora, reformed) women on the other.[98]

---

[93] *M'Kinnell* v. *Robinson* (1838) 3 M. & W. 434; *Cannan* v. *Bryce* (1819) 3 Barn. & Ald. 179: cases of loans for illegal stock-jobbing and gaming.
[94] *Lloyd* v. *Johnson* (1798) 1 Bos & Pull 340.
[95] *Pearce* v. *Brooks* (1866) LR 1 Exch. 213.
[96] *Wolfenden Report* s. 226 cf. 225.
[97] Annexed to the Resolution of the Fourth General Assembly of the UN of 2 Dec. 1949.
[98] Procopius, *Secret History* 17.5–6.

Before, then, we accept that prostitution is a social evil that should be ended it is worth glancing at the arguments in its favour. There are two. The first starts from the notion that it is a positive good to multiply pleasure and avoid frustration, a view which is called utilitarian. The second argument conceives of prostitution as a method of preserving families from strain. Something will be said of each in turn. If the test of sound social policy and, even, according to Bentham, of morality is whether the policy or conduct promotes the greatest pleasure of the greatest number, prostitutes must be among the most socially productive and even the most moral sections of the community. It was surely a step forward in civilisation when farmers learned to grow enough food not just for their own families but for others. A food market was organised and the buyers, freed from the toil of farming for themselves, turned their skill to metal working, art, government and war. Although sex is not as important to men as food, it certainly ranks high in the list of good things. So it must presumably rank as progress when a profession is set on foot by which some women provide sex not merely for a single husband but for dozens of men who either have no women of their own or are isolated or seek variety. If productivity is a sign of economic health, why not sexual productivity?

Neither market economists nor utilitarians generally draw these obvious conclusions from their own theories. Nevertheless it is clear that the male sex does not on the whole condemn prostitution. Men may not want their wives and daughters to be pros, but they are not against the profession as such. They do not look on the women who live by sex with the strong revulsion with which many regard homosexuals and pimps. The police, as many have noted, are often on friendly terms with the women they arrest for soliciting.

The explanation of this difference in attitude takes us to the second argument, which involves looking at prostitution in the light of family life. The man who goes with a prostitute is breaking the rules of family life and cheating his wife, but the prostitute is not cheating anyone. On the contrary the fact that she is available helps keep the family together. If her client had an affair with the wife of his next-door neighbour he might disrupt two families. By coming to her he threatens neither. 'Remove prostitutes from human affairs and you will pollute all things with

lust.'[99] The fact that a prostitute must be cool, that for the good
of her profession she must try not to become involved, makes for
impersonal, unexplosive sex. The trick and the pro do not look
for a deep relationship; what they want is rather an
unrelationship.

Prostitutes, then, do not threaten a social order based on the
family in the way in which homosexuals and pimps threaten it.
The latter opt out of the system by which men support women
and raise families. They either do not marry, or make women
support them. Prostitutes, on the other hand, help men who
accept the system to break one of its rules in the least harmful
way. That is a very different matter, and it explains why prostitutes are not reviled like the other groups.

That prostitution multiplies pleasure and indirectly keeps the
family intact has not been enough to commend it, at least for
the last century, as a useful social institution. Like slavery and the
possession of colonies it has fallen from the status of being necessary, though not ideal, to that of being, at least in establishment
opinion, undesirable and a social evil. It is viewed differently only
in that, in free societies, respect for liberty generally ensures that
a woman can choose to be a prostitute if she wants. Where, as in
Marxist states, freedom is not highly valued, especially if it takes
the form of private enterprise, prostitution is repressed, though
it has not so far been wiped out.

Why has it come to be thought that prostitution is a social
evil to be eliminated or at least discouraged to the extent that
respect for free choice allows? From a Protestant point of view,
inherited by Marxism, those activities which do not result in
material products are wasteful. From this point of view, contrary
to what was said earlier, sex, apart from the procreation of
children, is not to be counted as a form of production. A prostitute is not a productive worker.

But more important than the Protestant attitude to childless
sex has been the protest movement, led by respectable women,
which in the nineteenth century began a campaign against state
regulation of prostitutes and brothels. Its origin was largely
English. Harriet Martineau, Florence Nightingale, Josephine
Butler and others began with a trenchant protest against the
Contagious Diseases Acts of 1864 and 1869, which compelled

[99] Augustine, *De Ordine* II iv 12.

prostitutes in certain ports to undergo medical examination in order to restrict the spread of venereal disease.[100] The campaign has in the long run been successful both in the UK and internationally. Its fruits include the United Nations resolution of 1949, and the fact that France, the model country in regulating prostitution, abolished controls in 1946,[101] Italy in 1958.[102]

Though controls over brothels and prostitutes have a long history, which in England goes back at least to 1161,[103] the rise of state power and professional armies brought with it a more formal system by which the state took care that its armed forces were not made incapable by venereal disease or frustrated by the absence of women. So began a form of regulation by which prostitutes were registered, subjected to medical examinations and often lodged in brothels or camps. The system spread to civil life. The French, readier than others to follow an argument to its proper conclusion, were the model for other countries. A French city of 20,000 would before 1946 have, perhaps, three brothels catering for different classes. Each would have five to fifteen resident prostitutes. The client paid the establishment a rent, and the prostitute a fee. Unlicensed whores ('clandestines') were not allowed to trade.[104]

It was the attempt by the Contagious Diseases Acts of 1864 and 1869 to introduce parts of this system into England that set protest alight. Since the arguments against state control of prostitution lead into the arguments against prostitution itself, the two can be considered together.

The arguments against state control rest on respect for the prostitute's freedom of choice and on the bad example set by the state if it regulates a profession which is degrading to those who practise it and which encourages men to break their family obligations.

Respect for freedom is the first argument. The state, it is argued, should not stop a mature woman prostituting herself if she wants to. On the other hand it should in the name of freedom intervene to stop others exploiting her or forcing her to be a

---

[100] *Daily News,* 31 Dec. 1869, reprinted in: *Law and Morality,* ed. L. Blom-Cooper and G. Drewry (1976), 114.
[101] Law of 13 April 1946; Ordinance of 25 Nov. 1960.
[102] Law 75 of 20 Feb. 1958.
[103] T. E. James, *Prostitution and the Law* (1951) 38.
[104] Sicot 52.

prostitute against her will. In the first place, then, a woman should not need an official licence or card in order to practice as a prostitute, nor should there be a quota. But more important in the mind of the reformers was the conviction that official brothels undermine freedom by encouraging trade in women. These brothels are the market where the procurer can sell his wares. Their existence leads to women, often foreigners, being forced into prostitution, perhaps at an early age, to supply the demand.[105]

There is a good deal of evidence to support the reformers' analysis. But nowadays, perhaps in part because of the decline of regulation, it seems that, at least in Western countries, women are seldom coerced into becoming or remaining prostitutes.[106]

The second objection to state control therefore stands in the foreground nowadays. This rests on the view that prostitution is degrading, and that the state soils itself by making rules for it to be carried on.

What does it mean to say that prostitution is degrading? After all, to earn a living by the use of the body need not be a bad thing. Professional footballers are admired. To serve all customers indiscriminately is a feature of many jobs, like that of a waiter. What of the physical contact with the client? Hairdressers and dentists also make money from work that involves physical contact. Is the objection that no great skill is needed? Neither is it for work on a building site. Is it that disease and exhaustion mark the prostitute? The same is (or was) true of the coal miner. That it has no future? Teachers have found the same. The points listed are reasons (not necessarily the most important ones) why most people do not want their sisters or daughters to be prostitutes. They do not explain why they think the trade not just unwise, but base.

A more powerful argument against prostitution is that it involves a debased form of sex. Ideally the act of sex should be one of love or friendship. Sex with a prostitute generally excludes both and, though friendships between prostitutes and their clients are not uncommon, many prostitutes find what they do unpleasant. But there are other debased activities which do not lead to the people concerned being condemned. Street music is a

---

[105] M. Pearson, *The Age of Consent* (1972) 23f.
[106] *Wolfenden Report* s. 304–5.

debased form of music, but we do not think of it as a social evil or of street musicians as a debased group of people. It is probably because sex is more intimate than making music that commercial sex is condemned. As one prostitute put it, 'it is selling your soul not selling a service'.[107] This also explains, in part, the different attitude of the Wolfenden Committee to homosexuality and prostitution. Between people of the same sex love or at least friendship is possible. So homosexuality, even if immoral, need not, in their eyes, be something of which a civilised society need be ashamed. From the point of view of ideals, on the other hand, there is nothing to be said in favour of prostitution. It will always be on or below the level of street music.

To this we may add that to respectable women prostitution is apt to seem doubly distasteful. Since women are on the whole more inclined than men to see sexual relations in terms of love and security, a profession which rests on a quite different type of sexual relation is a denial of woman's nature. Moreover, the fact that it exists prompts awkward questions. Is marriage, behind the facade of love, the sale of sex for money and security? Does the prostitute strike a better bargain than her sister? Perhaps these disturbing thoughts account in part for the wish, so strong in the Wolfenden Report, to brush the dirt of prostitution under the carpet.

4. THE REFORM OF THE LAW

Prostitution is, in the view of many, degrading and it is often associated with gambling, drug pushing, theft and organised crime. Nevertheless, if we think that people have a right to sexual freedom (which is discussed in Chapter 7) and still more if we value private enterprise, we must accept that an adult may be a prostitute if he or she wishes and may resort to a prostitute for sexual pleasure if so minded. So far from being a social evil to be rooted out, prostitution is an expression of the fact that in a free society we may choose within limits to do what we like with our bodies and to earn our living as we like. Marxists, who are against free enterprise and personal freedom, naturally take a different view.

The law of England neither recognises nor denies the rights

[107] K. Millett, *The Prostitution Papers* (1975) 36.

mentioned. It is not criminal to be a prostitute, but soliciting either in the street or by advertisement is an offence, so that a law-abiding prostitute would have to use her own flat or house and to find tricks from her own circle of acquaintances. Quite apart from pimps, those who knowingly let premises to or supply services to prostitutes run considerable risks of being held to be living on the earnings of prostitution.

A right which is hedged round in this way can hardly be called an effective right. The object of law reform should be to secure that the right of an adult to be, and to resort to, a prostitute becomes a legally effective one. The first step to this end would be to allow prostitutes to solicit in the street or by advertisement. The Street Offences Act of 1959, passed as a result of the Wolfenden Report, was intended to clear the streets of prostitutes. To a large extent it succeeded in doing so, though the penalties are now inadequate for the purpose.[108] But that Report, and the debates which followed, never properly considered whether it is right to stop working-class women from earning their living by making contacts in the street when no nuisance or public inconvenience is proved.

It was class legislation, since the middle-class prostitute working from a flat or house was not affected, and it followed a bad legislative technique, namely that of trying to prevent soliciting to the annoyance of members of the public by forbidding soliciting altogether. It did so because annoyance is difficult to prove, but that does not make it good legislation. It would be fairer to allow soliciting in a street or public place unless annoyance is thereby caused to the person solicited (as was required in English law before 1957). The present state of the law puts arbitrary power in the hands of the police. The offence is in effect one of soliciting to the annoyance of the police, not that of members of the public. Even in the absence of annoyance to individuals, however, there is a case for allowing local authorities to ban soliciting in certain places, for instance residential areas, as is provided by the law of West Germany.[109] This makes it possible

---

[108] Home Office: *Report of the Working Party on Vagrancy and Street Offences* (1976) s. 77 proposes increases.

[109] West Germany: Penal code s. 184a (Law of 23 Nov. 1973). For France see Law of 13 Apr. 1946 and Crim. 1 Feb. 1956, Dalloz 1956. 365 (Violation of personal freedom for prefect totally to forbid prostitutes to circulate in public).

for those who are offended by seeing prostitutes to be sure of avoiding them.

Secondly, prostitutes should be allowed to advertise in shop windows or contact magazines without the fear of prosecution either for themselves or the shop or magazine owners. The advertisements must conform to the law of obscenity, but apart from this there is no reason why they should not invite kinky forms of sex. Indeed there is every reason why they should, since one of the functions of the profession is to cater for these forms of sex. The decision in *Shaw* v. *DPP*,[110] which held that a jury may find those who agree to publish such advertisements guilty of a conspiracy to corrupt public morals was well intended, but fails to take account of the fact that, if prostitution is to be really and not just notionally legal, prostitutes must have ways of making contact with clients.

Thirdly, the criminal and civil law about those who deal with prostitutes stands in need of reform. A prostitute must be able to live somewhere, eat, feed and clothe herself normally and, in general, be treated as an ordinary member of the community. It may be desirable to retain a crime of living on the earnings of prostitution. But it should surely not be given the wide scope it now has in England. It should be confined to cases in which two conditions are fulfilled : first, that the pimp or other accused person is wholly or largely supported from the proceeds of prostitution and, secondly, that he has used threats, undue influence or improper pressure in order to obtain this support. The fact that he has given little or nothing in return would be evidence of the use of threats or undue influence. It may well be that it would be difficult to prove that a pimp was guilty of the suggested offence. I am not sure that this would be a bad thing. The law about pimping at present illustrates once more the bad legislative habit of forbidding something which is not objectionable in order to strike at something which is—penalising pimps who are simply business managers or lovers in order to strike at those who exploit whores. The German legislation of 1973 goes half way in this direction by requiring either exploitation by the pimp or management for gain.[111]

---

[110] 1962 AC 220.
[111] Penal Code s. 181a (Law of 23 Nov. 1973) penalises those who exploit a prostitute or manage her for their own gain.

If the criminal law were amended along the lines proposed the law of contract would also need to be changed. While the contract between the prostitute and her client, like any contract providing for sexual relations, would be unenforceable, it would no longer be illegal. The prostitute who did her part of the bargain on credit could sue for a reasonable reward, of which the market and the agreement would provide evidence. Those who supplied her with goods or services knowing that she was a prostitute could sue for the agreed amount even if, just because she was a prostitute, they raised their prices. After all, no one thinks that an American tourist is not liable to pay the agreed price on a contract for the sale of knick-knacks simply because sellers increase their prices for American tourists.

In short, a prostitute would move from being a person who is legally treated as a helpless person closer to that of a normal member of society exercising a profession of which many disapprove, just as many disapprove of the army or the liquor trade. Though prostitution is never likely to become a highly organised profession with an effective trade union, it would be helped if associations relating to it were relieved of the stigma of being for an object which is illegal in civil law and possibly amounts to a conspiracy to corrupt public morals. The examples of the prostitutes of Lyons, who protested to some effect against police harassment, and of the American COYOTE campaign, shows that something can be achieved if prostitutes are able to organise. No doubt there will also, from their point of view, be drawbacks. If their contracts are not illegal their earnings must be subject to income tax.

There remain three points of lesser, but not negligible, importance : courtesy, the equality of the sexes, and state control. As to the first, it is surely not necessary for the legislator to use the phrase 'common prostitute'.[112] The phrase is in any case not appropriate, because a prostitute, unlike a 'common' innkeeper or carrier, is not bound to serve every customer who can pay. Indeed, even the term 'prostitute' carries a certain stigma and should be avoided when it properly can be, for instance in the definition of soliciting. As the law now stands this must be 'for

[112] Street Offences Act 1959 s. 1(1); Home Office Working Party, above n. 108, s. 85.

the purposes of prostitution'[113] whereas it is really only necessary to say 'persistently for sexual purposes'.

As regards equality between men and women, it is surely a good idea to aim at this whenever possible, even if in sex law complete equality is neither attainable nor desirable. The law about persistent soliciting in a street or public place for sexual purposes should be the same for both sexes, but for each should involve the proof of annoyance or that the place was one in which soliciting is specially prohibited. So kerb-crawling in a car for the purpose of soliciting would be an offence on the same footing as soliciting in the street by a prostitute walking or standing at the street corner. The system of police cautions could extend to soliciting by both sexes.

It will be objected that people will not come forward to give evidence of annoyance.[114] In so far as this is true, is it not an indication that they do not feel seriously annoyed?

State control or regulation of prostitution rouses hackles. Even such a professing liberal as John Stuart Mill argues that, if there is compulsory medical inspection of prostitutes to prevent VD 'it cannot but seem (to soldiers and ignorant persons) that legal precautions taken expressly to make that kind of indulgence safe are a licence to it.[115] There is no parallel case of any indulgence or pursuit avowedly disgraceful and immoral for which the government provides safeguards.' Yet in the case of some activities, like drinking, smoking and gambling, which are allowed but not encouraged by the state, it is agreed that the state can properly intervene to make sure that they are carried on with due regard to health, comfort and decency. If they are degrading, the state's intervention is designed to make them less so.

Is the same true of prostitution? Should the state licence brothels and prostitutes, provide for medical inspection to reduce the spread of venereal disease and take other measures of this sort? Many people think that it should not, and it seems to me that there is strong case, though not for the reasons usually advanced, against state regulation. In the case of drink, smoking

---

[113] Street Offences Act 1959 s. 1(1).

[114] Home Office Working Party s. 87.

[115] J. S. Mill and H. Taylor, *Letter to J. Nichol* of 29 Dec. 1879 para. 4 (Blom-Cooper and Drewry 119).

or gambling it is in general only excess that should be restrained. In the case of prostitution, however, most of the clients will inevitably be married, and by visiting a brothel or going with a prostitute will be breaking their duty to their wives. Although the state does not require the highest moral standard of its citizens it should arguably not encourage them to break their civil duties. If it controls prostitution it adopts the view that men cannot be expected to be faithful to their wives. It endorses Napoleon's blunt remark that for a man one woman is not enough.[116] Hence, though in the absence of control disease may spread and clients be overcharged, it is better for the state to stand aside.[117]

[116] Sicot 50.
[117] C. J. Tarring and others, *The State and Sexual Morality* (1921) 14.

6
Offenders and Trials

'You can check out any time you like, but you can never leave'

(Henley/Frey/Felder : *Hotel California*)

How many people offend against sex laws? How many are tried and convicted? What special rules are there for the trial of sex offences? What sort of punishment is inflicted on those found guilty? For how long? What are the prospects of curing sexual delinquency by medical treatment? This chapter gives a brief survey of the legal position of sex offenders, their numbers, trials punishments and treatments. The information may be of interest, especially to those who find themselves charged with a sex offence and want to know what to expect.

I.   NUMBERS

Most people find figures boring and hard to follow. A few, like the author, are excited by them. Whatever one's view, there is no escaping statistics in this chapter.[1] The first inquiry concerns the number of offenders. The number of people convicted either on indictment or in Magistrates' Courts of sex offences is quite small. It is perhaps best to set out the figures for three recent years for some typical sex crimes :

---

[1] Taken, unless otherwise stated, from *Criminal Statistics, England and Wales 1965, 1970 and 1975*. (Cmnd. 3037, 4708, 6566).

Offence	1965	1970	1975
Rape	169	305	343
Indecent assault on female	2,833	3,274	2,860
Sexual intercourse with girl under 13	76	87	136
Sexual intercourse with girl between 13 and 16	581	696	573
Gross indecency with child	306	375	373
Incest	146	115	188
Buggery	219	212	226
Attempted buggery, etc.	827	890	891
Indecency between men	483	857	1,507
Procuration	79	145	125
Brothel keeping	154	140	99
Aiding offence by prostitute	6	3	1
Living on prostitute's earnings	227	219	130
Soliciting, etc. by prostitute	1,532	2,347	3,292
Importuning by man	820	451	591
Indecent exposure	2,496	2,862	2,490
Total	10,954	12,978	13,830

Convictions for sex offences in England and Wales therefore rose by 19 per cent between 1965 and 1970 and 7 per cent between 1970 and 1975. Women made up 15 per cent of those convicted in 1965, 19 per cent in 1970 and 25 per cent in 1975. These figures can probably be interpreted in a straightforward way. The late sixties was a time of social upheaval, and there was some rise in reported sex crimes, among others. The seventies have been stable, but the relative position of women has changed.[2] They are more often charged with sex offences than they used to be. Though most of these are minor matters like soliciting by prostitutes and brothel-keeping, tried in the Magistrates' Court, it is perhaps significant of the changed position of women in society that the police and members of the public are now more willing to prosecute women. But they are still seldom charged with or convicted of serious sex crimes. Only 15,

[2] Sir L. Radzinowicz and J. King, *The Growth of Crime* (1977) 13.

14 and 23 women were convicted on indictment in the years 1965, 1970 and 1975.

Between 1965 and 1970 the proportion of offenders in the age group from 17 to 21 rose from 15 per cent of the total to just under 20 per cent. In 1975 it was still 20 per cent. Sex crimes are not the preserve of the young.

One point of interest which the figures suggest is that the Sexual Offences Act 1967 which made homosexual acts between consenting adults in private legal had little effect on the number of convictions for homosexual offences. Perhaps the impact of the Act was simply to reassure those homosexuals who would not have been arrested or tried anyway that they had nothing to fear.

Thirteen thousand convictions for sex offences in a year is not a large number. It amounts to one in 4,000 of the population. If this continued throughout a person's lifetime and he or she lived to be 70, his or her chances of being convicted of a sex offence at any time would not be more than one in fifty-seven, even if no one was convicted twice. In fact many sex crimes, especially the minor ones like soliciting, are frequently repeated and frequently prosecuted, so that one in fifty-seven is an over-estimate.[3]

But if the chances of a person being convicted of a sex offence are very low, the chances of his (or to a lesser extent her) committing one are much higher. Obviously there are lots of undetected offences against sex laws, as there are against other laws. For each person convicted how many get away with it?[4] One can make an estimate for the crime of sexual intercourse with a girl between 13 and 16. In 1975 573 men were found guilty of this offence. The number of girls of age 13, 14 and 15 in 1973 was about 1,062,600.[5] On Schofield's figures for 1965 about 5 per cent of girls had sexual intercourse under 16.[6] Suppose that this percentage has remained the same (if anything it has probably risen). Then about 53,130 girls of these ages will have had

[3] F. H. McClintock and N. H. Avison, *Crime in England and Wales* (1968) 303, make the risk one in 63 for a male by age 60.
[4] Radzinowicz and King 49.
[5] Registrar-General, *Statistical Review of England and Wales for the Year 1973* (1975) 11 4, gives 1,124,000 males and 1,062,000 females in this age group.
[6] Schofield, *Young People* 50.

sexual intercourse before they were 16. Suppose that the number of men who commit this offence is exactly the same as the number of girls with whom they commit it—that each girl does it with just one boy-friend and that no boy does it with more than one under-age girl. (Though both these assumptions are false they tend to cancel one another out.) Then in the three years in which a group of girls moves from 13 to 16 about 53,130 boys will commit the offence with them and about 1,700 will be convicted of it. The number of offences is around thirty times the number of convictions.

For some crimes like rape the proportion of cases reported to the police may be as high as a half and perhaps as many as a third of the offenders are convicted. For others like indecent assaults on children under 16 the rate is very low. On Schofield's figures about 30 per cent of boys under 16 fondle a girl's genitals and 10 per cent of the girls do the same to the boys. If the partner is under 16 also this is an indecent assault, since children under 16 cannot in law give their consent to such an act. So this crime is probably committed by 100,000 boys and 35,000 girls a year. The boys are liable to two years' imprisonment and the girls would be surprised to learn that they are liable to ten, since an indecent assault on a male is a more serious offence. Since only 440 boys and two girls under 17 were convicted of indecent assault of any sort in 1975, the ratio of offenders to those caught and tried must be much higher than 225 to 1 for the boys— perhaps closer to the figure of 15,000 to 1 which the calculations suggest for the girls.

The ratio of sex crimes committed to those which result in trial and conviction is clearly high, but varies from crime to crime. Most of these breaches of the criminal law do not come to light or, if they do, are kept to a narrow circle of family, friends or mates. If the police are told, they may caution the offender. It has been held proper to do this, for example, when a teenage boy has sexual intercourse with a girl under 16.[7] In 1975 more men under 21 and more women of all ages were cautioned than convicted for sex offences.[8] So far as soliciting by prostitutes is concerned, the police are indeed bound to give two cautions

[7] *Metropolitan Police Commissioner ex parte Blackburn* 1968 1 All ER 763, 771.
[8] Cmnd. 6566 p. 24; below p. 156.

before making a charge.[9] This police discretion, though it can lead to abuse, for instance to picking on certain prostitutes and letting others go, is necessary. A prosecution for a sex offence may disrupt a family whatever the outcome, and is not to be lightly undertaken.

2. TRIALS

In most respects a trial for a sex offence is like one for any other crime. Most sex offences are triable on indictment rather than summarily.[10] Charges of sexual intercourse with a girl under 16, or permitting her to use premises for that purpose, may, however, be tried either way, at the option of the accused, if he is 17 or over.[11] So may indecent assault on either sex, indecency between men, and procuring homosexual acts.[12] Soliciting for prostitution is tried summarily.[13] The offences of living on the earnings of prostitution, controlling a prostitute, and soliciting by a man[14] can be tried either summarily or on indictment, the maximum punishment being limited to six months in prison if the trial is by the Magistrates' Court. In these cases, apart from a charge of homosexual soliciting,[15] the accused cannot claim to be tried on indictment before a jury.[16] Charges of keeping a brothel, letting premises for use as a brothel, permitting premises to be used as a brothel and permitting them to be used for prostitution are tried summarily, but the accused, if he has been previously convicted, can insist on a jury.[17]

Indictments for rape, sexual intercourse with a girl under 13 and incest with a girl under 13 must be tried by a High Court judge unless the presiding judge of the circuit directs other-

---

[9] Home Office Circular 109/1959; Street Offences Act 1959 s. 2.

[10] SOA 1956 Second Schedule.

[11] Criminal Law Act 1977 s. 16(1) and 2nd schedule 17; SOA 1956 s. 6, 26.

[12] Criminal Law Act 1977 s. 16(2), (3) and 3rd schedule 23, 27, 32–5; SOA 1956 s. 13, 14, 15; SOA 1967 s. 4(1).

[13] Street Offences Act 1959 s. 1(2).

[14] SOA 1956 Second Schedule 30–2.

[15] SOA 1967 s. 9.

[16] Above, n. 10.

[17] SOA 1956 Second Schedule 33–6.

wise.[18] Charges of sexual intercourse with a girl under 16 or attempted intercourse with her must be prosecuted within twelve months of the offence alleged.[19] The sanction of the Attorney-General or Director of Public Prosecutions is needed for a prosecution for incest or attempted incest.[20] The Director of Public Prosecutions must give his consent to prosecutions for buggery or gross indecency between men if either was under 21 at the time of the alleged offence. The same is true for attempts to commit these crimes, and for aiding, counselling or procuring their commission.[21]

Two rules of the law of evidence are of general importance in the trial of sex offences, and two others are of special concern when a rape offence is charged.

(i) The first rule of general importance is that, when a sex offence is tried by jury, the jury must be directed that it is not safe to convict on the evidence of the victim who lays the complaint unless it is *corroborated*.[22] If the jury are not told this and the accused is convicted, the Court of Appeal will normally allow the appeal.[23] On the other hand, if the jury are told of the danger, but proceed to convict because, though there is no corroboration, they are satisfied that the complaint is true, they are entitled to do so. Jack may therefore in a clear case be convicted of rape merely on the evidence of Jill who states that he had intercourse with her without her consent. But the prosecution will and should try to produce other evidence which can count as corroboration. This might take the form of testimony which tends to show that Jack not John was the man who was alone in the room with her or that Jack ran away just after she screamed. It must point to Jack as the culprit, not just to the fact that Jill has been raped by someone.[25] So Sue may give evidence that she saw Jack enter or leave or, if Jill claims to have scratched Jack's nose in the struggle, that Sue saw it bleeding. Any of these might amount to corroboration.

[18] Cross and Jones, *Introduction to Criminal Law* (7th ed. 1972) Appendix D.
[19] SOA 1956 Second Schedule 10(a) and (b).
[20] SOA 1956 Second Schedule 14(a) and (b).
[21] SOA 1967 s. 8.
[22] Cross, *Evidence* (4th ed. 1974) 181–2.
[23] *Trigg* 1963 1 All ER 490.
[24] *O'Reilly* 1967 2 QB 722.
[25] *James* (1971) 55 CAR 299.

It is not only about the evidence of the victim that the jury must be warned. The same is true of the evidence of accomplices.[26] This is important in certain sex crimes such as buggery and gross indecency between men, because if the act is done by consent each is an accomplice in the other's crime.[27] In these cases the jury need not necessarily be told that it is 'dangerous' to convict in the absence of corroboration, nor need the word 'corroboration' always be used, but the judge must convey to them the need to consider whether there is independent evidence which in some material particular points to the accused as the culprit.[28] So if Tom, aged 17, complains that he was buggered by George, the head of his college, and that he allowed George to do this in the hope of being let through an examination, the judge should warn the jury at George's trial that there are two reasons why they should look for some confirmation of Tom's evidence before convicting—the fact that he is the complainant in a sexual offence and the fact that he is an accomplice in the crime of buggery.

Children may give sworn evidence in criminal trials, provided that the judge is satisfied that they understand the nature of an oath.[29] If they do so, the jury must be warned in similar terms about the risk of acting on their evidence unless it is corroborated in some material point which implicates the accused.[30]

In the three types of case mentioned (the evidence of victims in sexual cases, accomplices, sworn evidence of children) the jury may, after due warning, convict even if the evidence is not corroborated, provided they are satisfied of its truth. In two other instances, however, which have a bearing on sex offences, corroboration is a legal requirement. Hence, if there is no corroboration of the evidence, the jury are not entitled to convict, however much they may believe it, and, if they do, the conviction will be set aside.[31] A person charged with the offences of procuring a woman to have sexual intercourse by threats or false pretences, of causing the prostitution of a woman or of procuring a girl under 21 for unlawful sexual intercourse cannot be convicted on

---

[26] Cross, *Evidence* 174–81.
[27] Stephen, *Digest* art. 221; Smith and Hogan 357.
[28] *O'Reilly* 1967 2 QB 722, 727; Cross 178.
[29] Cross 182–3.
[30] *Cleal* 1942 1 All ER 203.
[31] Cross 169–74.

the evidence of a single witness unless the witness is corroborated in some material particular by evidence implicating the accused.[32] Lastly, a child of sufficient intelligence who understands the duty of speaking the truth can give unsworn evidence in criminal cases.[33] But the accused is, on the House of Lords reading of a badly drafted provision of the Children and Young Persons Act, not liable to be convicted unless the unsworn evidence of the child is corroborated by some other evidence, which must not be the unsworn evidence of another child.[34]

Corroboration is therefore important in the trial of sex offences. Certainly the evidence of accomplices and perhaps that of children needs to be regarded with caution. Is the same true of the evidence of those, mainly women, who claim to be the victims of sex offences? Is their evidence any less reliable than that of, say, a man who claims to have been defrauded? Is the rule that their evidence should be corroborated anything more than an item of male bias?

(ii) The other rule of evidence which is of special concern to those who are charged with sex offences is the rule relating to *similar fact evidence*.[35] Generally speaking, if a person is charged with a crime, evidence must not be given which merely tends to show that he has a tendency to wrongdoing in general or to that particular sort of wrongdoing. So, on a charge of rape, evidence is not admitted, generally speaking, that the accused has convictions for theft or is of bad character or even that he has previously been convicted of indecent assault, or that he committed a different rape on the same day. But evidence which shows a tendency to commit a crime by a specific method or in certain special conditions may be admitted if the court does not think that the value of the evidence is outweighed by the danger that it will prejudice the minds of the jury, who may take it at more than it is worth. So evidence was admitted that a person accused of strangling a small girl whom he had not interfered with sexually had done the same to two other small girls without interfering with them either.[36]

This type of evidence is in no way confined to sex offences;

---

[32] SOA 1956 s. 2(2), 3(2), 22(2), 23(2).
[33] Children and Young Persons Act 1933 s. 38.
[34] *Director of Public Prosecutions* v. *Hester* 1973 AC 296.
[35] Cross 319–45.
[36] *Straffen* 1952 2 QB 911.

but in practice it is more often admitted in these than in other cases because of the tendency of people to conform to a pattern in their sexual behaviour—to have sex with the same partner, or to perform the same sort of sexual act, or to do it in the same surroundings. This is especially true of kinky forms of sex. Hence evidence which tends to show that the accused person did much the same thing on another occasion as is now alleged may have a special value in showing that he is rightly identified as the culprit in this case, or that his defence that he was just being friendly to or innocently associating with the victim is untrue.[37]

Hence, on a charge of gross indecency with boys evidence has been admitted that the accused had powder puffs and obscene photographs in his room. This tended to show that the boys rightly identified him later as the man with whom they had made an appointment on a previous occasion.[38] In another case of gross indecency where the accused was alleged to have masqueraded as a medical man attached to an institution of people interested in the occult, and to have taken advantage of young men who visited the institution, by pretending to give them medical treatment, it was held that the evidence of two young men to this effect could be admitted to confirm evidence to the same effect by a third, whom the accused said he had never met.[39] In another case the accused was charged with homosexual offences with two groups of boys aged between 9 and 12 who gave evidence that they had been invited to his house and given refreshments, comics, and a chance to take the puppy for a walk. The accused had then used much the same sexual technique with nearly all of them. It was held that the evidence of the different boys could be admitted in relation to the charges of indecency not merely with other members of the same group but with the boys in the other group.[40] Finally, when the headmaster of a school was accused of buggery with a boy of 16 in the school and with inciting another boy of 17, also a pupil, to commit buggery with him and both boys gave evidence that the accused had asked them to bugger him, it was held that the evidence of each could be admitted as tending to prove the charge of an offence with the

---

[37] Cross 330, 335.
[38] *Thompson* 1918 AC 221.
[39] *Hall* 1952 1 KB 302.
[40] *Director of Public Prosecutions* v. *Kilbourne* 1973 AC 729, 751.

other. The evidence of one also corroborated the evidence of the other.[41]

It might be thought from these four examples relating to homosexual charges that in a case of this sort any evidence tending to show that the accused is a homosexual will be admitted. This is not so.[42] The opinion of Lord Sumner that homosexuals are stamped by their perverted lust 'with the hallmark of a specialised and extraordinary class, as much as if they carried on their bodies some physical peculiarity' is no longer accepted.[43] Though the decisions are tangled, the principle is that the evidence may be admitted only when it shows that the accused likes a particular technique, such as being passive rather than active, or a particular approach, such as pretending to give medical treatment. Even so the evidence must bear on an issue in the case, such as the identity of the accused, and its value must not be outweighed by the prejudice it is likely to arouse in the minds of the jury.

(iii) There are two further rules which must be shortly mentioned because they are important in the trial of sex offences, especially rape. The first is the rule of the Criminal Evidence Act 1898 s. 1(f).

If an accused person gives evidence in his own defence he cannot be asked questions in order to show that he has previous convictions or has been charged in the past, or has done similar things in the past to what is now charged, or has a bad character. But if he or his lawyer asks questions of the prosecution witnesses to show that he has a *good* character, or if he himself in his evidence says so, or if his defence is conducted in such a way as to make imputations on the character of the prosecutor or the prosecution witnesses, it is different. In that case he can be asked both about his character in general and about convictions or incidents in the past which are similar to what is now charged.

The difficulty from the point of view of the accused person is to defend himself convincingly and deny the charges without casting imputations or aspersions on the prosecutor or the prosecution witnesses. Suppose that on a charge of rape he gives

[41] *Boardman* v. *DPP* 1975 AC 421.
[42] *Chandor* 1959 1 QB 545.
[43] *Thompson* 1918 AC 221, 235 but *Boardman* v. *DPP* 1975 AC 421, 443, 450, 458.

evidence that the woman consented and adds that she offered
to masturbate him? Suppose that on a charge of buggery the
accused gives evidence that the person who makes the charge is
a male prostitute to whom he and others have given money in
return for sex? The layman might think that these defences both
involved imputations on the character of the supposed victim.
It has, however, been held that in the first case the accused cannot be cross-examined about his past,[44] while in the second he
can.[45] To deny consent on a rape charge is simply to deny that
the prosecution has to prove, namely sexual intercourse without
consent. To accuse the person bringing the charge of being a
prostitute is to go beyond a mere denial, and it lets in the record
of the accused even if this is the only way in which he can conduct a proper defence.

(iv) The last rule of evidence which is of special interest in the
trial of sex offences is the rule about *complaints* by the victim or
alleged victim.[46] If the case is not one of rape or a sexual assault,
it adds nothing, generally speaking, to a person's evidence that he
or she told the same story to Tom, Dick or Harry as he is now
telling in court. There is no reason to suppose that the more
often a person says something the more likely he is to be speaking
the truth. So evidence of what he said to others is excluded.

But it is different if the complaint is of rape or a sexual assault.
A woman is expected not to take rape lying down. In general,
the victim of a sex offence, whether man or woman, can be
expected to complain at the first reasonable opportunity. Evidence that she (or he) did so is admitted, since it tends to confirm
that she is truthful.[47] This is so whether, as in rape and most
cases of indecent assault, consent would be a defence, or whether,
as in the case of an assault on a child under 16 or gross indecency
with a child under 14, it would not be.[48] In all these cases it
would be natural for the victim to complain.

The law therefore admits evidence of the complaint, provided
it was made freely and at the first reasonable opportunity.[49] A

---

[44] *Turner* 1944 KB 463.
[45] *Selvey* v. *Director of Public Prosecutions* 1970 AC 304.
[46] *Roberts* 1942 1 All ER 187; Cross, *Evidence* 207.
[47] *Lillyman* 1896 2 QB 167; *Osborne* 1905 1 KB 551; *Camelleri* 1922
1 KB 122 (boy of 15).
[48] *Osborne* 1905 1 KB 551.
[49] *Osborne* 1905 1 KB 551, 561.

complaint made as much as a week later has been admitted.[50]
Obviously the victim cannot be expected to tell the first stranger
she meets. If Millie's mother puts pressure on her by asking 'Did
Steve force you?', and she says Yes, the complaint will not be
regarded as free. She must not be asked leading questions, but
there is no reason why she should not be questioned about her
distressed state and invited to explain it.[51]

The rule about evidence of the victim's character (e.g. that she
has had sexual intercourse with other men) is discussed in
Chapter 3.[52]

3.   SENTENCES

In dealing with the sentences for sexual offences it will be convenient to discuss, first, the maximum sentences : secondly, the
actual sentences imposed for the various sex offences in the Crown
Court and the Magistrates' Court; and thirdly, the principles
laid down by the Court of Appeal when it hears appeals against
sentence. The last is important because by its judgments the
Court of Appeal makes known what it thinks are the proper
sentences for the gravest instances of rape and the other crimes,
and what general standards should be observed by judges in
sentencing.

Legislation

The maximum sentences are normally set out by Parliament in
statutes. For sex offences they are often on the high side, but not
consistently so. Sometimes they reflect the conditions of a past
age. There is life imprisonment for rape, intercourse with a girl
under 13 (1885) or permitting her to use premises for intercourse
(1885), for buggery of a boy under 16, a woman or an animal
(1861), and for incest by a man with a girl under 13 (1908).[53]

In 1975 there were only eight life sentences for sex offences,
five for rape and three for buggery. This is not many, but some
will think it wrong that there should be any. Though people

---

[50] *Hedges* (1909) 3 CAR 280.
[51] Cross, *Evidence* 211.
[52] Above, p. 64.
[53] SOA 1956 Second Schedule 1, 2(a), 3(a), 14(a).

sentenced in this way are usually released after a certain number of years, they have no guarantee that they will ever be freed. It is not clear that anything, other than a grave threat to the safety of the state, could justify us in putting one of our fellow citizens in that position. But, assuming that we shall continue to do so, the most serious sex offences are surely those involving either violence or sex with children under the age of puberty. These are for the most part included in the list given above, along with others (buggery with a woman with her consent, or with an animal) which should not be criminal at all.

There are also some freakish differences as regards maximum fixed terms of imprisonment. Parliament wants to mark the difference between homosexual and heterosexual crimes. One way in which it has done this is to make the punishment for indecent assault on a man ten years as against two for a woman and five for a girl under 13.[54] Apart from the fact that women can assault men or other women, this is surely to legislate by passion rather than reason. It is indeed in order for Parliament to show that it prefers heterosexual acts, but not to make the maximum penalty five times as great in one case as the other.

For sexual intercourse with a girl between 13 and 16 the maximum is two years in prison, for a man over 21 who is guilty of indecency with a man under that age five years is the limit.[55] This gives a ratio, still too high, of two and a half to one. Another penalty fixed by indignation rather than cool reflection is the seven-year maximum for incest by a man or woman.[56] It is difficult to see any point in a prison sentence in these harrowing cases other than to allow the family of the offender to regroup in his absence; and this does not require him, still less her, to be away for more than a year or so.

Finally, the offences of living on the earnings of prostitution and controlling a prostitute carry a maximum of seven years in prison,[57] which again reflects a sense of outrage rather than an attempt to weigh the comparative gravity of pimping and crimes of violence. In all these instances it is a wrong sense of proportion, not a wrong sense of values that has led Parliament astray.

[54] SOA 1956 Second Schedule 17, 18.
[55] SOA 1956 Second Schedule 10(a); SOA 1967 s. 3(1)(b).
[56] SOA 1956 Second Schedule 14(a), 15(a).
[57] SOA 1956 Second Schedule 30, 31.

Sentencing practice

A person arrested for a sex offence will want to know what is likely to happen to him or her. Naturally much turns on the age of the supposed offender and the seriousness of the supposed offence. On the 1975 figures, however, a woman is likely to be cautioned and a man over 21 to be tried and convicted. A man under 21 is likely to be cautioned. The details are as follows[58] :

	% Cautioned	% Found guilty
Males under 14	73	27
Males from 14 to 17	68	32
Males from 17 to 21	56	44
Males from 21 upwards	12	88
Females under 14	100	0
Females from 14 to 17	75	25
Females from 17 to 21	60	40
Females from 21 upwards	53	47
Males of all ages	34	66
Females of all ages	61	39

Suppose that the offender is tried and found guilty in the Crown Court or the Magistrates' Court. What sentence is he or she likely to receive? The figures for those convicted in the Crown Court in 1975 for the various sex offences, together with the numbers who received different sorts of sentence for each type of offence, were as shown on p. 157 (percentages in brackets).

For certain offences, such as rape, the offender is pretty certain to be sentenced to custody of some sort (prison, detention centre, approved school, Borstal, or a hospital order). Indeed he has a 91 per cent chance on a conviction for rape of being sentenced to some sort of custody. The risk of custody is also high for procuring (75 per cent), incest (69), buggery (63) attempted buggery (56), indecent assault on a woman (54), and sexual intercourse with a girl under 13 (50). But it is lower for gross indecency with children (42 per cent) and quite low for sexual intercourse with a girl between 13 and 16 (20) and for indecency between men (17).

58 Cmnd. 6566 p. 24.

Offence	Total	Prison	Borstal etc.†	Fine	Suspended sentence	Probation	Discharge etc.*	Medical‡	Others§
Rape	328	241 (73)	51 (16)	3 (1)	19 (6)	3 (1)	4 (1)	5 (2)	2 (1)
Indecent assault on woman	524	233 (44)	40 (8)	60 (11)	93 (18)	54 (10)	21 (4)	13 (2)	10 (2)
Sexual intercourse with girl under 13	118	48 (41)	10 (8)	7 (6)	26 (22)	13 (11)	10 (8)	1 (1)	3 (3)
Sexual intercourse with girl between 13 and 16	540	84 (16)	20 (4)	163 (30)	103 (19)	69 (13)	87 (16)	0 (0)	14 (3)
Gross indecency with children	55	22 (40)	0 (0)	3 (5)	7 (13)	16 (29)	5 (9)	1 (2)	1 (2)
Incest	181	120 (66)	5 (3)	0 (0)	24 (13)	26 (14)	2 (2)	1 (0)	2 (1)
Buggery	217	125 (58)	3 (1)	17 (8)	37 (17)	18 (8)	7 (3)	8 (4)	2 (1)
Attempted buggery, etc.	252	122 (48)	7 (3)	17 (7)	43 (17)	39 (15)	10 (4)	12 (5)	2 (1)
Indecency between men	115	19 (16)	1 (1)	36 (31)	26 (23)	18 (16)	15 (13)	0 (0)	2 (1)
Procuration	96	69 (72)	3 (3)	5 (5)	13 (14)	5 (5)	1 (1)	0 (0)	0 (0)
Total	2426 (100)	1083 (44.6)	140 (5.7)	311 (12.8)	391 (16.1)	261 (10.8)	163 (6.7)	41 (1.7)	36 (1.5)

* Absolute or conditional discharge or release upon recognisances.
† Detention centre order, approved school or Borstal.
‡ Hospital order under s. 60 Mental Health Act 1959 or Restriction order under s. 65.
§ Care or supervision order, preventive detention, extended sentence, etc.

This tells us to what extent the Crown Court thinks that the different offences deserve prison sentences or other forms of custody. But the offender will be equally interested in knowing what length of sentence he is likely to get if he is sentenced to prison. The next table sets out the median sentences in the Crown Court for the years 1965, 1970 and 1975. The median sentence is the one which is intermediate between the longest and the shortest (the second longest of three, the third longest of five and so on). The sentence 3–2 means a sentence of over two years but not over 3, etc.

Crown Court Sentences

Offence	1965 Years	1970 Years	1975 Years
Rape	4–3	3–2	4–3
Indecent assault on woman	2–1	2–1	$1\frac{1}{2}$–1
Sexual intercourse with girl under 13	2–1	3–2	3–2
Sexual intercourse with girl between 13 and 16	1–$\frac{1}{2}$	1–$\frac{1}{2}$	1–$\frac{1}{2}$
Gross indecency with children	1–$\frac{1}{2}$	2–1	1
Incest	3–2	3–2	3–2
Buggery	3–2	3–2	2–$1\frac{1}{2}$
Attempted buggery, etc.	2–1	2–1	2–$1\frac{1}{2}$
Indecency between men	$\frac{1}{2}$	1–$\frac{1}{2}$	$1\frac{1}{2}$–1
Procuration		2–1	$1\frac{1}{2}$–1

In the Magistrates' Court the chances of a prison sentence are naturally much lower. The figures for 1975 which follow are something of a mixed bag, since they include a certain number of cases in which children under 17 have been formally charged with sexual offences, including serious offences like rape, buggery and incest. In this table the total number of persons found guilty is set out, together with the numbers sentenced to each type of punishment or order, but no percentages are given.

Offence	Total guilty	Prison	Approved school etc.†	Committed to Crown Court	Fine	Suspended sentence	Care or supervision	Probation	Discharge, etc.*	Medical‡	Other
Rape	15	0	4	5	1	0	3	0	2	0	0
Indecent assault on woman	2,336	87	70	54	904	152	243	418	384	13	11
Sexual intercourse with girl under 13	18	0	1	1	5	0	11	0	0	0	0
Sexual intercourse with girl between 13 and 16	33	0	1	2	5	0	13	0	12	0	0
Gross indecency with child	318	11	0	9	111	27	13	105	41	0	1
Incest	7	0	0	0	0	0	7	0	0	0	0
Buggery	9	0	0	0	0	0	7	0	2	0	0
Attempted buggery, etc.	639	31	6	38	227	47	43	151	89	6	1
Indecency between men	1,392	8	1	4	1,199	21	0	42	108	2	7
Procuration	29	0	0	0	18	3	2	5	1	0	0
Brothel-keeping	99	9	0	0	44	18	1	12	15	0	0
Living on prostitute's earnings	130	17	0	1	71	17	0	5	17	0	2
Aiding offence by prostitute	1	0	0	0	1	0	0	0	0	0	0
Soliciting, etc. by prostitute	3,292	160	0	19	1,651	272	6	336	619	1	228
Indecent exposure	2,495	57	10	3	1,348	86	110	423	407	15	36
Male importuning	591	6	0	2	446	5	0	25	107	0	36
	11,404 (100)	386 (3.4)	93 (0.8)	138 (1.2)	6,031 (52.9)	648 (5.7)	459 (4.0)	1,522 (13.3)	1,804 (15.8)	37 (0.3)	286 (2.5)

* Absolute or conditional discharge or release on recognisances.
† Attendance centre, detention centre or approved school.
‡ Hospital order under s. 60 Medical Health Act.

Sentencing policy

So far we have concentrated on averages—the chances of an offender receiving a given type of sentence or length of sentence if found guilty of a sex offence. Nothing has been said of the principles which are supposed to govern sentencing. It is to these that I now turn.

When the Court of Appeal hears appeals against sentence it has a chance to set aside sentences which it thinks are seriously out of line and to substitute what it considers to be the proper sentence in the case. In this way a body of principles is gradually built up. From the court's decisions it is possible to construct a scale or tariff which relates the length of sentence to the seriousness of the offence. It is also possible to discover what factors the court regards as making the particular case more serious than the normal one of its type (aggravating) or less serious (mitigating).

There is a valuable study by Thomas[59] of the 'tariff' of the Court of Appeal, which will now be summarised. It should be remembered that the cases which come to the court are likely to be the more serious ones, since the longer the sentence the more likely is the offender to want to appeal.

Thomas points out that rape is different from most sex offences in that the main concern of the judge who sentences in a rape case should, in the view of the Court of Appeal, be to deter.[60] In fact, as we saw, over 90 per cent of those found guilty of rape in the Crown Court in 1975 were sentenced to some form of custody. The range of sentences is between two and ten years. Sentences tend to be in the upper part of the range if serious violence is used, as opposed to a mere threat, in cases of gang rape and when the offender breaks into the victim's home. The lower part of the range operates when the victim is to some extent at fault, for instance by going alone with a man into his room. For an indecent assault[61] on a woman which involves serious violence the approach is similar to that for rape, but the tariff is much lower and reflects the idea, perhaps carried too far, that, from the point of view of a woman who does not consent, intercourse is in a completely different class from other sexual acts.

[59] D. A. Thomas, *Principles of Sentencing* (1970) 108–27.
[60] Thomas 108–11.
[61] Thomas 119; R. Hood, *Sentencing in Magistrates' Courts: a study of variations in policy* (1962) 104–17.

Buggery is an exception and is put on much the same level as rape.[62] Ten years has been upheld for forcible buggery of a youth of seventeen. The crime attracted a sentence of thirty months in prison even when the offender had been drinking and the victim was his wife.[63] Where the offender has intercourse with a girl under 13[64] three to five years is the tariff, with a tendency towards the upper end of the scale when he abuses his authority, for example if the girl 'looks on him as a father'. A sentence below three years is more likely if he is a youngster.

For indecent assaults on young girls[65] prison sentences vary between less than a year and six years, and some attention is given to the mental condition of the man on the one hand and the need for prevention in the case of repeated offences on the other. Finally, in the cases where there is in fact consent,[66] such as sexual intercourse with a girl between 13 and 16, or indecent so-called assault on a girl under 16 (who actually consents), there is a clear distinction between teenage experiments and cases involving older men. For the youngster a modest fine or discharge is generally substituted. For older men a sentence in the region of six months' imprisonment is often thought appropriate. It must be remembered that a girl under 16 may take the initiative even with an older man. If a mature man repeats the offence he may find that the maximum of two years is confirmed by the Court of Appeal, and the same is true as the offender's age creeps upwards into the thirties and forties.

So far as homosexual offences committed by men are concerned the tariff varies according to whether the offence takes the form of a nuisance, such as an act by consenting adults in public, or is done with a boy or teenager.[67] In the first sort of case a fine or prison sentence of a few months is thought appropriate. In the second sort of case one must distinguish between buggery and indecent assault. Sentences of seven to ten years for buggery tend to be upheld when the offence involves the use of force or abuse of authority (for example by a step-father) or when the victim is very young. Five years is an approved sentence when,

[62] Thomas 118.
[63] *Mountney* 1967 *Crim. L.R.* 185.
[64] Thomas 116–17.
[65] Thomas 120–2.
[66] Thomas 113–16, 120.
[67] Thomas 123–6.

without these factors, the boy is under puberty, and three when he is 13 to 15 and has not been corrupted by the offender. For the youth of 17 or 18 two years will generally be upheld. Four or five years seems to be the conventional maximum for indecent assaults on boys short of buggery. The approach is similar to that for buggery, but the scale is lower. In case both of buggery and of indecent assault a sentence of life imprisonment or a very long term is sometimes passed for preventive reasons when the offender has a long record of homosexual offences, and the Court of Appeal sometimes substitutes Borstal or a hospital order for a prison sentence when it thinks there is a chance of suitable treatment.

As in the case of rape, one may doubt whether the importance attached by the courts to actual penetration (and so to buggery as against indecent assault) is fully justified.

So far as sentences for living on the earnings of prostitution are concerned,[68] the appellate tariff is five to seven years for the pimp who induces the woman to take up or return to prostitution or coerces her, and two or three for the offender who, without putting pressure on her, takes money from a woman who is already a prostitute.

The general level of sentences for sex offences, taking them as a whole, seems reasonable. Only in the graver cases of incest, procuring and buggery does an occasional judge seem from time to time to be carried away by his emotions instead of reflecting coolly on the impact of the sentence he imposes. A prison term is never lightly to be given. Most of us would resent losing our freedom for five hours, let alone five months or five years. If we are to lose it we must be firmly persuaded of the justice of the cause.

4. TREATMENTS

Some of the sexual behaviour which society dislikes falls off as the people concerned get older and find that their sex drive is reduced, that they can control themselves better, or that they can find a stable partner. In other cases fear of publicity and punishment makes the person who would like to offend cautious. A man who is bold in his twenties is often not so bold in his thirties.

---

[68] Thomas 126-7.

But, apart from rape and sexual violence, sex offences do not fall off with age to the same extent as, say, burglary. A certain number of offenders (recidivists) are convicted of sexual offences two, three or more times. For instance of those convicted on indictment of sexual offences in 1962 when they were 17 years old or more[69] :

59 per cent had no previous conviction
13 per cent had one previous conviction
16 per cent had two to four previous convictions
13 per cent had five or more previous convictions

There is enough recidivism to make us ask whether, alongside nature and the law, there is some third way in which sex crimes can be prevented. What about medicine and psychology? Can doctors and scientists change people's sex lives?

The idea that many out-of-the-way sexual habits stem from mental disorders has a long history. It was forcefully expressed in Krafft-Ebing's *Psychopathia Sexualis*,[70] published in 1886. This treats sexual fetishes, like having an erection at the sight of a woman's handkerchief, homosexuality, and excitement connected with giving or suffering pain (sadism and masochism), as forms of mental disorder. Another type of behaviour which could plausibly be put down to some mental twist is indecent exposure. The men who show their private parts to women they do not know seem to be suffering from some affliction which might with luck be cured.

The attempt to find a cure for sexual misdeeds therefore seems sensible, at least for some types of behaviour. Bancroft gives a sober account of the various methods that have been tried, none with any great success.[71] Hypnosis was the earliest. Then there was a fashion for aversion therapy—giving the patient unpleasant drugs or electric shocks—and more recently for trying to change his sexual fantasies, so that if, for instance, he is a man who has images of other men, he comes to picture women instead. Injecting the patient with hormones to change his sexual balance is

---

[69] McClintock and Avison, *Crime in England and Wales* 234, 238.
[70] On R. von Krafft-Ebing see E. M. Brecher. *The Sex Researchers* (1972 ed.) 72.
[71] J. Bancroft, *Deviant Sexual Behaviour: Modification and Assessment* (1974) 32–51.

another method that has been tried, a rather dangerous one, it seems.[72]

Perhaps one of the troubles concerns the notion of cure. There cannot be a cure without a disease. If a car breaks down it can be repaired. If it merely runs on a different oil from that available at the moment it is no use asking the garage to repair it, though it can perhaps be converted to take the other sort of oil.

Conversion is not repair. It is for the car owner after weighing the cost to decide whether conversion is technically possible and worth while. It does not help him to decide freely if he is locked in the garage until he makes up his mind, still less if he thinks that the garage owner will be more likely to let him out if he agrees to the conversion.

To what extent is sexual misbehaviour a sign of mental disease, of a disrepair or bad functioning of the brain? Clearly it may be so. But the great majority of sex offenders have brains which are in good order. Their conduct is no more due to mental disease than is that of the smash-and-grab man who snatches the diamonds from the jeweller's window. The thief likes jewels or money and is ready to break rules to get them. The sex offender likes sex, or sex of a certain type and is prepared to break rules to get it.

The debate is about the middle ground between mental disease and ordinary rule-breaking. It is occupied by some very messy words. There are, it is said, people whose sexual behaviour is 'deviant'.[73] Some of them suffer from a 'mental disorder'.[74] One group of these are 'psychopaths',[75] or 'sexual psychopaths'.[76] But do these words describe anything beyond the simple fact that there are people who keep on breaking, or have a tendency to keep on breaking, the rules of society and the law about sexual behaviour?

'Deviance' is a bad word, because, while literally it suggests

[72] L. O. Gostin, *A Human Condition: The Law relating to mentally abnormal offenders: Observations, analysis and proposals for reform* vol. 2 (1977) 89–91.

[73] The word is widely used, mostly without definition: e.g. A. Storr, *Sexual Deviation* (1964).

[74] Mental Health Act (hereafter MHA) 1959 s. 4(1).

[75] MHA 1959 s. 4(4).

[76] *State* v. *Probate Court of Ramsey County* 287 N.W. 297, 299 (Minn. 1939 has a mental disorder), *U.S.* v. *Gill* 204 F. 2d 740, 744 (Ind. 1953 unstable personality).

the act of a person who takes a different road (from the majority),
it is used in sociology in a way which implies that the majority
are justified in putting pressure on the deviant to return to the
main road. Merely to do something different from the majority
is not, surely, to let oneself in for 'cure' or 'treatment'. Is a non-
drinker 'deviant' because the majority drink? Is a Jehovah's
Witness deviant because he does not share the views of the
majority about religion? Presumably not. Non-conformity is not
in itself deviance. The deviant breaks the rules, not just the practices of society or the law. Even so, is a man who keeps parking
in a no-parking area deviant? Hardly. For a person to be deviant
the rules broken must be important and their breach must rouse
anger or indignation. On this view someone who sexually molests
children under the age of puberty (a paedophile) is deviant. So is
the exhibitionist who exposes his private parts. The father who
has sex with his teenage daughter would still be deviant if there
were no crime of incest, since his behaviour would run against
the rules of society and would cause outrage to many.

The case of the homosexual brings out the drawbacks of deviance as a notion for describing sexual behaviour. Homosexual
acts between men break social if not legal rules. They annoy and
disgust many people. But homosexuals are not just scattered
individuals like paedophiles or incestuous fathers. They form a
group of their own, a sub-culture. From their point of view they
are not deviating but striking out on an alternative route, no
doubt a minor country road rather than the main highway. Is
this really deviance or is it rather dissent? Is there any better
reason for trying to 'cure' them of their attitudes than for 'curing'
a man who is conservative in politics of his conservative beliefs,
or a Jehovah's Witness or his? No doubt all these people can, if
society is ruthless enough, be *brainwashed* into adopting a different attitude. But brainwashing is not cure. Nor would it make
any difference if these groupings of opinion were illegal, as of
course in Marxist states they are.

If 'deviance' is a slippery eel, 'mental disorder' and 'psychopath' are no better. According to the Mental Health Act 1959[77] a
'psychopathic disorder' is a persistent disorder or disability of
mind which results in abnormally aggressive or seriously irresponsible conduct on the part of the patient, and requires, or is

[77] S. 4(4).

susceptible to, medical treatment. Suppose that we can agree on what sexual behaviour is 'seriously irresponsible'. How do we know whether the behaviour is the result of a persistent disorder or disability of mind? The legislator has written into the statute a certain theory of human behaviour (incidentally one which denies free will), though there is nothing in our knowledge of the way the brain works to support it.[78] It is true that Parliament has said that a person is not to be treated as suffering from mental disorder by reason only of promiscuity or other immoral conduct.[79] So the prostitute is not, just because of her profession, a psychopath. But what, again, of the homosexual? Is he just guilty of 'immoral conduct' (notice how Parliament thinks that immorality must be sexual). Or is he 'seriously irresponsible'? And does his condition 'require medical treatment'?

The question is important because the homosexual is in the greatest danger of being classed as a sexual psychopath and treated accordingly, though the exhibitionist may be in peril too. The result of being called a psychopath can be more serious for the person concerned than if he were simply convicted and sentenced for his crime.

Many US states have laws under which those who are classed as sexual psychopaths can be detained for treatment, sometimes without trial, until they are 'cured'.[80] It has been held constitutional in the US to detain a sexual psychopath for treatment for a longer time than that for which he might have been sentenced on conviction if he were not a psychopath.[81] In England a conviction for an offence punishable with imprisonment is normally required.[82] But thereafter, if two medical men are prepared to give evidence (even orally) that the offender suffers from a psychopathic disorder which warrants his detention in a hospital

[78] H. Brown, *Brain and Behaviour* (1976) 271.

[79] MHA 1959 s. 4(5).

[80] Ploscowe, *Sex and the Law* (1951) 225–41; S. J. Brakel and R. S. Rock, *The Mentally Disabled and the Law* (1971 ed.) 341–75 (table of definitions and procedures 362 f.).

[81] *Trueblood* v. *Tinsley* 148 Col. 503, 366 P. 2nd 655 (1961).

[82] MHA 1959 s. 60 requires that the offender must be convicted before the Crown Court of an offence for which the punishment is not fixed by law (e.g. not murder) or before the Magistrates' Court of an offence punishable on summary conviction with imprisonment. But if the Magistrates's Court is satisfied that the offender did the act charged it can send him to hospital without convicting him: s. 60(2).

for medical treatment, the court may make a hospital order and (in the case of the Crown Court) couple this with a restriction order.[83]

For a hospital order the court must be of the opinion both that, on the evidence of two doctors, he has a mental disorder and that in all the circumstances of the case including the nature of the offence, the character and background of the offender, and the other possible ways of dealing with him, a hospital order is the most suitable way of disposing of the case.[84] (There is surely something sick about a language in which people are 'cases' and the way they are treated on conviction is 'disposal'.) Once an offender is detained in hospital he can only be released on the order of the responsible medical officer or the managers of the hospital.[85] The Mental Health Review Tribunal may also order his release.[86] To prevent his release in this way the Crown Court may, if it thinks it necessary for the protection of the public, add to the hospital order a restriction order.[87] This reserves to the Home Secretary the power to allow the offender's discharge. Whatever length of treatment he has served in hospital, there is no way in which the offender can force the authorities to release him if they choose not to. His can be a life sentence.

Are the dangers imaginary? Apparently not. Gostin[88] mentions Robert's case. In 1966 Robert was convicted of indecent assault on a male. Two doctors gave evidence that he was a psychopath and he was detained in Broadmoor under a hospital order coupled with a restriction order for an unlimited period. In 1971 he was persuaded to take part in a programme of treatment by sex hormone transplants. The treatment gave him feminine breasts, one of which had to be removed by operation. After ten years, he is deformed and still detained. Ten years in prison is, of course, the maximum sentence for indecent assault on a male person. Even in the worst case, and with loss of all remission, an offender who was not classed as a psychopath could not be kept in jail for longer.

[83] MHA 1959 s. 60(1), 65(1).
[84] MHA 1959 s. 60(1)(b).
[85] MHA 1959 s. 47(2)(b), 63(3)(a).
[86] MHA 1959 s. 3, 122–4.
[87] MHA 1959 s. 65(1).
[88] L. O. Gostin, *A Human Condition* (above, n, 72) 89.

The Butler committee[89] have suggested amending the Mental Health Act so that a psychopathic disorder consisting of sexual deviation alone should not be a ground for a hospital order. In my opinion no one should be subject to a hospital order until the court has fixed a term of confinement. The hospital order would operate in lieu of imprisonment. It could not last for longer than the sentence, and the patient, if well behaved, would be entitled to remission of his period of treatment to the same extent as he would have been entitled to remission to his prison sentence. We have no need to imitate those Marxist states in which dissent or deviance is dealt with by compulsory medical treatment.

In recent years the number of hospital orders, especially those made by Magistrates' Courts, has grown less. The number of hospital and restriction orders for sexual offences made by English courts in 1965, 1970 and 1975 was:

	1965	1970	1975
Hospital order	139	114	56
Restriction order	19	41	22
Total	158	155	78

The reason for the sharp decline is not obvious. Is it too much to hope that the courts have seen through the pretensions of the medical profession to be able to 'cure' sexual misbehaviour?

[89] *Report of the Committee on Mentally Abnormal Offenders* (Butler Committee Cmnd. 6244, 1975) ch. 5.

7

Trends, Rights and Limits

'And I've just got to be me'
(Deniece Williams: *Free*)

I. TRENDS

During the seventies the relative power of men and women has
changed. The two sexes have at the same time become more like
one another. This is shown, first, by the decline in the birthrate.[1]
Partly as a result of the contraceptive pill, women are now in a
better position to decide whether they will have children, and,
if so, how many and when. In the past, when contraception was
avoided by some, while others used a method such as the sheath
which was under the control of the man, the power to decide
about children rested largely with men. Now many women will
marry young, postpone having a family in order to continue with
their careers and perhaps in the end decide that they are too old
to start or have become used to a different way of life. The
balance of power has shifted, and men no longer rule to quite
the same extent. Just for this reason, some try to prevent their
wives using the pill, or to control their use of it.[2]

Women are asserting themselves by deciding whether to have
children and, if so, at what age. This is not the only way in which
they are taking the offensive. As the criminal statistics show, they
are now being convicted of more serious crimes than before, and
of a greater number in comparison with men. These include

[1] From 8.6 per 1,000 in 1972 to 7.8 per 1,000 in 1974: see C.S.O. Annual
Abstract of Statistics 1974, Table 22.

[2] Ann Whitehead, 'Sexual antagonism in Herefordshire', in *Independence
and Exploitation in Work and Marriage* by D. L. Barker and S. Allen (1976)
169, 203.

crimes of violence.[3] Either women are becoming more aggressive, or else men are now readier to report them to the police, because women are more inclined to assert themselves, and men resent it.

True, there is still a wide gap between the sexes. Men are still convicted on indictment of twelve times as many crimes of violence against the person as women.[4] But the gap is narrowing, and we may expect it to narrow still further as those conventions crumble which kept women from doing things which were thought of in the past as a male preserve, and as women, partly through changes in the law about the property of husbands and wives,[5] acquire more economic power. If it becomes less easy for women to find work, if they are the first to be laid off as unemployment increases, the trend to equality will slow down but not stop. How far it will in the end go depends on social changes which we cannot now foresee and on the extent, largely unknown, to which the differences between the sexes in drive, ambition and aggression depend on genetic or physical factors.

We live, then, in an age which is moving in the direction of violence and equality. Is it also a sexually permissive age? This is not an easy question to answer, partly because the idea of permissiveness is hazy, and partly because the facts are not easy to unearth. The sexually permissive society is not, presumably, one in which people indulge in sex to excess, where they are sexual gluttons, but one in which others allow, or at least do not forbid, them to do as they please. It is surely wrong to view the English scene by asking whether it is in this sense sexually permissive. Many people take the view that the sex life of other adults is their own business, that they are entitled to do their own thing, that no one is entitled to dictate their choice of partner or erotic act. Others are not prepared to concede this. The second group is not permissive, but neither is the first. The first is rather saying that we have a right to sexual freedom or self-expression or self-rule (the choice is largely a matter of terms) and that no one has the right in the name of population policy or the institution of marriage or the need for women to be supported to permit or forbid us to act as we please. In sexual morality permissive-

---

[3] Above, ch. 3 n. 10.
[4] Above, ch. 3 n. 9.
[5] Married Women's Property Act 1964 s. 1; Matrimonial Homes Act 1970 s. 1(1); Matrimonial Proceedings and Property Act 1970 s. 37.

ness comes into play only when the immature or incapable are concerned. Parents can be permissive towards children, or they can be restrictive. Which are they in practice?

Once again the best evidence I can find comes from Schofield's 1965 study of teenage sex. He found that a quarter of the parents of teenage boys (15 to 19) did not insist on knowing where they were when they went out in the evening. The figure for girls was only a third of this, 8 per cent.[6] So parents still discriminated a great deal in the way they supervised girls and boys. About a third of the parents of teenage boys and a sixth of those of teenage girls did not insist on their being in at a particular hour at week-ends.[7] These figures would probably be higher today and they do not directly measure sexual permissiveness. Nevertheless they are some guide to the proportion of parents who would not object to their children having sexual experience, at any rate if they, the parents, were not directly involved and were not told. To judge by these figures, and allowing for some increase since 1965, less than half of all parents have a permissive attitude towards the sexual experience of their teenage sons, let alone their daughters.

So far as adult sex is concerned the question is not whether society is permissive but whether it is self-ruling. Do we live in an age in which it is admitted that adults can direct themselves in these matters, that they have, in the language of politics and of the West German penal code, the right of sexual self-determination?

It is easy but of little value to try to guess the answer. Some help may be drawn from a National Opinion Poll survey of 1970.[8] In interpreting it one has to bear in mind the difference between what members of the public themselves think and what they think other people think. Of those with a definite opinion in this survey 55 per cent thought it morally wrong to have an illegitimate child, but 85 per cent thought that an illegitimate child is no longer looked down on. He or she does not suffer a social stigma.[9] Forty-four per cent thought it morally right for all

---

[6] Schofield, *Young People* 129 (24 per cent of boys' parents and 8 per cent of girls').

[7] Schofield, *Young People* 121 (35 per cent of boys' parents and 17 per cent of girls').

[8] National Opinion Polls Market Research Ltd: *Report on Attitudes towards Crime, Violence and Permissiveness in Society* (1970).

[9] NOP (above, n. 8) 65–7.

women to use the pill, 39 per cent right only for married women and 16 per cent wrong for all women.[10] Fifty-four per cent of those who had a definite opinion were in favour of homosexual acts being legal between consenting adults, but a majority of all men, of all poorer people and of all people over 45, were against this.[11] Though on this question women are more prepared than men to recognise self-rule in matters of sex, the researchers remarked that in general, on any question which has sexual overtones, women are more restrictive than men. This extends to the youngest group included in the survey, those from 16 to 24.[12]

It may be that self-rule in sexual matters is now more readily and widely admitted than it was in 1965. But the likely conclusion to be drawn from these figures is that English people divide fairly evenly in their moral opinions, that neither the liberals nor the conservatives have a clear majority. This has some importance from the point of view of the question whether there is a right of sexual freedom or self-expression.

2. RIGHTS

If there is a positive right to sexual freedom, and not just a claim resting on disputed moral arguments, it must be based on a legal text or on the fact that we live in society and have wants which may conflict with the wants of others. One way of reconciling these conflicts is to admit that each person has an equal claim to satisfy his want. At least when the want is urgent and deeply felt, it makes for social peace to recognise these equal claims. A right is a recognised claim of this sort, and equal claims give rise to equal rights. Since law is, among other things, a technique of social harmony and justice,[13] in which special importance attaches to the values of peace and equality, one of the duties of lawyers and legislators is to give effect in their respective sphere to those equal rights which society admits.

But it is a question of fact whether in a given society, like present-day England, a right such as a right to sexual freedom is

---

[10] NOP 56–9.
[11] NOP 68–70.
[12] NOP Introductory Section.
[13] Honoré, *Tribonian* (1978) 30–6.

actually recognised. Can we say that it is, and that the law should therefore give effect to it? I do not think so. Opinion, we have seen, is fairly equally divided on the point, and since rights do not exist in the air, but only when supported by convention, or by a specific text, there is at most the embryo of a right to sexual self-expression in England today.

Suppose, however, that such a right were to receive general assent, how ought we to conceive it? No right to sexual freedom is mentioned in so many words in the Bills of Rights which abound in the world's constitutions and are in general treated as so many scraps of paper. In the US, which has a tradition of taking rights seriously, the courts have tried to give effect to sexual self-expression under the umbrella of privacy. In *Griswold* v. *Connecticut*[14] the Supreme Court ruled that for a state to forbid the sale of contraceptives was an invasion of the privacy of married people. But quite apart from the fact that the sale of contraceptives takes place in public and only their use is private, the mere fact that an act occurs in private, even in the privacy of the home, is no reason why the law should not regulate it. We are more likely to be murdered in the kitchen than the street, but to kill your wife with the carving knife is no better, indeed probably worse, than to gun down your enemy in the market.

Although, therefore, sex should and generally does take place in private, the right to sex is best treated as something different from the right to privacy. It has its own distinct features. This is the view which the legislator adopted in West Germany, where the 1973 legislation[15] reformed the law about sexual offences and grouped them under the heading of offences against sexual self-determination. Just as nations like Scotland or Quebec have the right to settle their own destiny and to manage their own homeland if they prefer, so people of a certain maturity have on this view the right to decide for themselves what form of sex, if any, they want and with whom they want it.

In England, lacking a Bill of Rights, one might start from the right of bodily integrity which has long been protected by the law of trespass. It is a civil wrong, a trespass, for anyone to touch another, at any rate in a hostile manner, without consent.[16] If, however, consent is given, no trespass is committed. What is

[14] 381 US 479 (1965).
[15] Law of 23 Nov. 1973 (BGB1. 1973.1.1725).

needed in order to construct a right of sexual self-expression is the idea that each of us may use his body as he pleases provided he or she she does not touch another without their consent. This simple idea, that human beings have the right to use their bodies as they choose, and to touch others with their consent, is all that is needed to furnish a technical basis for the right to sexual freedom.

In its social setting the idea of sexual freedom goes much deeper than merely touching and being touched. It is not merely physical. It is my right to express myself and my personality in a certain intimate way which involves the use of my body but reaches beyond it, or may if I am lucky do so. It embraces the right to love, to be loved and to express love or, in some cases, just friendship. For this reason, and because sex can be physically so intense, many people value it more highly than, say, religion, though freedom of worship, unlike sexual freedom, has long been listed as a basic human right.

Because sex is something physical and something more, it would be wise, if a right of sexual freedom comes to be generally accepted, that it should be listed in any Bill of Rights which may be enacted in England. To do so will be to ensure that the law protects something beyond sheer physical contact : in particular that it gives freedom to those who wish to contact one another, for example by advertisement, to do so, that it ensures access to contraceptives and that it asserts the right of those who live in rented accommodation to invite visitors to their rooms. The details may be quite difficult to work out, but the principle will clearly be that the right of physical contact needs to be supplemented by rules ensuring access to means and opportunity.

The principles which should guide legislators and lawyers who want to give effect to a right of sexual freedom are therefore mainly three :

(a) The right to sexual freedom consists in the right to use our bodies as we choose and to touch others with their consent, together with accessory rights designed to ensure reasonable sexual opportunities.

(b) Sexual freedom may be exercised by those who have

---

[16] *Bravery* v. *Bravery* 1954 1 WLR 1169; P. Devlin, *Samples of Lawmaking* (1962) 84–5.

reached maturity. The age of maturity is also the age of full responsibility. In giving effect to this principle I have argued[17] that the age of maturity should be 18. Below this there may be restrictions on certain forms of sexual activity, for example homosexual acts, but those under 18 should be exempt from liability for acts that can be regarded as teenage experiments.[18]

(c) The principle of sexual freedom or self-rule is a principle of conduct, not of education. In education parents, teachers, officials and, so far as concerns them, courts are entitled to give effect to the moral preferences of society.[19] These include the preference for marriage over living together and for heterosexual over homosexual conduct. So when courts decide issues of custody or consent to adoption, while they have no business 'to condemn or tolerate the way in which adults choose, legally, to live',[20] they may, if other factors are not decisive, prefer the more regular home, not because the parent who lives in it has behaved unimpeachably,[21] but in the interests of the child.[21a]

The second and third principles point to the limits of sexual freedom as a potential legal principle. Something remains to be said about these.

3. LIMITS

The right to sexual freedom will not apply, or not fully, to animals, children and young people, defectives, prisoners. Those who are crippled or for other reasons immobile will have difficulty in exercising it. This section tries to sketch what the limits to the right of sexual freedom would be if such a right were recognised, and how far they agree with the existing law.

A first point to be noticed about the right to sexual freedom

[17] Above, ch. 4, nn. 89–93.
[18] Above ch. 4, nn. 94–5; ch. 3, p. 83.
[19] Above, ch. 4, p. 106.
[20] *Re D* 1977 2 WLR 79, 87 per Lord Wilberforce.
[21] *J.* v. *C.* 1970 AC 668, not following *Re L* 1962 1 WLR 886a; *S(BD)* v. *S(DJ)* 1977 Fam. 109.
[21a] *Re D* 1977 2 WLR 79, 87, 98 (consent of homosexual father to adoption: the majority of the House of Lords decided the case on another point).

is that it does not extend to animals. Whether animals have rights at all is debated. In my opinion, since they cannot put forward any claim, they do not, but supposing that the contrary view prevails,[22] their rights will be limited to the right not to be killed as food for human beings and not to be treated with cruelty. They cannot claim not to be touched.

Hence there is no satisfactory reason for retaining in the modern law a crime of buggery with animals, that is of having sexual relations with an animal which involve some penetration of its body.[23] This crime has a respectable ancestry; it is mentioned in and historically drawn from the Bible.[24] It raised and perhaps still raises fierce passions, and was one of the last crimes for which the death penalty was abolished. It has become pointless, since any rational object that it might seek to achieve can be better reached in another way. If the animal is treated with cruelty in the course of a sexual attack the crime of cruelty to animals can be charged.[25] If what is complained of is the inroad on the property right of the owner, he has a civil remedy for trespass to his goods. If the tale of woe concerns the farmhand who has sex with the sheep when he should be feeding the pigs, this amounts to a breach of the contract of employment for which a warning and, if repeated, a dismissal might be justified. If, again, as in the bizarre case of *Bourne*,[26] a man forces his wife to submit to a dog, the conduct may well amount to an indecent assault; at any rate the wrong is by husband to wife, not by wife to dog. Though the law books will be poorer if they cease to mention Coke's great lady who committed buggery with a baboon and conceived by it,[27] the crime of buggery with animals should, I fear, be consigned to the scrapheap, and the great lady left to enjoy her kinky pleasures.

Children and young people do not have the right of sexual freedom to its full extent. In sex law it is best to use 'child' to refer to someone under the age of puberty and 'young person' to refer to those over puberty but not yet of full age. The age of

[22] S. R. L. Clark, *The Moral Status of Animals* (1977).
[23] *Brown* (1889) 24 QBD 357.
[24] E.g. Leviticus 18.23.
[25] Protection of Animals Act 1911 s. 1.
[26] (1952) 36 CAR 125.
[27] Coke, 3 *Inst.* 59.

puberty for girls is now between 12 and 13.[28] Sexual attraction
to children under puberty, generally called paedophilia, presents
a different problem from that of sexual attraction to teenagers.
Paedophiles are given to deceiving themselves and others about
their condition. Here, though cure would be in point, the prospects of successful treatment are dim.[29]

At the moment a man who has unlawful sexual intercourse
with a girl under 13 is liable to life imprisonment.[30] The girl's
consent, even if it can be taken seriously, does not have any legal
effect. The penalty for indecent assault is also higher if the
assault alleged is on a girl under 13.[31] So far as boys are concerned, 16 is the age chosen by the legislator. Under this age
buggery carries a maximum of life imprisonment.[32] Finally, the
Indecency with Children Act 1960 selects 14 for both sexes as
the age under which punishment is provided for sexual acts and
invitations which are not otherwise punishable.[33] This branch of
the law surely needs tidying up, so that paedophiles are seen as
a separate class of offender, whether they molest boys or girls and
whether they have sexual intercourse or commit buggery or resort
to some other sexual contact with them. The offence should be
that of committing a sexual act with a child or inviting the child
to commit a sexual act with the invitor or a third person. The age
chosen, taking account of the current age of puberty might be
13 or 14. Two of our EEC neighbours opt for 14.[34]

Whether and to what extent these sexual contacts by older
people, including teenagers, harm young children is debated.
Often, it is said, they are soon forgotten unless the child's parents
or other adults show that they attach a great deal of importance
to them.[35] However this may be, they clearly cannot be allowed.
A child under puberty is not sexless. One survey found that about

[28] Schofield, *Promiscuity* 13.
[29] J. Bancroft, *Deviant Sexual Behaviour* (1974) 156–7; J. W. Mohr,
R. E. Turner and M. B. Jerry, *Pedophilia and Exhibitionism* (1964) 38–74,
193.
[30] SOA 1956 Second Schedule 2.
[31] SOA 1956 Second Schedule 17.
[32] SOA 1956 Second Schedule 3.
[33] Indecency with Children Act 1960 s. 1(1).
[34] Italian Penal Code art. 524; Belgian Penal Code art. 375(4); but Netherlands Penal Code art. 244—twelve; French Penal Code art. 331(1); Danish
Penal Code art. 222(1)—both fifteen.
[35] Wolfenden Report (Cmnd 247 of 1957) s. 38; Schofield, *Homosexuality* 154–5; Barnett 165.

half the men and women interviewed remembered sex play before puberty.[36] But a child of this age needs not sexual adventures but to learn the facts of life in good time. The best way to learn is probably not via the mixture of fact and fiction gleaned from friends—in practice the main source—nor the embarrassed mumbling of parents but rather through teaching at school.[37] It seems that though about five-sixths of girls receive some sex education at school only about half the boys do so. Even when they do, the instruction is not always thorough or given in good time, nor is there enough repetition. Hence, for example, boys grow up not understanding about girls' periods.[38] In our defective education, this is one of the blotches.

Young people, from the point of view of a law of sexual freedom, would be those between 13 or 14, whichever age is chosen, and 18, which would be the age of majority, including sexual majority. Most parents would agree that this is the age group which presents the greatest problems and most teenagers would, from their own point of view, think the same. They would, in a world in which sexual freedom was admitted, be in a position of limited rights and responsibilities. To begin with the latter, a young person in this group would not commit a crime by having sexual relations with one of his or her own age group or with an older person.[39] It would not matter whether the other person was of the opposite or the same sex. There would, however, be criminal liability for rape, or any sexual act involving the use of force or threats, for sexual acts with those under 13 or 14 and for inviting them to indulge in sexual acts. As to rights, this group would be entitled to instruction at school, particularly about contraception, venereal disease, the differing attitudes of men and women to the emotions connected with sex and the exhilaration and agony that may come, unwanted and unasked, from sexual experience. Some instruction is certainly needed, for of the teenagers who have sexual intercourse about half take no precautions and for the most part have hardly thought about the need for any.[40] It is true that there are practical difficulties. While a young man can either withdraw before he is ready to come or buy a sheath at a

[36] Schofield, *Promiscuity* 159.
[37] Schofield, *Young People* 82–4.
[38] Schofield, *Young People* 86.
[39] Above, pp. 174–5.
[40] Schofield, *Young People* 93.

chemist or barber, a girl will have to go to the doctor for a coil or for the contraceptive pill. She will generally hesitate to do this, especially if the doctor is a man and knows her parents. The doctor in turn may think that to help her with contraceptive advice, if she is under 16 at least, is to be accessory to the crime of unlawful sexual intercourse. The fear seems not to be justified. The girl under 16 who has unlawful sexual intercourse commits no crime to which the doctor could be an accessory.[41] But, apart from the legal position, the doctor may simply disapprove of her conduct. He may also think that her parents should be consulted. This is legally correct, since the parents have the right to consent to medical treatment being carried out on a child under 16.[42]

A girl in this position, if she has a feeling of responsibility, may therefore prefer to consult a family planning clinic, if there is one near by, or in the biggest towns, one of the Brook Advisory Centres.[43] A girl over 16, whether married or single, has a right to birth control advice and supplies from her local family planning clinic.[44] In practice most teenage girls who are having sexual intercourse, if they are alert to the need, rely on the boy to take precautions.[45] Sheaths are, luckily, easy to buy and quite effective. The danger of unwanted pregnancies comes from the couple who do not think of the possible consequences, or who do think, but take the (mistaken) view that any contraceptive spoils the fun. Promiscuous girls are less likely to worry about taking precautions than those who are going steady, and are more likely to have an unwanted baby. Their need is greater, and it is unfortunate, though only to be expected, that they are treated with less sympathy by doctors and clinics than their steadier sisters.

Mental defectives are not at the moment allowed sexual freedom, since though they commit no offence themselves, anyone apart from their husband or wife who has sexual intercourse with them is guilty of a crime.[46] It may not be easy for a defective to marry, and this means that, if the law is observed, they are cut off from all chance of a satisfactory sex life. Yet a mental defective may not be physically defective. He or she may, like other

---

[41] *Thornton* v. *Mitchell* 1940 1 All ER 339.
[42] Family Law Reform Act 1969 s. 8; P. D. G. Skegg 36 MLR (1973) 370.
[43] A. Coote and T. Gill, *Women's Rights: a Practical Guide* (1974) 133–4.
[44] Coote and Gill 135.
[45] Schofield, *Young People* 92.
[46] SOA 1956 s. 7.

people, have strong sexual needs. If a right to sexual freedom is recognised something will have to be done for these people, whose position is all the more helpless because if they are in an institution it is a particularly serious offence for an official or employee of the institution to have sex with them. No offence is of course committed if one defective has sexual relations with another, but for this to be possible those running the institution must be prepared to allow it. The problem, both in and out of institutions for the mentally handicapped, is a hard one. Suppose someone is prepared to look after, but not to marry, a defective. Should it not be possible for him to be licensed to have sexual relations with her? It may certainly be necessary to try to ensure that no unwanted pregnancy occurs. The problem is a tangled one, but perhaps there is an exceptional case here for the licensing of sexual relations by the state.

Almost as irksome is the position of the person who is not defective but is physically handicapped, a cripple or immobile. Like the defective, his or her sexual needs are not reduced by the misfortune. Indeed they may be rather increased, since the cripple cannot take refuge in manual work, or sport. Rather than brothels run by the medical services,[47] to which there are serious objections,[48] or by kindly volunteers (called by Ullerstam 'erotic Samaritans'),[49] what is needed is a form of prostitution which will cater for the wants of these people marooned on their lonely islands.

In sum, the changes in the law which would be needed to give effect to a right of sexual freedom or self-rule are numerous but not radical. The right itself, however, waits on public opinion; and public opinion, I guess, is slowly shifting towards it, at least in England. The threat to sexual freedom comes not from that source but from the source that threatens all other freedoms, namely Marxism, which, wherever it seizes power, uses it to thwart private initiative, to suppress brothels, and to turn men's minds from personal happiness to the production of material goods. In the last resort, sexual freedom depends on other freedoms, and political tyranny will mean sexual repression.

[47] Schofield, *Promiscuity*, 223–7.
[48] Above, ch. 5 p. 141–2.
[49] L. Ullerstam, *The Erotic Minorities* (1967).

Bibliography

American Law Institute (1962) — Model Penal Code. Philadelphia: American Law Institute.

Amir, M. (1971) — Patterns in Forcible Rape. Chicago, London: Chicago University Press.

Amos, S. (1877) — Laws in Force for the Prohibition, Regulation and Licensing of Vice in England and Other Countries. London: Stevens.

Atkinson, R. T. (1965) — Sexual Morality. New York: Harcourt, Brace and World.

Baker, R. and Elliston, F. ed. (1975) — Philosophy and Sex. Buffalo, New York: Prometheus Books.

Bancroft, J. (1974) — Deviant Sexual Behaviour: Modification and Assessment. Oxford: Clarendon Press.

Baker, D. L. and Allen, S. (1976) — Independence and Exploitation in Work and Marriage. London and New York: Longman.

Barnett, W. (1973) — Sexual Freedom and the Constitution. Albuquerque: University of New Mexico Press.

Beach, F. A. ed. (1965) — Sex and Behaviour. New York: Wiley.

Bernard, J. (1976 ed.) — The Future of Marriage. Harmondsworth, Middlesex: Penguin Books.

Blom-Cooper, L. and Drewry, G. ed. (1976) — Law and Morality. London: Duckworth.

Brakel, S. J. and Rock, R. S. (1971 ed.) — The Mentally Disabled and the Law. Chicago, London: University of Chicago Press.

Brecher, E. M. (1972 ed.) — The Sex Researchers. London: Granada Publishing.

Brown, H. (1976) — Brain and Behaviour. New York, London, Toronto: Oxford University Press.

Brownmiller, S. (1975) — *Against Our Will: Men, Women and Rape.* London: Secker and Warburg.

Central Statistical Office (1975) — *Annual Abstract of Statistics 1974.* London: H.M. Stationery Office.

Clark, H. (1968) — *The Law of Domestic Relations in the United States.* St. Paul, Minnesota: West Publishing Co.

Clark, S. R. L. (1977) — *The Moral Status of Animals.* Oxford: Clarendon Press.

Cole, G. (1975) — The Legal Implications of Cohabitation. *Poly Law Review,* 1, 28.

Collias, N. E. (1944) — Agressive Behaviour among Vertebrate Mammals. *Physiological Zoology* 17, 83.

Coote, A. and Gill, T. (1974) — *Women's Rights: A Practical Guide.* Harmondsworth, Middlesex: Penguin Books.

Corbin, A. L. (1950-63) — *Corbin on Contracts: A Comprehensive Treatise on the Rules of Contract Law.* St. Paul, Minnesota: West Publishing Co.

Cretney, S. (2nd ed. 1976) — *Principles of Family Law.* London: Sweet and Maxwell.

Cross, R. (4th ed. 1974) — *Evidence.* London: Butterworth.

Cross, R. (1975) — Centenary Reflections on Prince's Case. *Law Quart. Rev.* 91, 540.

Cross, R. and Jones, A. (7th ed. 1972) — *Introduction to Criminal Law.* London: Butterworth.

Curley, E. M. (1976) — Excusing Rape. *Philosophy and Public Affairs* 5, 325.

Dalloz (Publisher) (1963) — *Encyclopédie juridique: répertoire de droit pénal et de procedure pénale.* Paris: Jurisprudence Générale Dalloz.

Davidson, K. M., Ginsberg, R. B. and Kay, H. H. — *Text, Cases and Materials on Sex-Based Discrimination.* St. Paul, Minnesota: West Publishing Co.

Devlin, P. A. (1962) — *Samples of Law-making.* London, New York, Toronto: Oxford University Press.

Devlin, P. A. (1965) — *The Enforcement of Morals.* London, New York, Toronto: Oxford University Press.

Eidelberg, L. (1961)   *The Dark Urge.* New York: Pyramid Books.

Evans, A. E. (1923-4)   Property Interests arising from Quasi-marital Relations. *Cornell Law Quart.* 9, 246.

Flood, P. (1962)   *The Dissolution of Marriage: Non-Consummation as a Ground for Annulment or Dissolution of Marriage.* London: Burns and Oates.

Freedland, M. R. (1976)   *The Contract of Employment.* Oxford: Clarendon Press.

Friday, N. (1973)   *My Secret Garden.* London: Virago.

Gagnon, J. H. (1968)   Sexual Deviation: Social Aspects. *International Encyclopedia of the Social Sciences* 14, 219.

Gallon, R. T. (1967)   Wive's Legal Rights. New York: Dell.

Gebhard, P. H. (1969)   Misconceptions about Female Prostitution. *Medical Aspects of Human Sexuality* 3, 24.

Geis, G. (1972)   *Not the Law's Business: An Examination of Homosexuality, Abortion, Prostitution, Narcotics and Gambling in the United States.* Rockville, Maryland: National Institute of Mental Health.

Gillespie, D. L. (1972)   Who has the Power? The Marital Struggle. In Dreitzel, H. P. ed. *Family, Marriage and the Struggle of the Sexes.* New York: Macmillan.

Glick, P. C. and Norton, A. J. (1973)   Perspectives on the Recent Upturn in Divorce and Remarriage. *Demography* 10, 301.

Glover, E. (1969)   *The Psychopathology of Prostitution.* London: Institute for the Scientific Treatment of Delinquency.

Gostin, L. O. (1977)   *A Human Condition: The Law relating to Mentally Abnormal Offenders, Observations, Analysis and Proposals for Reform.* London: National Association for Mental Health (Mind).

Hart, H. L. A. (1963)   *Law, Liberty and Morality*. London: Oxford University Press.

Home Office (1957)   *Report of the Committee on Homosexual Offences and Prostitution*. (Command 247). London: H.M. Stationery Office.

Home Office (1961)   *Criminal Statistics for England and Wales 1960* (Command 1437). London: H.M. Stationery Office.

Home Office (1966)   *Criminal Statistics for England and Wales 1965* (Command 3037). London: H.M. Stationery Office.

Home Office (1971)   *Criminal Statistics for England and Wales 1970* (Command 4708). London: H.M. Stationery Office.

Home Office (1976)   *Criminal Statistics for England and Wales 1975* (Command 6566). London: H.M. Stationery Office.

Home Office (1975)   *Report of the Committee on Mentally Abnormal Offenders* (Command 6244). London: H.M. Stationery Office.

Home Office (1975)   *Report of the Advisory Group on the Law of Rape* (Command 6352). London: H.M. Stationery Office.

Home Office (1976)   *Report of the Working Party on Vagrancy and Street Offences*. London: H.M. Stationery Office.

Honoré, T. (1978)   *Tribonian*. London: Duckworth.

Hood, R. (1962)   *Sentencing in Magistrate's Courts: A Study of Variations in Policy*. London: Stevens and Sons.

Humphreys, L. (1970)   *Tearoom Trade*. London: Duckworth.

Hutt, C. (1972)   *Males and Females*. Harmondsworth, Middlesex: Penguin Books.

Jackson, J. (2nd ed. 1969)   *The Formation and Annulment of Marriage*. London: Butterworth.

James, T. E. (1951)   *Prostitution and the Law*. London: Heinemann.

Kinsey, A. C., Pomeroy, W. B. and Martin, C. E. (1948)   *Sexual Behaviour in the Human Male*. London, Philadelphia: Saunders.

Kinsey, A. C., Pomeroy, W. B., Martin, C. E. and Gebhard, P. H. (1953) — *Sexual Behaviour in the Human Female.* London, Philadelphia: Saunders.

Koh, K. H. (1968) — Consent and Responsibility in Sexual Cases. *Criminal Law Rev.* 1968, 81.

Kolnai, A. T. (1930) — *Sexualethik.* Padeborn: Schöningh.

Law Commission for England and Wales (1966) — *Reform of the Grounds of Divorce: The Field of Choice* (Command 3123). London: H.M. Stationery Office.

Law Commission for England and Wales Working Paper No. 77 (1976) — *Family Law; Report on Matrimonial Proceedings.* London: H.M. Stationery Office.

Leigh, L. H. (1976) — Sado-masochism, Consent and the Reform of the Criminal Law. *Modern Law Rev.* 39, 130.

le Moal, P. (1965) — *Etude sur la prostitution des mineurs: problèmes sociaux, psychologiques et psychiatriques observés auprès de cent prostituées mineures.* Paris: Les éditions sociales françaises.

Leslie, G. R. (3rd ed. 1976) — *The Family in Social Context.* New York, London, Toronto: Oxford, University Press.

Licht, H. (1953) — *Sexual Life in Ancient Greece.* New York: Barnes and Noble.

Lombroso, C. and Ferrero, E. G. (1893) — *La donna delinquente, la prostituta e la donna normale.* Turin, Rome: Roux & Co.

Lorenz, K. Z. (1952) — *King Soloman's Ring: New Light on Animal Ways* (tr. M. K. Wilson). London: Methuen.

McClintock, F. H. and Avison, N. H. (1968) — *Crime in England and Wales.* London: Heinemann.

Magee, B. (1968 ed.) — *One in Twenty: A Study of Homosexuality in Men and Women.* London: Corgi Books.

Merton, R. K. and Nisbet, R. A. ed. (1966) — *Contemporary Social Problems.* New York: Harcourt, Brace and World.

Millett, K. (1975) — *The Prostitution Papers.* Frogmore, St. Albans: Granada Publishing.

Milner, C. A. and R. B. (1973) — *Black Players: The Secret World of Black Pimps.* London: Michael Joseph.

Mohr, J. W., Turner, R. E. and Jerry, M. B. (1964)
Pedophilia and Exhibitionism. Toronto: University of Toronto Press.

Money, J. (1970)
Sexual dimorphism and homosexual gender identity. Psychological Bulletin 74, 428.

Mussen, P. H. ed. (3rd ed. 1970)
Carmichael's Manual of Child Psychology. New York, London, Sydney, Toronto: Wiley.

National Opinion Polls Market Research Ltd. (1970)
Report on Attitudes towards Crime, Violence and Permissiveness in Society. Prepared for the Daily Mail, London.

Needham, R. (1974)
Remarks and Inventions: Skeptical Essays about Kinship. London: Tavistock.

Nygh, P. E. (1975)
Guide to the Family Law Act 1975. Sydney, Chatswood: Butterworth.

Office of Population Censuses and Surveys (1975)
Registrar-general's Statistical Review of England and Wales for the Year 1973. London: H.M. Stationery Office.

O'Neill, N. and G. (1972)
Open Marriage: A New Life Style for Couples. New York: Evans.

Patai, R. (1959)
Sex and Family in the Bible and the Middle East. New York: Free Press.

Pearson, M. (1972)
The Age of Consent. Newton Abbot, Devon: David and Charles.

Perkins, R. M. (2nd ed. 1969)
Criminal Law. Mineola, New York: Foundation Press.

Ploscowe, M. (1951)
Sex and the Law. New York: Prentice-Hall.

Radzinowicz, L. and King J. (1977)
The Growth of Crime: The International Experience. London: Hamish Hamilton.

Rayden (1974)
Law and Practice in Divorce and Family Matters (12th ed., by J. Jackson and others). London: Butterworth.

Rivière, P. G. (1971)
Marriage: A Reassessment. In Needham, R. ed. *Rethinking Marriage and Kinship.* London: Tavistock.

Rolph, C. H. ed. (=Hewitt, C. R.) (1955)
Women of the Streets: A Sociological Study of the Common Prostitute. London: Secker and Warburg.

Runciman, J. C. S. (1947)   *The Medieval Manichee: A Study of the Christian Dualist Heresy.* Cambridge: Cambridge University Press.

Sapirstein, M. R. (1948)   *Emotional Security.* New York: Crown.

Scheingold, L. D. and Wagner, N. N. (1974)   *Sound Sex and the Ageing Heart.* New York: Behavioral Publications.

Schofield, M. (1965)   *Sociological Aspects of Homosexuality: A Comparative Study of Three Types of Homosexual.* London: Longman.

Schofield, M. (1968 ed.)   *The Sexual Behaviour of Young People.* Harmondsworth, Middlesex: Penguin Books.

Schofield, M. (1976)   *Promiscuity.* London: Gollancz.

Shepher, J. (1971)   Mate Selection among Second Generation Kibbuts Adolescents and Adults. *Archives of Sexual Behaviour* 1, 293.

Shorter, E. L. (1976)   *The Making of the Modern Family.* London: Collins.

Sicot, M. (1964)   *La prostitution dans le monde.* Paris: Hachette.

Skegg, P. D. G. (1973)   Consent to Medical Procedures on Minors. *Modern Law Rev.* 36, 370.

Slater, P. E. (1968)   Some Social Consequences of Temporary Systems. *The Temporary Society.* New York: Harper and Row.

Smith, D K (1971)   Transsexualism, Sex Reassignment, Surgery and the Law. *Cornell Law Rev.* 56, 963.

Smith, J. C. and Hogan, B. (3rd ed. 1973)   *Criminal Law.* London: Butterworth.

Stephen, J. F. (4th ed. 1887)   *A Digest of the Criminal Law (Crimes and Punishment).* London, New York: Macmillan.

Thomas, D. A. (1970)   *Principles of Sentencing: The Sentencing Policy of the Court of Appeal Criminal Division.* London: Heinemann.

Treitel, G. H. (4th ed. 1975)   *The Law of Contract.* London: Stevens.

Tripp, C. A. (1975)   *The Homosexual Matrix.* London, Melbourne, New York: Quartet.

Ullerstam, L. (1967)   *The Erotic Minorities: A Sexual Bill of Rights.* New York: Grove Press.

Weitzman (1974)   Legal Regulation of Marriage: Tradition and Change. *California Law Rev.* 62, 1122.

West, D. J. (1977)   *Homosexuality Re-examined.* London: Duckworth.

Westermarck, E. A. (1939)   *Christianity and morals.* London: Kegan Paul.

Westermarck, E. A. (5th ed. 1922)   *The History of Human Marriage.* New York: Allerton.

Williams, G. (1964)   Victims as Parties to Crimes—A Further Comment. *Criminal Law Rev.* 1964, 686.

Wimperis, V. (1960)   *The Unmarried Mother and her Child.* London: Allen and Unwin.

Wolff, C. (1971)   *Love between Women.* London: Duckworth.

Yeger, S. (1976)   Whoring on the Side. *New Society* 24 June.

Index of statutes

References to page numbers in this book are in bold type

Index of cases

References to page numbers in this book are in bold type

General Index